CHILDREN'S LANGUAGE AND COMMUNICATION DIFFICULTIES

D0921317

Also available from Cassell:

D. Child: *Psychology and the Teacher*, 6th edition
B. Copley and B. Forryan: *Therapeutic Work with Children and Young People*
J. Collins: *The Quiet Child*
J. Corbett: *Special Educational Needs in the Twentieth Century*
J. Edwards: *The Scars of Dyslexia*
P. Farrel: *Teaching Pupils with Learning Difficulties*
J. Osmond: *The Reality of Dyslexia*
P. Salmon: *Handbook for Psychology in the Classroom*

Children's Language and Communication Difficulties

Understanding, Identification and Intervention

Julie Dockrell and David Messer

CASSELL
London and New York

Cassell
Wellington House
125 Strand
London WC2R 0BB

370 Lexington Avenue
New York
NY 10017–6550

www.cassell.co.uk

© Julie Dockrell and David Messer 1999

First published 1999

British Library Cataloguing-in-Publication Data
A catalogue record for this book is available from the British Library.

ISBN   0-304-33657-2 (hardback)
         0-304-33658-0 (paperback)

Typeset by Kenneth Burnley, Wirral, Cheshire.
Printed and bound in Great Britain by TJ International Ltd, Padstow, Cornwall.

Contents

*This book is dedicated to the many children
who struggle daily to express their
feelings, knowledge and beliefs.
We owe the children a debt of gratitude
for forcing us to reconsider
the role of language and communication
in development.*

Acknowledgements

We are grateful for the support and help of the many teachers and children who have participated in studies funded by the Wellcome Trust and the Gatsby Foundation. A number of our colleagues have spent time reading and commenting on chapters. We are indebted to Bryan Dockrell, Nicola Grove, Jon Gilmartin, Liz Kilbey, Geoff Lindsay, Constanza Moreno, Victoria Murphy, Sarah Norgate, Stuart Powell, Mina Ralli and Nick Wood. Ann Locke read and commented on the first draft of this book and her comments have been very helpful.

Our respective families have offered support and tolerance while we tackled this project. We hope they are pleased with the finished product.

Preface

Stop for a moment and think what life would be like without the ability to use language. Almost every aspect of our activities would be made more difficult, and in many cases we would not be able to carry out activities that we routinely perform. Similarly, children's difficulties with language can have widespread effects on the way that they live their lives. It can affect their social interaction and their entertainment, as well as their ability to think and learn. If you know a child with language difficulties then these issues will be readily apparent to you, and even if you do not know such a child it should be quickly obvious that language pervades most of the activities in which we as humans engage.

Given the impact of language difficulties and the widespread interest in this topic, our book has been written for professionals, teachers and parents who are interested in finding out about:

- research results concerning typical language development;
- theorists' claims about the process of language development;
- present-day knowledge about children who have difficulties with communication and language;
- the principles that should underlie attempts to assist the development of children who have communication and language difficulties.

The book is designed for the 'informed reader'. We hope it will be of interest to those who know little about psychological, linguistics or educational research and as a result we have attempted to make it as accessible as possible without compromising the information that is presented. We are deeply committed to research as a way of assisting the development of children with language difficulties. One basic aspect of this approach is that people should be able to check and read further about a topic. For this reason, after some long discussions about this issue, we have followed the conventions of research publications and include the names of investigators and the date when their article was published. We know the inclusion of these names and dates can be off-putting to those not familiar with the research tradition. However, in the end we decided to include this information so that those who are interested can follow up on the material that we present; this also is the reason why we have included some selected further reading for those who want to know more about a particular topic.

Many of the potential readers of this book will be interested in finding out ways in which they can help a particular child. Unfortunately, we will not be providing instant 'cook book' solutions to particular communication and language difficulties. Instead, we will be trying to give you an appreciation of the

- complexities of language development;
- characteristics and needs of various groups of children;
- principles that should underlie help and intervention.

In this book we will be trying to present you with up-to-date information about language disabilities, and in doing this we will need to identify and discuss alternative views about the development of communication. The range of explanations provided by researchers often results in practitioners feeling frustrated because they usually want a clear message about the best way to conduct an intervention, or the best theory about explaining a particular condition. Unfortunately, research workers usually want to complicate matters, they want to put forward their own theory or disagree with another person's ideas! Such controversy is the essence of developing new under-standings about any issue, but can be seen as unhelpful by those who want to apply the latest research findings. However, we believe that an awareness of conflicting viewpoints can be helpful in thinking about and intervening with children who have language disabilities. The conflicting theories can assist understanding of different features of a disability, and in general there is a move away from attempting to apply one solution or theory to all cases; rather a more pragmatic problem-solving approach is becoming increasingly favoured in attempts at intervention. Thus, in discussing theories and explanations we will not necessarily be emphasizing one particular view over another to say which is 'correct'.

When thinking about interventions concerned with language it is useful to make some comparisons with medical interventions when a person has a medical condition such as an infectious disease. Medical science has accumulated a wealth of understanding of how diseases are transmitted, how to treat a disease and what the consequences of having a disease are, but even here there will be uncertainties such as those about the precise outcome. This wealth of understanding is a result of intensive research over a long period, and the target of the investigations is often a relatively simple organism affecting the biological functioning of a more advanced organism. Clearly when we are dealing with complex psychological processes involving a person's mind and their environment, as well as trying to understand why language is delayed or different, then the task is much more complex; consequently we should expect that the results of interventions are less predictable. Furthermore, given the diversity of the human mind, any intervention needs to take account of this diversity. Unlike the relatively simple and uniform disease, interventions designed to affect the human mind need to be adapted to the particular characteristics of the child and the particular situation in which the child is developing.

Our book begins with an outline of the development of communication and language in typical children. This provides a scaffold for later discussion of the development of children who have language difficulties. The next chapter considers the major theoretical viewpoints about language development, and although these debates usually do not directly influence the process of intervention, the theories have a powerful influence on the research agenda of investigators. The third chapter discusses children with specific speech and language disorders. The major features of the format of this chapter are duplicated in the subsequent chapters about children who have other communication and language disabilities. In these chapters there is a consideration of the issue of identifying the condition, the prevalence of the condition, the nature of the language problems, associated factors, and the wider impact of the language difficulty. The subsequent chapters consider children with learning disabilities (Chapter 4), sensory isolation and visual impairments (Chapter 5), and hearing impairments (Chapter 6). The next two chapters discuss issues related to identifying and assessing language problems (Chapter 7) and the process of intervention (Chapter 8). In both these chapters we give emphasis to the general principles which should underlie these processes rather than dealing with specific techniques. In the last chapter we draw some general conclusions from the material we have presented in the previous chapters.

FURTHER READING

Beveridge, M. and Conti-Ramsden, G. (1987) *Children with Language Disabilities*. Milton Keynes: Open University Press.

Bishop, D. (1987) *Uncommon Understanding: Development and Disorders of Language Comprehension in Children*. Hove: Psychology Press.

Dockrell, J. and McShane, J. (1993) *Children's Learning Difficulties: Cognitive Approach*. Oxford: Blackwell.

Donaldon, M. (1995) *Children with Language Impairments*. London: Jessica Kingsley.

Messer, D. J. (1994) *The Development of Communication*. Chichester: Wiley.

Useful Websites for parents and professionals:
disabilitynet. co. uk

Net for connections for communication disorders:
Http://www. mankato. msus. edu/dept/comdis/kuster/welcome. html
parentsinfo. html

Chapter 1

The Development of Communication and Language

One of the most obvious places to start a book about children's language is with a discussion of the growth of communication in the early years of life. In this chapter we concentrate on describing the process of typical development and relating this to difficulties other children can face. Thus, the chapter will describe some of the major milestones in the development of communication and also discuss different perspectives about why infants can so easily acquire language. The main purpose of the chapter is to familiarize you with the more obvious milestones in development, to alert you to issues which we will return to in subsequent chapters, and to introduce some theoretical issues.

THE BEGINNINGS OF COMMUNICATION

Infants are, from the moment of birth, an important topic of communication between and among their family. Babies can affect adults by their cries, gaze, movements and facial expressions. These are powerful signals and most adults attend and react to them. Cries are especially aversive and give rise to concern, soothing and attempts to reduce the infant's distress. Later on, at about six weeks, infants reliably produce smiles, which are a powerful positive behaviour for others and give an indication of what a baby likes and enjoys.

Infants come into the world with predispositions to attend to human beings. They find human faces more interesting than other comparable stimuli, they prefer to listen to speech than many other sounds, and we know that older infants show a preference for the movements of humans (see Box 1.1 for a more detailed review). More surprisingly, new-born babies have been found to prefer their own mother's voice to that of another female, prefer to look at their mother's face than that of another female, and within ten days prefer the odour of their own mother to that of another female. Consequently, infants are almost immediately attuned to the person who is likely to be the most important provider of care and communication.

During the first four or five months of life, social interaction between babies

Preferences have been identified for:

Human faces – new-borns	Goren et al., 1975
Human speech – new-borns	Cooper and Aslin, 1990
Mother's face – new-borns	Bushnell et al., 1989
Mother's speech – new-borns	DeCasper and Fifer, 1980
Mother's odour – 7–10 days	Macfarlane, 1975
Human movement – 3–4 months	Bertenthal and Proffitt, 1986

Box 1.1: The investigation of new-born babies' preference for humans

and caregivers in Western and many other cultures usually revolves around the activities of the participants. There may be body games and long periods of mutual gaze, caregivers often comment on the baby's facial expression or how the baby might be feeling (see Box 1.2). A striking feature of this interaction is that adults usually break the rules of social interaction. For example, there can be long periods of mutual gaze, close physical proximity, the use of exaggerated facial expressions and the use of a sing-song voice. Many of these features fit in with infant attentional preferences, so that these modifications to usual adult interaction help capture and sustain infant interest.

There are different views about what is happening during this period. Some theorists, such as Kenneth Kaye, regard this as a time of mutual adjustment between baby and adult. He believes that adults fit their behaviour around that of the baby to give the appearance of adult conversation. A good example of this is vocal turn-taking. If you listen to a mother and child interacting together it often has the appearance of an adult conversation; with the baby making a sound and the adult answering afterwards, the infant

Both mother and infant are looking at one another until the infant turns away; the mother is in close proximity to her baby.

Mother	Infant
'How are you today?'	
(Mother moves face to and away from baby)	Infant's eyes widen
'How are you?'	Infant keeps interest in mother
(Mother moves face in same way, and smiles)	
'Don't you want to talk?'	Infant smiles
(Mother puts her head to one side)	
'That's better'	Infant then looks away

Box 1.2: An example of a conversation between a mother and her three-month-old infant

producing another sound and the adult making another reply. Careful analysis of these patterns suggests that it is adults fitting in their speech among the vocalizations of children which gives the appearance of a turn-taking conversation. It has even been suggested that it is not until 2–3 years that children time their vocalizations to avoid speaking at the same time as another person (Davis, 1978). However, not all early vocal interaction involves turn-taking. Sometimes, there are periods of 'chorusing' when both adult and baby vocalize together. Such chorusing often gives adults a strong feeling of 'togetherness' with the baby. On other occasions simultaneous vocalizations may occur when caregivers are trying to soothe a baby.

Another important component of interaction is eye gaze. Adults infer from infant eye gaze that the baby is interested in something, and a lack of interest is deduced from a lack of sustained eye gaze. The presence of mutual eye gaze between carers and infants is often treated as something very special by the adult. Mothers speak about the way it seems to register that the baby 'knows them' and can relate to them. Analyses of the pattern of eye gaze during early social interaction suggests that mothers tend to promote periods of mutual gaze, by returning the infant's gaze if they are already looking at her, and sustaining their gaze at infants when mutual gaze is occurring. Infants do not show the same strong patterns in their behaviour and this suggests that what is occurring is the mother structuring her behaviour around the infant. As we will see in Chapter 6, social interaction with children who have visual impairments involves other channels to support effective communication.

During the first few months of life adults and infants are getting to know one another and the baby is becoming enmeshed in a reasonably predictable pattern of social interaction which is structured around his or her capabilities. There have been suggestions that the experience of early interaction sets up rhythms and patterns of social behaviour which are utilized in later verbal conversations (e.g. vocal turn-taking leading to turn-taking in speech). Certainly a strong case can be made for these early interactions contributing to later communicative processes. However, there is no certainty that the absence of such early experiences would prevent the later development of communicative abilities; it is possible that a child isolated from humans for the first few months of life may still develop social and language abilities (see Chapter 6).

Not everyone thinks that infants are passive partners in the process of early social interaction as suggested by Kenneth Kaye (1982). Some believe that even young infants have some rudimentary understanding that they are involved in a process of communication. Colwyn Trevarthen (1979) has for a long time claimed that even in early social exchanges infants show a desire to influence others and make their own feelings apparent to another person. He calls this ability *intersubjectivity*. Evidence he uses is the way infants will move their limbs when excited, as if trying to influence another person. He has also observed what he terms 'pre-speech' mouth movements where young babies will move their lips and tongue in an apparent attempt to communicate something to someone else (see Figure 1.1).

The views of Kaye and Trevarthen nicely illustrate opposite

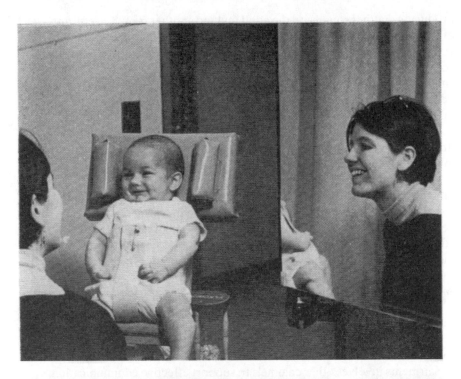

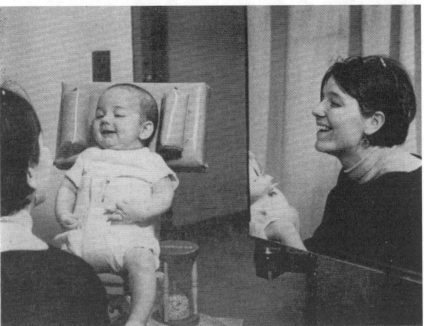

Figure 1.1: Pre-speech communication. Source: Schaffer (1977)

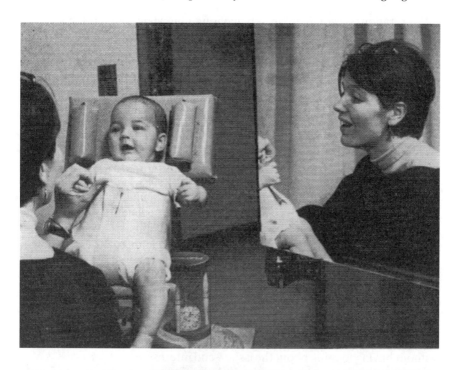

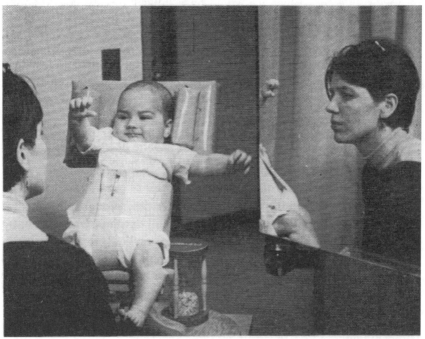

Figure 1.1: Pre-speech communication (continued)

interpretations of young infants' behaviour. One view is that infants learn to communicate through apprenticeship with their more expert caregivers. Through this apprenticeship, babies eventually learn to use their behaviours to achieve objectives and influence other people, in other words to communicate in the fullest sense of the term. However, a difficulty with this view is that it is not clear how infants change from merely taking part in the social process to understanding that they are playing an active part in it. Another issue is how the apprenticeship allows infants to become aware that they are communicating with beings that move, have intentions and respond to communication.

A provocative view about this achievement has been put forward by Andrew Meltzoff and Alison Gopnik (1993). They claim that infants are, from a very early age, perhaps even at birth, able to appreciate that people are not just a collection of interesting stimuli, but are animate beings similar to themselves. To some this might seem a surprising claim, to others an obvious statement of their own experience. The idea of infants being able to appreciate that people are 'like me' draws on the idea of *direct perception*. This involves the ability to categorize or recognize something without having to think about the issues; one simply 'knows'. A good example of direct perception is identifying the *faces* of people as male or female. We all can do this with a very high degree of accuracy; we simply know whether a person is male or female without having to think about the issue – and interestingly, the process is based on very subtle cues which we would have difficulty explaining to another person (it would seem that young infants also are able to distinguish between male and female faces). Thus, the claim is that infants directly perceive other people not as a collection of stimuli, but as something that is animate and something that they can respond to in a social way. As we will see in Chapter 4 these arguments are important in forming the basis of explanations about the cause of autism.

There are various forms of evidence to support the idea of infants possessing intersubjectivity. The first comes from observations of interaction in which investigators such as Colwyn Trevarthen (1979) have recorded the fine timing of responses between infants and adults, where one individual appears to anticipate and complement the behaviour of their partner. Other evidence comes from the studies of imitation by Andrew Meltzoff and his colleagues (Meltzoff and Gopnik, 1993; see Figure 1.2). If young infants can imitate the actions of adults then one explanation is that they do so because they can relate the actions of others to their own self. A third source of evidence is the way that young infants respond to emotion, and the way children with autism fail to make these responses (Hobson, 1986; but for an alternative explanation see Baron-Cohen, 1991). However, none of the findings are conclusive. As a result, one cannot be certain whether infants respond to people in an intersubjective or mechanistic way, and because of this there continues to be a debate about these issues.

In contrast to early social abilities, infants' access to and control of their physical environment is limited by poor vision and poor manipulative abilities

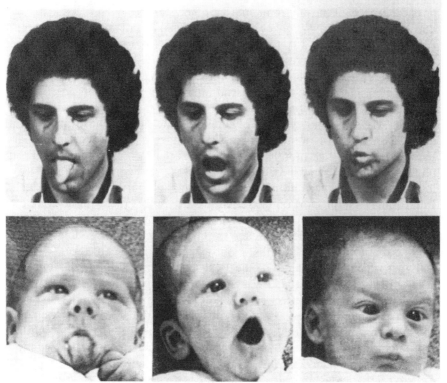

Figure 1.2: Imitation in a 2- to 3-week-old infant. Source: Meltzoff and Moore (1977)

(though they have good hearing). Thus, various theorists have characterized the first five or six months as a period when caregiver and infant interact with one another, and largely ignore the wider physical world. Social interaction with adults is about each other and their reactions to each other. Such a period may be important in allowing mutual knowledge to develop, and for infants to start to become attuned to some of the characteristics of their culture. For example, even by three months there are differences in the interaction of American and Japanese mother–infant pairs which seem to reflect the wider characteristics of their culture (Fogel *et al.*, 1988). In addition, it is important to bear in mind that these early interactions may be part of the process of attachment formation, and may influence the type of attachment that is formed. Another issue which we will consider in Chapters 5 and 7 is the adaptations that occur to enable social interaction to take place with children who have disabilities, such as blindness or deafness.

INTERACTING WITH THE PHYSICAL WORLD

At about five or six months there seems to be a change in the form of social interactions between infants and adults. This involves a greater interest in physical aspects of the environment (e.g. objects). It has been speculated that this is associated with advances in postural, visual and manipulative abilities. Adults tend to respond to this change by talking more about the physical environment. Several investigations have documented these changes. As will be shown in Chapter 5, it is also apparent that when children have disabilities adults often adapt their style of social interaction to maintain an effective channel of communication.

Ben Sylvester-Bradley and Colwyn Trevarthen (1978) have provided a detailed investigation of these progressive changes in one mother–infant pair between two and five months that illustrates the increased salience of the physical world. There was a decline in infant sociability in terms of positive looking at the mother and an increase in the amount of maternal speech. Interestingly, the proportion of contentless utterances (i.e. with no concrete referent such as 'hello') increased up to four months, and then declined. Robyn Penman and her colleagues (1983) provide similar findings from a larger sample. At three months about a quarter of the time was spent in activities which were related to objects, at six months about half the time was spent in this way. There also was a corresponding change in the topic of maternal speech from affect-related utterances at three months to information-giving utterances at six months. In addition, other research has reported that maternal utterances to three-month-olds concern mood and physiological activity, those to seven-month-olds concern perception, volition and psychological activity, while utterance to ten-month-olds are about goal-directed activities (Rabain-Jamin and Sabeau-Jouannet, 1989).

At around nine months there seems to be a further change in the nature of social interaction. For one thing this is the age at which children are developing attachments to particular people and sometimes showing wariness of strangers. Such changes mean that children are starting not only to make perceptual discrimination between different people, but are also making clear affectional discrimination as well. These developments influence the nature of social interaction. At around this age children start to show *social referencing*, they will check to see the reactions of familiar adults to unusual or threatening events, and will of course be monitoring these adults to check where they are and what they are doing.

At about this age children also start to produce conventional *gestures*, such as pointing, and they clearly use communication as a means of achieving certain objectives. At first, children appear to use gestures like pointing without fully understanding their communicative significance. For example, a child might point with both hands in different directions, or may leave their hand suspended in the air while looking at something else. In addition, children at about nine months have difficulties following points which involve a large distance between the index finger and the target object. Although the development of gestures is clearly a significant advance in communicative abilities, it is not clear whether such capacities need to be in place for the development of language. As we will see, some individuals who cannot use gesture because of motor disabilities acquire language.

There have been differences of opinion about the development of communicative gestures like pointing. One approach is to suppose that children will produce actions in a fairly random manner, and some of these behaviours will be responded to by adults, with important consequences for communication and development. For example, a child might lift her arms up, and when this happens adults respond to the child's actions by picking her up. As a result of such experiences children start to learn that they can affect others (Lock, 1980). A different possibility is that observational learning plays a part in the emergence of gestures, as some children clearly imitate gestures without understanding their significance.

However, there is an explanation which takes a very different perspective and involves the idea that there is a general cognitive advance. Jean Piaget (1932; 1962) supposed that at about eight to nine months children start to identify new ways to achieve their objectives. This might be in tasks such as learning to reach for a toy around a visible perspex barrier, or in using people to help them achieve an objective. During this period infants start to produce sounds which are associated with particular circumstances, such as wanting something, or dislike. A useful illustration of all this is the changes in the way children will try to take an object from a carer. At seven months a child will usually try to grab the object, they will not look at the adult's face, and will not vocalize. In contrast, by ten months, children will look at the adult's face and may make pleading noises at the same time.

Thus, infants seem to be learning to use new and less direct behaviours to achieve their objectives, and learning that they can use the help of adults to achieve what they want. It is often supposed that these new communicative abilities will provide a starting point for later pragmatic skills (the ability to achieve particular goals through using communication), and form the basis of the motivation for using language. For some investigators this represents a very important transition from *pre-intentional* to *intentional* communication. However, others like Colwyn Trevarthen argue that some form of communicative intentions are present before this age. Such differences of opinion are difficult to resolve given that we cannot be sure how a baby is thinking, and because much depends on the way we define terms such as 'intentional communication'. Although there are differences of interpretation, most authorities would agree that at around nine months there are important changes in the nature of adult–infant communication, both in the type of communicative demands that are made by infants and because of their greater awareness of the communication of other people.

THE FIRST USE OF WORDS

Various methods have been used to collect information about the development of communication. Much of the research on early non-verbal social interaction has video recorded interactions and this was followed by painstaking coding of movements and behaviour. Research on child language has involved a number of famous examples of detailed diary records being kept by researchers who are parents. This has provided important descriptions and insights which have been of great value, but there is always the difficulty of knowing how typical any one child is. A recent development has been the MacArthur Communicative Inventories (CDI), a standardized checklist that can be given to parents to record the words their children understand and produce. This has allowed much more extensive data collection about children's language abilities and has revealed considerable variability in children's speech (see Box 1.3).

The use of the CDI on over 1,000 children has provided extensive information about early word use (Bates et al.,1994; 1995). One set of findings has concerned the production of speech, that is what children actually say, another set of findings concerns comprehension, that is what words and utterances children understand. Often children can understand more than they can say, but it is easy to overestimate children's verbal comprehension because they will often use contextual information to help them work out the meaning of words.

The findings from research using the CDI indicate that the average number of different words reported as comprehended and produced at eight months are 36 and 2 (respectively), at ten months 67 and 12, at 16 months 191 and 64; by 30 months children are reported to produce 534 words. Caution is needed when interpreting findings on comprehension because parents may have different interpretations of what they consider 'understanding'. In addition, it should be emphasized that there is great variation in the rate of vocabulary development. For example the range in the number of different words that were produced at 12 months was between 0 and 52 words, at 16 months between 0 and 347, and at 30 months between 208 and 675 words. Furthermore, at 16 months, 10 per cent of children had vocabularies of 179–347 words, while another 10 per cent had vocabularies below eight words; this range was more reduced at 30 months with 10 per cent having vocabularies of between 654 and 675 words, and another 10 per cent having vocabularies between 208 and 262 words. It is also striking that most of children's first 200 words are common nouns.

Box 1.3: Findings from the CDI about early vocabularies

THE STUDY OF COMMUNICATION – WORDS AND LANGUAGE

Communicating involves many skills. Often the study of communication is considered to involve the following sub-areas, and the terms referring to these sub-areas are the ones which are used in our book.

Phonology

Each language has its own range of sounds, and the sounds used in a language to make up words follow predictable patterns. When infants babble these sounds they follow the sounds of their mother tongue. A phoneme is the smallest unit of sound which can be identified in language.

Semantics

The meaning associated with words and utterances. Semantics involves the meaning of individual words, but these can change depending on the structure and context of the utterance.

Pragmatics

The expression of intentions and the ability to accomplish objectives by the use of speech. Sometimes this involves being aware of conventions and the use of language in a way appropriate for the context. Pragmatics can involve non-verbal communication.

Syntax and morphology

A morpheme is the smallest unit of meaning in a language. These can be whole words such as 'cat' which is termed a 'free morpheme' because it can be said by itself, or parts of words which mark a grammatical function, such as the plural '-s'. These are termed 'bound morphemes' because they are usually part of another word. Children need to learn the appropriate rules underlying the use of morphemes. Syntax is another set of linguistic rules that children acquire, these involve the ordering of words into phrases. The term 'morpho-syntax' is used to refer to the grammatical rules about word order and morpheme use.

Producing grammatically acceptable speech involves both organizing the order of words in the sentence and making sure that the words have the necessary grammatical endings. Linguists use the term 'grammar' in a general way to refer to rules about the way speech is produced and comprehended, this even includes the organization of sounds in speech. They often distinguish between syntax, which are the rules about the order of words (i.e. 'the sat cat on mat' violates the rules of English), and morphology, which is the organization of grammatical elements which are attached to words (e.g. the '-ed' which is used to signal the past tense). However, for the sake of simplicity we will use the term 'grammar' to refer to both these aspects.

One of the necessary steps involved in discussing a subject like language is to define what we mean by the term. There is sometimes confusion in everyday speech between the words 'communication' and 'language'. Occasionally, animals, such as bees, dolphins or monkeys, are said to use language. We will use the word 'language' to describe a form of communication in which different elements can be identified, and in which the arrangement of these elements influences the meaning of the message. Most forms of animal communication do not meet these criteria (e.g. the growl of a dog conveys a threat, but there does not seem to be any special arrangement of the sequence of sounds in a growl which would convey different messages). If we wanted to be more strict in our definition, and thereby exclude many of the remaining forms of animal communication, then we could propose that language has to involve *structural dependency,* that is a set of relations between different elements (e.g. between the subject and a verb of a sentence). It is important to recognize that although there is a reasonable consensus in the academic community about what is language and what is communication, there can be disagreements over the fine detail. Arguments over the fine details can be important in deciding whether or not we consider a particular form of communication a language.

SOCIAL INTERACTION AND VOCABULARY DEVELOPMENT

There has been a long-standing interest in the way that social interaction has an impact on vocabulary development. Research indicates that infants are provided with a rich source of non-verbal information which helps them understand the speech spoken to them. One of the most obvious forms of assistance is pointing. As already mentioned, infants can follow points, and adult speech invariably refers to objects identified by infant or adult points. However, to acquire an extensive vocabulary infants need other ways of identifying the referent of adult speech. Observation of adult–infant interaction has revealed that speech is usually about an object that the infant is looking at, or which the adult or child is handling. In addition, children often hear a series of utterances about the same referent. The series tends to be marked by a longer-than-usual pause, by the manipulation of a new object and by the naming of the object. Thus, the immediate structure of social interaction provides very useful cues that can help children identify the physical referent of speech. Interestingly, a slightly different pattern of behaviour appears to be relevant for the identification of actions. Action words tend to be said before the relevant event or after the event has occurred. A number of experimental studies confirm that this link between speech and visual attention provides a basis for the development of vocabulary (see Tomasello and Farrar, 1986).

It is also possible that the participation in social routines, such as the exchange of objects or games like peek-a-boo, helps children to understand the place of speech within a well-learned format. Furthermore, as children become older, they seem to become more able to utilize contextual information to help them understand the meaning of a word. As we will see in Chapters 5 and 6, the vocabulary development of children with visual, hearing and other disabilities appears to rely on other forms of matching between speech and non-verbal information.

Children's first words often are closely tied to a specific context. A child might only say 'chuff-chuff' when running his train over the living-room floor. However, with experience the use of the expression becomes more general so that it applies to other trains and in other circumstances. Observations such as this raise questions about whether infants are using words in exactly the same way as adults.

Cognitive processes and vocabulary development – semantics

Being able to use and understand words involves much more than associating a word with its referent. For one thing, even if a referent can be identified by non-verbal means, there is usually uncertainty about the precise link between word and object. Does the word refer to the whole object, the colour of the object, or what the object is doing? The list could be almost endless. An associated problem concerns categorizing the world in a way that allows a child to use words appropriately. We will use the term 'category' to refer to a group of things (or more formally entities) which share something in common and which can be distinguished from other entities (e.g. birds make up a category of types of animals). We will use the term 'concept' to refer to the knowledge a person has about a category of things (e.g. we might know that most birds build nests). It might seem that it is a reasonably simple process to form a category. However, to form a category the infant needs to notice a similarity which is common to all members of the category and disregard any features which are dissimilar. They need to notice that dogs bark and wag their tails, although they vary in size, colour and shape. It has been pointed out that, given the number of ways in which things can be similar and dissimilar, the task of forming categories would seem to be almost impossible.

There has been a move away from supposing that categories are based on precise definitions such as one would find in a dictionary. Most of us do not know the formal biological definitions of the category of dog, and whether this includes dingos or wolves. Consequently, in some cases formal definitions of words have to be left to experts, but most of the population has a reasonably good idea of what is included in a category. It should also be acknowledged that there are some words where there is much more uncertainty about a term, for example, what is a 'hero' and who can be considered a 'hero'? There will of course be differences of opinion in the answers to such questions. All this serves to illustrate that the things that are referred to by words are to some extent open to negotiation and debate; they vary across people and across time.

A number of attempts have been made to describe the way categories are formed by infants. Prototype theory has become a very popular explanation of this. A child notices the characteristics of a set of things and by some process of averaging forms a prototype which contains many of the characteristics of these things, and few of the characteristics of related categories. So a prototype of a bird might be something like a robin after seeing a sparrow, a crow, a thrush and so on, but is unlikely to look like a penguin or ostrich.

A study which neatly illustrates this process was conducted by Younger and Cohen (1983). They showed ten-month-old infants pictures of make-believe animals and found evidence that infants reacted in a way predicted by prototype theory (see Figure 1.3). Make-believe animals were made by using three different sets of attributes (e.g. club, web or hoof feet) for each of the regions of the animal's body (ears, body, legs, feet and tail). Thus, each region

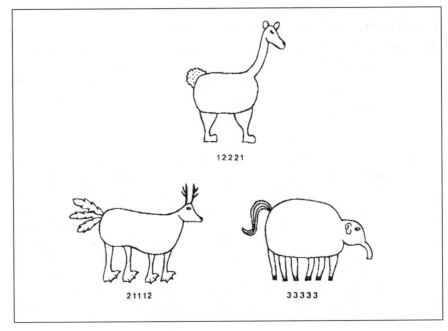

12221

21112   33333

Figure 1.3: The stimuli used by Younger and Cohen. Source: Younger and Cohen (1983) © Society for Research in Child Development. Used with permission

could have one of three different forms. Infants were shown a set of animals and then shown one of the following:

1. An animal which had characteristics in a similar combination to that seen before
2. An animal which had the characteristics seen before, but in a new combination, or
3. A completely new animal.

The infants treated the animal with a new combination of attributes in the same way as the completely new animal. This suggests that the infants were processing, not just how many times they have seen certain forms, but also how often they see these forms in certain combinations. This indicates that ten-month-old infants are not simply processing whether or not a feature is present, but are also attending to the relationship between the features.

There is support for the idea that children's categories are based on prototypes from studies which have asked them to pick out a referent from a range of similar objects. The children tend to pick out the referent which is central to the category and is therefore likely to be similar to any prototype. However, one difficulty with prototype theory is that it is not clear how any 'averaging' process occurs, and given the range of things that children encounter, it is difficult to understand how they achieve this complex computational process.

In an attempt to explain the way children are able to acquire the meaning of words, there have been proposals that children are operating within a set of constraints and assumptions. The result of this is that young children only consider one or a limited number of possible meanings of a word. The advantage of such proposals is that they provide an explanation of how children are able to acquire the meaning of words when there are so many uncertainties about the nature of the referent. One of the most widely discussed proposals is the *whole object assumption*, in which children are seen as treating a word as referring to the whole object rather than part of the object or some attribute of the object. In this way many uncertainties about reference are eliminated. An example of this is a child mistakingly using 'hot' to refer to an oven, probably as a result of having been told 'it's hot'. This proposal about constraints explains why children can learn the meaning of words with apparent ease. However, there have been a number of questions about this process. For one thing, it is not clear whether these (and other) assumptions are the result of some innate predisposition, or a result of experience of social interaction which leads children to make inferences about speech. There is experimental evidence which indicates that children do not always use the whole object assumption; sometimes they will interpret a word as referring to the substance an object is made from, rather than the object itself. In addition, there is a difficulty in explaining how children acquire verbs if they are using only the whole object assumption.

The use of one-word utterances – pragmatics

A remarkable feature of early speech is that for a comparatively long time children only produce one-word utterances; this lasts from about nine to twelve months until around eighteen to twenty months. However, during this time there are considerable changes in the way that words are used. It is often difficult to know whether a nine-month-old is merely imitating a sound they have heard; in contrast, an eighteen-month-old appears to use one-word utterances for a whole range of different purposes. As we will see, there is considerable debate about what is the status of one-word utterances, a debate that is fuelled by the uncertainty about what an infant is wanting to communicate. On the one hand there have been claims that one-word utterances stand for a complete sentence of several words; on the other hand it is supposed that this speech is not language proper but a more primitive form of communication.

John Dore (1978) suggested that one-word speech involves *primitive speech acts* which are not the same as adult words. The primitive speech acts have a method of referring to an entity, together with a device, such as intonation, to indicate the force of the communication and these include: labelling, repeating, answering, requesting an action, requesting an answer, calling, greeting, etc. Thus, Dore suggested that a range of functions can be identified in one-word speech. Dore believed that innate mechanisms allow these primitive speech acts to become more similar to adult speech acts, and so allow multi-word utterances to emerge.

A slightly different analysis has been provided by Halliday (1975) who identified four pragmatic functions which occur in non-verbal and sometimes verbal communication:

1. *Instrumental:* to obtain an objective, e.g. obtain a toy.
2. *Regulatory:* to influence the actions of others, e.g. play a game.
3. *Interactional:* to form a relationship, e.g. greetings.
4. *Personal:* to express feelings, e.g. crying or protesting.

Halliday (1975) claims, on the basis of observations of his son Nigel, that pre-verbal vocalizations can fulfil these four functions, and later single-word utterances will fulfil the same functions. Additional functions emerge slightly later; when a child can use word combinations and engage in dialogue, an informative function emerges to communicate information.

Attempts to classify the intent and pragmatic aspects of communication have encountered problems. This coding has to employ detective work in order to be able to classify a word on the basis of the context in which it occurs. Such difficulties illustrate the serious problems of investigating this period of development, and should make us aware of the difficulties and pitfalls of too ready an interpretation of what a young child is saying.

Different styles of speech and individual variation

An interesting idea is that, even at this early stage, there are differences between children in the way they use speech. Katherine Nelson (1973) suggested that *referential* infants have a vocabulary that is predominantly composed of object names, they are early talkers, and social interaction with adults often involves objects. In contrast, *social expressive* infants have fewer object names in their vocabulary, having instead many words which fulfil a role in regulating social interaction (e.g. bye-bye, ta, etc.), and they sometimes use formulas (words which tend to occur together, e.g. all-gone). There is evidence that referential children tend to have mothers who produce more utterances per event, more descriptions and fewer directives. In addition, the referential style of maternal speech appears to be prevalent among first-borns which may be related to the more tutorial style of interaction often employed with such children.

When Katherine Nelson classified children's first 50 words she used information from maternal diaries about the type of words and the context of use. Referential words were considered to involve the labelling of objects. However, a problem with this is that children sometimes use object words in a functional way (e. g. the referential word 'drink' is used when asking for some liquid). Consequently, Katherine Nelson's classification of speech is partly based on the way words are used in adult speech, not on the children's intentions, and so the same word could be used for both social and referential purposes (see Pine, 1992).

Two other styles of speech have been identified by Elizabeth Bates (1988);

she terms these *analytic* and *holistic* styles (sometimes termed rote style). The analytic style involves a high percentage of referential words in children's one-word vocabularies, frequent naming of objects in two-word utterances, and the later over-generalization of grammatical rules. These children often appear to learn words faster, are female, are first-born and come from higher socio-economic status families. The holistic style involves the use of intonation during babbling, many expressive words at the one-word stage, the use of formulas in two-word speech (copied phrases), and later under-generalization and inconsistent application of rules. However, although it is easy to think of children in terms of these styles, later research by Elizabeth Bates (1995) has made her doubt that children can be so neatly categorized in this way.

The vocabulary burst

One dramatic feature of children's one-word speech is the *vocabulary burst* when there appears to be a rapid expansion of the number of words which are produced. This seems to occur at about eighteen to twenty months when a vocabulary of between 30 and 50 words has been reached. In a few weeks the vocabulary expands to several hundred words. As the vocabulary expands there is an increase in the number and proportion of verbs, adjectives and adverbs in children's vocabulary. There is also evidence that a 50–100-word vocabulary is associated with the beginning of two-word speech. It may be that some 'critical mass' is necessary for two-word utterances.

Several researchers have suggested that the vocabulary burst is a product of children's more advanced understanding of the nature of words, and signals the use of words in an adult way. Katherine Nelson (1988) proposes that this involves understanding that words can be used to refer to categories of objects and events. Underlying the advance is believed to be a new insight that all concepts have a relevant word, and all words refer to a concept. John Dore (1978) has termed this the *naming insight*, an understanding of the relation between words and objects.

There have, however, been questions raised about the vocabulary burst. For one thing not all children appear to go through a vocabulary burst, some seem to show a gradual increase in vocabulary. It has also been suggested that the vocabulary burst is nothing more than the steepest part of the exponential curve which makes up the expansion of children's vocabulary (Bates, 1995).

TWO-WORD UTTERANCES

The use of one-word speech appears to be followed by several months when children's speech mostly consists of two-word utterances. It is suggested that this speech can fulfil a number of communicative functions such as those shown in Table 1.1. These were identified in a classic study by Brown (1973), and were thought to be common in children learning a range of different languages. This and similar schemes rely on contextual information to identify the semantic role of the words, a problem already discussed in relation to one-word speech.

Agent	+	Action	John kick
Action	+	Object	Kick ball
Agent	+	Object	John ball
Action	+	Location	Kick there
Entity	+	Location	John there
Possessor	+	Possessed	Adam ball
Entity	+	Attribute	Ball fast
Demonstrative	+	Entity	That ball

Table 1.1: Meaning in two-word utterances

Suggestions about the way children change from using one- to two-word utterances have taken a variety of forms. Some have suggested that children will produce what are termed 'vertical constructions' where their reply to an adult utterance provides more than an answer as it also involves an extension of the topic (e.g. Mother: 'Do you want cereal?' Child: 'Milk'; here the child does not simply answer 'Yes' but seems to be adding information that she wants both cereal and milk, see Scollen, 1976). Another suggestion is that children start to produce words that could form a two-word utterance, but there is a pause between these words.

It is unclear why children's speech is restricted to two-word utterances for a period of time (see also Chapters 3 and 4). This does not seem to be a mechanical problem of producing the sounds. A Hungarian study reported that children can produce one-word utterances containing a number of syllables, but are unable to produce two-word utterances containing the same number of syllables. In addition, some children produce *formulas*, that is multi-word utterances ('Hello Daddy') where the words are rarely if ever used separately.

One way to explain the use of two-word speech is in terms of a general cognitive change that allows children to combine different ideas in a single utterance. Interestingly at about this age there are a number of other cognitive changes including the start of pretend play, the ability to sort objects into different groups, and the development of various imitative abilities. With such a flurry of cognitive developments it is not too surprising that there are developments in speech at about the same age.

These cognitive changes have been interpreted as indicating that children are developing the ability to use symbols, that is they can form mental representations of things, and these representations are no longer tied to seeing or acting on the thing. Being able to pretend a banana is a telephone is a well-known example of early symbolic activity. It is also suggested that the ability to use symbols means that children start to use words in a much more flexible way because the words are no longer treated as being directly linked to their referent. Such changes represent a development from *pre-symbolic* to *symbolic* speech.

EARLY MULTI-WORD UTTERANCES

Early multi-word utterances do not contain certain types of words, such as pronouns, articles and auxiliary verbs. Because of this such utterances are sometimes referred to as 'telegraphic speech'. In some languages which have more varied word endings than English, children at this level are able to acquire this aspect of language. Telegraphic speech appears to be a transition to what is generally agreed to be a proper language. There are a number of descriptive systems which capture this transition. A classification of early multi-word speech which has proved to be popular has been that of Courtney Cazden (1968) and Roger Brown (1973). This is based on the type of morphemes that are used and the *mean length of utterances* (MLU). The MLU is usually calculated from the mean number of morphemes in a sample of 100 utterances of a child. Because morphemes are counted instead of words, it is possible for there to be more morphemes than words in an utterance (e.g. 'He kick-ed ball' consists of four morphemes). Although MLU is a widely used measure it has some deficiencies. For one thing the MLU may be very different depending on the language being acquired; in some languages it seems easier to develop a long MLU at an early age. Another problem is that the sample of 100 utterances is quite small to form the basis of the assessment of a child's language development, particularly when one considers the way that the context might influence children's speech.

Cazden and Brown identified a number of stages in the development of multi-word utterances on the basis of the study of three children who were given the pseudonyms of Adam, Eve and Sara. Stage I was considered to involve utterances below 2 to 2.5 morphemes, the utterances mostly contain nouns and adjectives, with few inflections being used (i.e. the addition of morphemes such as -s to signal plurals). The first morphemes were acquired between twenty-one and thirty-four months, and the sixth morpheme by twenty-three to thirty-eight months (see Table 1.2). In this study, both verbal and non-verbal information was used to help establish whether a particular morpheme should have been used (e.g. 'the doll' is appropriate if there is only one doll, but the use of this expression when there are several dolls reveals that the child was not using the morpheme '-s', needed for most plural nouns). Although there was variability in age of acquisition, the order was similar in the three children. Despite the small sample, subsequent studies have tended to report similar findings.

English is a language in which word order is important in conveying meaning, and the use of inflections is less important. The language of the Greenlandic Inuit involves the use of a complex morphological system where a word may have a large number of affixes: up to eight morphemes can accompany a word. One observation of a 2-year-old child by Fortescue (1984/5) revealed that in half an hour 40 separate inflections were produced, with the longest single-word utterances containing several elements of meaning. Thus, the rate of language acquisition is clearly influenced by the structure of the language being acquired. Findings like this have led Dan

1.	Present progressive verb	+ -ing
2/3.	Prepositions	in/on
4.	Plurals	noun + -s
5.	Irregular past tense	went, swam
6.	Possessive	hers
7.	Uncontracted copula (verb to be)	she was good
8.	Articles	the, a
9.	Regular past tense	looked, talked
10.	Third person present tense Irregular	she has
11.	Third person present tense Regular	she talks
12.	Uncontracted auxiliary (verb to be)	she was talking
13.	Contracted copula	she's good
14.	Contracted auxiliary	she's talking

A copula involves the use of the verb 'to be' as the main verb of an utterance; it can be used either in the uncontracted (full) form (e.g. 'She is good') or in the contracted form (e.g. 'She's good'). An auxiliary verb is not the main verb of an utterance and it is used in the presence of another verb, e.g. 'She is talking'. It can be used in its uncontracted form, or in a contracted form (e.g. 'She's talking').

Table 1.2: The sequence of acquisition of fourteen morphemes investigated by Roger Brown

Slobin (1985) to suggest that semantic and syntactic complexity influences the age a morpheme will be acquired.

LATER LANGUAGE DEVELOPMENT

A quick look through many books on child language would suggest that most significant developments are accomplished by 3 years of age. However, a little thought indicates that language development does not end in the pre-school years, and although the developments in later years often are less dramatic, nonetheless the progress made in the school years makes a vital contribution to adult communicative competence. In relation to this, Kevin Durkin (1986) has forcefully argued that important developments in vocabulary, syntax and phonology continue through the school years and often beyond.

There is a doubling of children's vocabulary size between starting at school and reaching the middle years of secondary school. Furthermore, we continue to expand our vocabularies throughout our life, albeit at a much slower rate than in the early years. A number of investigations indicate that vocabulary expansion in later childhood (and beyond) is accomplished because the meaning of a new words can be abstracted from very limited contextual information.

A number of grammatical forms are not fully mastered until the school years. An interesting example of this is the use of passive sentences (e. g. the passive form of 'The truck pushes the bus' is 'The bus is being pushed by the truck'). Children of 3 or 4 years of age seem to use word order to help them understand speech and this leads to errors when they have to understand passive utterances or carry out instructions which involve passive utterances (when young children are asked to act out the passive utterance from the example that has been just given, they will make the blue truck push the bus). Another grammatical form that is usually mastered in the school years is the understanding that the indefinite articles (i.e. 'a') should be used to introduce a new subject rather the definite article (i.e. 'the') as well as the appropriate use of reflexive and non-reflexive pronouns (i.e. themselves, himself, herself, him, her). In addition, during the primary school years children's use of clauses becomes more complex. Subordinate clauses are used to express temporal relations and the use of these can be a good index of language complexity. Some of the most complex grammatical forms are only mastered in the adolescent years; these include the use of relative clauses, and the use of expressions in written material such as 'moreover' and 'conversely'.

Further developments in language are not confined to grammatical rules. During the school years there also are important changes in the way that children learn to construct narratives, to use intonation, to use language to interact with others, to use language to persuade or bully others, and to use language to convey humour and tell jokes. There is also increasing metalinguistic awareness, that is awareness of language itself. Such awareness can involve the ability to identify words and also a move from understanding language as an implicit set of rules which are used without conscious thought to a more formal understanding of the rules of language.

SUMMARY

The change from non-verbal to linguistic communication which occurs in the first few years of life is dramatic and largely unaided by formal teaching. A few minutes' thought about the communication of a three-month-old infant and that of a thirty-month-old shows that there is a massive change in the form of communication. These changes involve all aspects of communication; the thirty-month-old can produce the words of their mother tongue and imitate words they hear with comparative ease, they are much more sophisticated in using language to achieve their pragmatic goals, they understand the semantics of speech and non-verbal communication, and they are able to use many grammatical rules. The changes may not be as extreme but language development continues to adolescence and beyond. In the next chapter we consider theories about language development. This involves an examination of ideas about why children are able to acquire language in such a short space of time when their other cognitive processes are still very limited in capacity.

Chapter 2

Mechanisms of Language Development

The ability to use language is a skill that has had a profound impact on human beings. It has had an impact in the historical sense of allowing us to effectively communicate with one another and develop skills which go far beyond those found in other species. It also has a profound impact in the individual sense of allowing children to communicate, think and learn in a very efficient way that is not tied to the here-and-now of everyday experience. Given the importance of language to us as a species, it is not surprising that the subject attracts a vast amount of research interest, debate and controversy.

This chapter discusses the way that children become able to use linguistic communication that involves a system of grammatical rules. Much of the research on early child language concentrates on this issue, partly because in many ways this is the most difficult aspect of language development to be explained (for a discussion of the other communicative skills used in language see Chapter 1). Although our phonological abilities in producing sounds are sophisticated and complex, some other species such as birds learn to develop the appropriate set of sounds to communicate with other members of their species. Similarly, one can argue that although our conceptual system and use of semantics is sophisticated, other animals appear to have concepts of the world around them and their communication can be considered to have 'meaning'. It is also the case that the pragmatics of communication are not uniquely human, for example chimpanzees are reported to use deceit in order to achieve a particular goal. However, no other species uses a system of grammatical rules to produce such a range of communication.

Virtually all experts agree that humans would not be able to accomplish use of complex grammatical rules if we did not possess certain innate cognitive abilities which we have inherited as human beings, in the same way that we have inherited our ability to walk upright. However, there are major disagreements about two inter-related issues: the precise form of our inherited language ability and whether environmental experiences assist language acquisition. This chapter considers these issues in some detail as they have implications for the type of interventions that should be used with children, but as we will see, experts are still some way from agreeing about the answers. Before addressing these questions, in the next section we will briefly consider an issue which is often ignored in child language research – the way children can break into the language code.

THE CHANGE FROM NON-LINGUISTIC TO LINGUISTIC COMMUNICATION

How do children identify the different grammatical classes of words (nouns, verbs, etc.) when these are not clearly marked in the speech they hear? For example, in English, there does not seem to be any consistent linguistic clue which will enable children to identify nouns. A noun can appear at various positions in an utterance, and there is no word ending which only identifies nouns – the plural for nouns is '-s', but '-s' is also an ending for some verbs and adjectives.

Proposals about the way meaning (i.e. semantics) provides a basis for this process were made by a variety of investigators in the early 1980s. Steven Pinker's (1987; 1989) proposals about semantic bootstrapping, that is pulling oneself up by the bootstraps, is one of the most detailed and widely known. He proposed that the meanings of many words are acquired from hearing them used in particular settings, and he proposed that children can understand the meaning of an utterance from the context and the meaning of individual words. Thus, he supposed that working out the meaning of words provides the first steps in being able to work out the grammar of a language. He also suggested that identifying grammatical classes of words is helped because children instinctively know that the meaning of some words is related to their grammatical function; for example, names for concrete objects and people are universally nouns. Another feature of Pinker's explanation is that once a child has identified the way that a particular grammatical group of words is used, then if an unknown word is used in a similar way, children will use their existing grammatical knowledge when they use the unknown word in new circumstances. This explains how children are able to take an unknown word like 'wug' when shown one object, and produce an appropriate plural when shown two objects, even though the children have never heard the word 'wugs' (Berko, 1958).

Pinker admits there are problems with the semantic bootstrapping idea, such as: not all links between meaning and grammar are universal; speech to children may include a number of complex utterances which would make semantic bootstrapping much more difficult; the incorrect interpretation of contextual information may produce grammatical errors; and no account is taken of individual differences. Pinker's later proposals have included other types of information such as the sound pattern and word order providing clues about grammar. In addition, he favours a process which involves both a top down (working with given assumptions about language structure) and bottom up (working with the elements of language and trying to work out the overall pattern of rules) processing of information to explain how children make progress with this very difficult problem.

Unfortunately, it is still the case that the change from non-linguistic communication to language is not well understood. However, research and theory should alert us to the potential difficulty that some children have in progressing to using grammatical rules. As we will discuss in Chapter 4, some children, such as those with Down syndrome, seem to have difficulties with mastering this aspect of language.

COMMONSENSE EXPLANATIONS OF LANGUAGE ACQUISITION

Often if you ask people how children are able to learn to speak, they say it is because children learn to imitate the speech they hear. Obviously there is a relation between the speech children hear and the speech they produce, but current research and theory does not indicate that imitation plays a major role. For one thing, as we have already pointed out, language allows the production of an infinite number of sentences, many of which a child has never heard. Consequently, imitation does not explain how children are able to be creative in their use of language. There are also a number of reports of the difficulty of teaching children language by asking them to imitate. The following is a famous example of this:

Child:	Nobody don't like me.
Mother:	No, say 'Nobody likes me.'
Child:	Nobody don't like me.

This sequence was repeated eight times.

Mother:	Now listen carefully, say 'NOBODY LIKES ME.'
Child:	Oh! Nobody don't like*S* me. (McNeil, 1966)

Another explanation is that children simply learn the rules of language from hearing the speech around them. Researchers have two quite different views about the way this might occur. According to one view, children are able to use language because they have inherited information about the grammatical structure of all human languages. Their own grammar develops as they identify each rule of their mother tongue from the range of all possibilities. The other view claims that children work out the grammatical rules of language from the speech they hear because they possess general capacities for the processing of complex information. An associated claim is that the way we speak to children makes this task less difficult.

GRAMMATICAL RULES AS AN INHERITED CAPACITY

Noam Chomsky has been very influential in setting the theoretical agenda for research in child language and in developing views about the way inherited abilities enable humans to acquire language. One important feature of his argument is that language is a rule-governed behaviour which involves the capacity to use a finite number of elements (i.e. words) to produce an infinite number of messages; this is achieved by using different combinations of the elements. Furthermore, Chomsky (1965; 1986) supposes that language acquisition is possible because children have inherited knowledge about the grammars which form a basis for human language. His views caused a move away from environmental explanations of language learning in favour of innate (i.e. inherited) processes which require little in the way of special help from adults, and from ignoring children's internal cognitive processes to putting these at the centre of theory.

Research and discussion in the 1960s and 1970s was strongly influenced by these ideas. One of the important proposals was that children possess a *language acquisition device* (LAD) which enables them to identify the grammatical rules that are in the speech they hear. The LAD was not described in any detail; however, fundamental to its operation was having access to the grammatical rules of all human languages. This was termed the access to a *universal grammar*. Consequently, it was believed that the difficulty children faced in acquiring language was not in working out the grammatical rules from first principles, but in working out which set of rules is present in the language they hear. These proposals were put forward because the grammars of language were seen as such a complex set of rules that it would be impossible for children to work these out from scratch, especially as children do not seem to receive any formal teaching about the language they hear.

There were also important proposals about the structures which enable humans to put together words and make a grammatically correct sentence. The most important of these were the *deep structure* and the *surface structure components*. Deep structure can be thought of as the incompletely formed utterance; it contains the elements of speech (words and other linguistic elements) which can be put together to make a grammatical sentence by the use of the appropriate rules. In some ways the deep structure representation can be seen as being similar to the basic meaning of an utterance. The grammatically correct sentence is a surface structure representation which is then changed into the set of sounds involved in speech. Comprehension was believed to involve the reverse of this whole process. This distinction was made because sometimes the same surface structure as in 'Flying planes are dangerous', can have two different meanings, and this could be accounted for by different representations in the deep structure. There can also be different surface structures which have the same deep structure, as in 'The boy kicked the ball' and 'The ball was kicked by the boy'.

RECENT PROPOSALS ABOUT INNATE CAPACITIES

The proposals about a LAD generated considerable interest, and experiments were conducted to evaluate the ideas. Gradually it became apparent that there were problems with these and related ideas. As a result, a new theory was developed using some of the ideas that have just been described. The new set of proposals has been termed *government and binding theory* (from the title of a book by Chomsky, 1981) or *principles and parameters theory* (PPT, from the terms used in the theory). This theory still claims that children possess inherited abilities which allow them to acquire language, but provides more details about the mechanism of language acquisition.

The new theory was influenced by the assumption that some features of language are universal across the world; these are claimed to be represented by a set of linguistic principles (e.g. it is thought that all languages contain nouns), whereas other features of languages differ in the rules that they contain. Obviously languages differ in the words that they employ, but their linguistic rules also differ, so that some languages like English use a subject–verb–object word order, other languages like Japanese use a subject–object–verb word order. Such differences in linguistic organization are termed *parametric variation*. According to the new theory, acquiring language involves identifying the correct parameter from a range of innately specified possibilities. This process is seen to be similar to setting a switch to one of several positions, much as you might switch a light on or off. In other words, children are supposed to match the language they hear with models of speech that they already possess. When they find a match for a particular feature of language then they start to use this form of speech. This process is termed *parameter setting*. As there is a large number of dimensions on which languages vary, it has been supposed that there can be a number of parameters waiting to be set. It is also claimed that in some instances the setting of a parameter will have an effect on other parts of the language system, that other characteristics which are associated with the parameter are also set and used by children.

The fact that children's early speech is not grammatically correct and the fact that their language develops over time has resulted in debate about the precise nature of the parameter setting process. Discussion has focused on two different mechanisms. In one case it is supposed that children have all the principles and parameters available from the very beginning of language learning, but peripheral problems (such as identifying parts of speech and memory limitations) prevent children from fully utilizing this knowledge (Clahsen, 1992). As a result, children's speech is an imperfect version of adult speech, but it gradually becomes closer to the adult form as with increasing age these peripheral problems are overcome. This is sometimes known as the *continuity hypothesis.*

An alternative proposal is that initially children do not have access to all their inherited linguistic knowledge, but principles and parameters become available to be set as children become older (Felix, 1992). This has been termed the *maturation hypothesis.* The predictions from both these models are very similar; however, they are based on quite different mechanisms. An example of the type of research and discussion of such issues is given in Box 2.1. We also should note that there are indications that the parameter setting account is being replaced. The newer ideas suggest that children learn the grammatical rules associated with individual words and that this provides the basis for their ability to produce speech.

The telegraphic speech of children speaking English usually does not contain the subject of the utterance (e.g. 'want milk' is spoken rather than 'I want milk'). In some other languages this is an acceptable form of speech (e.g. in Italian). Parameter setting was applied to these findings with a proposal that when English-speaking children start to use language they assume that their mother tongue is like Italian. This was coupled with a claim that if children cannot yet make a decision about which parameter setting should be used then they will employ a 'default' parameter. Thus, the use of a default parameter in English-speaking children would result in the use of telegraphic speech which is similar in grammatical structure to Italian. The possibility was also considered that this might occur in children learning other languages. Subsequent research has, however, shown that matters are more complex than this. For one thing, Italian has word endings which indicate the subject of an utterance. In addition, although subjectless utterances are rare in English-speaking children, they are used sometimes, and used more often than in Italian-speaking children. Thus, although the idea of a default parameter is still an interesting idea, subsequent research findings have not provided convincing support.

A different and interesting alternative view has been put forward by Andrew Radford. He supposes that the telegraphic speech of young children is due to their only having several parameters which are set, and that the blossoming of language between two and two-and-a-half years is because more parameters become able to be set at these ages.

Box 2.1: Explanations about the telegraphic speech

A problem facing the parameter setting explanation is how to account for the acquisition of sign languages. These contain grammatical rules which are the same as those present in spoken language (see Chapter 6). Thus, a comprehensive version of parameter setting has to suppose that children are able to identify the linguistic structure in both speech and in hand movements, and then relate this to a set of universal grammatical principles. Although this is logically possible, it does seem to considerably increase the amount of information which has to be genetically coded. There is also an issue about the way bilingual children are able to acquire two or more languages and whether the same parameter can be set in different positions for two different languages.

Most of the research about parameter setting has concerned typical children, but there have been some attempts to use these ideas to account for children's language difficulties. One suggestion is that children with specific language impairments (see Chapter 3) are not able to set some of the language parameters and this results in their language problems. For example a great deal of interest was generated by the claim that a number of members of a family who had language problems could produce the irregular past tense form of verbs (e. g. 'go' → 'went'), but were not able to produce the regular form ('kiss' → 'kissed'). This was consistent with the idea that these people were not able to set the parameter required for these and other operations. However, since these claims have been made there has been controversy about whether the language problems are as neatly defined as was first supposed; if there are more general language problems then this weakens the claim that problems with parameter setting is the cause of the language impairments.

At a more general level, it is not particularly clear from the work on parameter setting how children with language difficulties should be assisted. At one extreme it might be maintained that in the absence of a parameter then there is little that can be done. However, it might also be claimed that increasing the language input of the grammatical forms which should be acquired next is the most sensible form of assistance.

As we have seen, the idea of parameter setting has been very influential in providing the agenda in research about language acquisition. However, opinions about PPT have tended to be polarized. Advocates of the theory see it as providing a framework for understanding language acquisition and of providing a direction for research. They argue that it gives a coherent theory about the acquisition of grammatical rules which is lacking in most other approaches. Furthermore, it makes sense that humans have a set of cognitive operations which allow them to acquire any human language. However we, like others, worry about the plausibility of the parameter setting approach, in biological and physiological terms. It is difficult to think of a realistic biological model that operates in the brain for the process which involves a considerable amount of innate information that can be set in operation merely by hearing the speech of others. Furthermore, it is possible that children may be provided with more help than the parameter setting account supposes, and as a result perhaps such a powerful innate device is unnecessary. We turn to this issue in the next sections.

DOES SPEECH TO YOUNG CHILDREN HELP THEIR LANGUAGE DEVELOPMENT?

Some of the claims made about the LAD supposed that it was such a powerful process that children could simply listen to any human speech and acquire language. The speech between adults is often difficult to process, it has numerous pauses which distort the grammatical structure, it is abstract in nature and employs a wide range of grammatical rules. However, speech to young children is simplified in a number of ways when compared to adult-to-adult speech. Look at the two short examples of speech below: it is easy to see which example comes from speech to children and which from speech to an adult; in both cases the pair have just finished watching a television programme.

Adult 1 with child or adult?	*Adult 2 with child or adult?*
'Was that fun?'	'What do you think about that?'
'Which bit did you like the best?'	'Tell me, er, what were the best bits for you?'
A reply from child/adult.	*A reply from child/adult.*
'I thought that was fun as well.'	'Yea, I suppose I liked that, it was good.'

There have also been numerous investigations which have documented the way that adults alter their speech to young children. The general findings from these studies are summarized in Table 2.1. All the characteristics of child directed speech (CDS) should make the grammar less complex and the processing of the speech much easier.

Shorter utterances	Three- or four-word utterances common in CDS
Restricted vocabulary	Smaller range of words and these often refer to common objects, activities or actions, fewer adjectives and adverbs
Pauses at end of sentences	The structure of CDS is more clearly marked by pauses than adult-to-adult speech
Slower	Speech to children is about half as fast as speech among adults
Repetitions	About one-fifth of speech to young children involves repetitions of previous utterances
Emphasis of words	Words important for the meaning of speech are emphasized
Verbs usually in the present tense	Morphosyntax is less complex as past and future events rarely talked about with young children
Fewer conjunctions (e.g. 'and', 'with')	Lack of conjunctions makes speech grammatically more simple

Table 2.1: The characteristics of adult speech to young children (CDS)

Research also has revealed that much of the speech to young children consists of small, well-formed phrases with the ends of phrases being marked by the lengthening of vowels, by longer pauses, by the loudness of words and by a change in the pitch of the sounds (how high or low the sounds are). It has even been shown that eight- to ten-month-old infants prefer to listen to speech which has pauses which are inserted at speech boundaries rather than at other positions. Thus, children are given subtle forms of help which could enable the identification of the linguistic boundaries in speech. We do not yet know whether children do in fact make use of this information or whether it is provided in all cultures. However, such non-linguistic information could be of fundamental help in locating the beginning and end of sentences and clauses and thereby providing a first step for the analysis of the grammatical rules of speech.

It is now accepted that we speak differently to children than to other adults; however, there is disagreement about whether these modifications help language acquisition. In an attempt to answer these questions studies have been conducted to find out if mothers who make more simplifications to their speech have children whose language is more advanced (Furrow and Nelson, 1986; Barnes *et al.*, 1983; Scarborough and Wyckoff, 1986; Murray *et al.*, 1990). However, the research has produced mixed findings, with some studies reporting positive effects of simplified speech, while others have reported very few, if any, positive effects. In addition, because these studies were not true experiments it is difficult to draw any firm conclusions about positive findings. Obviously, it was not possible to conduct an experiment where children are randomly given either child-directed speech or adult speech. From an experiment we could be reasonably certain that any differences in children's language was due to the speech that they had heard. The studies that have been conducted have compared families where mothers simplified their speech a lot or simplified it a little. Even if mothers who simplify their speech a lot tend to have children who have more advanced language when they are older, we cannot be certain that the simplifications cause this, because it is possible that the mother's speech might be a consequence rather than a cause of the child being linguistically advanced.

One piece of evidence that suggests that just hearing speech is not sufficient for language acquisition comes from reports of children whose main source of speech is television, either because their parents are deaf or because they watch the programmes from a different country (Sachs and Johnson, 1976; Snow, 1977). In these cases the children make little or no progress with the language they hear on television. However, the lack of progress may be as much due to this speech not occurring during an active social exchange, as to the speech not being simplified for children.

Questions have also been raised about the universality of the simplifications in speech to young children. Studies by Eleanor Ochs and Bambi Schieffelin (1984; 1995) suggest that there are groups of people who do not modify their interaction with infants in the same way that we do in the West. For example the Kaluli of Papua New Guinea are described as talking for their young infant rather than treating the child as a conversational partner. A typical interaction involves a baby sitting on her mother's lap and facing outwards, the mother will then speak to other people as if she is the infant. In this way the infant is treated as establishing social relationships with other people. Furthermore, the mother's speech is not related to the activities of the infant as it is in most Western families. Later, when a child starts to use the words for mother and breast, they are considered sufficiently developed to be formally taught language. This involves the adult saying a model utterance and the child being told to repeat it. The important point about these observations is that the same types of simplification seen in Western families do not always seem to be present in other cultures.

However, these cross-cultural observations and the conclusion that children do not need a modified environment in which to acquire language are not accepted without question. For one thing, modifications of adult speech to children are found in a number of different language groups (ranging from Apache to Arabic), and even children as young as four years of age will simplify their speech to an infant (Ferguson, 1964; Shatz and Gelman, 1973). It would also seem that many of the modifications of speech to young children are very well adapted to infant capacities, as infants prefer to listen to speech which is higher in pitch and has a more sing-song quality (Fernald *et al.,* 1989). Furthermore, there have been concerns with the accuracy of cross-cultural studies as translators often need to be employed, and whether infants might receive some simplified speech in these cultures from, for example, other children (Harris, 1992).

These findings about CDS raise an obvious question about whether we should modify our speech to young children. There is no easy answer to this as the research findings are not conclusive. Our own belief is that if a culture is using a certain pattern of early social interaction then it should only be changed if there are extremely good reasons based on research findings or other arguments. As we will see in the next section, there is even more difficulty in deciding whether and in what way we should speak to children with language delays.

THE CHARACTERISTICS OF SPEECH TO CHILDREN WITH LANGUAGE DELAYS

Adults' speech to children with both physical and language delays and learning difficulties tends to differ from that to other children. The adults' speech, although it is modified to the children's level of language or cognitive functioning, has often been observed to be more directive and less responsive than to children without learning disabilities (Maurer and Sherrod, 1987). Broadly speaking, directiveness involves the use of instructions and commands, responsiveness concerns the replies to child communication. There has been discussion about whether this phenomenon is an appropriate or inappropriate adaptation to children's needs, whether it is caused by the lack of conversational responsiveness and inattention on the child's part, and whether the lack of child responsiveness is the result of the adults' conversational style (Marfo, 1990).

A more directive style of speech in typical children is associated with poorer vocabulary development (Tomasello and Farrar, 1986). An implication of this is that a directive style will have the same effect on children with learning disabilities. Not everyone agrees with this conclusion and arguments have been put forward against a too ready acceptance of the idea that directive styles are an inappropriate and harmful aspect of interaction with children who have disabilities, especially as we have good evidence that, in general, carers are sensitive to the communicative needs of their children (Marfo, 1990). There is also the argument that we should always be cautious in taking findings from typical children and unquestioningly extrapolating them to other children. A further complication is that the effects of these forms of speech may depend on the abilities of the child, and what may be appropriate for less able children may be inappropriate with more able children.

The global characterization of speech to children as directive has given way to more detailed observations. For instance, some researchers have found directives tended to be used to encourage appropriate object-related play and compliance. As children with learning disabilities are less likely to sustain attention in a topic and less likely to initiate conversation, these characteristics are likely to result in adult directiveness. However, it should be noted that in a study of children who are deaf, that a directive style had effects on their conversational abilities (Power, Wood and Wood, 1990). An intervention which reduced the directiveness of teachers of deaf children had the effect of increasing child initiatives and preparedness to talk.

Thus, there is still uncertainty about whether a directive style of interaction is an inappropriate strategy with children who have learning disabilities and whether such a style impairs development. Like the study of the effects of adult–child speech, it is going to be difficult to obtain an answer to these seemingly simple questions. It is also clear that such answers are important for giving advice to parents and for the design of intervention programmes. For the moment it may be that the best advice is to observe the particular child and note the ways in which he/she responds to different styles of speech (see Chapter 7), and at the same time bear in mind that children with disabilities may need more time and encouragement if they are to take part and gain from verbal exchanges.

THE ROLE OF FEEDBACK

One of the assumptions made in parameter setting theories is that children are only supplied with examples of language and not given any feedback about the mistakes they make. It is further argued that the lack of feedback, or as it is sometimes termed *negative evidence*, makes it impossible to acquire language without the possession of extra innate information. This is because a child might choose an incorrect grammatical rule, and as they would never be told that this is incorrect, they would never change their grammar. Such reasoning has been used to support arguments that language acquisition cannot be accomplished merely on the basis of information from the environment.

A classic study by Roger Brown and Camille Hanlon (1970) examined the reactions of adults to ungrammatical speech produced by young children. They found that any overt correction of grammatical errors was extremely rare, if a child said 'He goed', adults were likely to accept this and not reply 'That's incorrect, you should say "He went"'. Adults were much more likely to provide overt corrections to semantic errors which concerned factual matters (e.g. the use of a wrong name). Thus, the study appeared to confirm that children do not receive corrections about grammatical errors, and as a result this supported arguments about a need for innate knowledge.

A series of studies in the 1980s confirmed these findings, but also indicated that adults make different replies to grammatically correct and incorrect children's utterances (Hirsch-Pasek *et al.*, 1984; Demetras *et al.*, 1986; Penner, 1987; Bohannon and Stanowicz, 1988; Bohannon *et al.*, 1990). In general it was found that if children made a grammatical mistake then the adult was likely to follow this with a question or an expansion of the child's utterance which might very well include the correct form of the utterance. On the other hand, if the utterance was grammatically correct the adult was more likely to follow this with a continuation of the topic of conversation. It was argued that these different reactions provided an important source of feedback to children. It was also argued that the interruption of the flow of conversation by asking questions and expanding on the child's speech might put pressure on children to produce utterances which allowed conversation to proceed smoothly. Another feature that was noted in several studies was that although adults' exact repetitions of children's speech were comparatively rare, these usually followed a grammatically correct child utterance. This, it can be argued, sends an implicit message that the utterance was correct. In addition, children have been found to be more likely to repeat the parents' expansions than other parental utterances.

The idea that such feedback can be an aid to language acquisition has been dismissed by some investigators (Morgan and Travis, 1989; Pinker, 1989). They argue that the probabilistic nature of the feedback means that even if children are aware that the adult response conveys relevant information, they cannot be sure from an adult's reply whether a particular utterance was grammatically correct or incorrect. It also has been argued that it is unlikely that children can store all their own utterances together with adults' reactions, and this would be necessary to make full use of the information that is provided. In addition, questions have been raised about whether this is a universal process which occurs in all human societies; if it does not occur in some societies then it cannot be essential for language acquisition. Even here there is disagreement about whether or not such processes are universal.

Some investigations have revealed that children are more likely to repeat an adult utterance which is an expansion than other utterances (Farrar, 1991). This, at the very least, indicates that children are processing the information in the adult expansion. More convincing support for the benefit of expansions comes from Matthew Saxton (1997). He has been able to show, in an experiment using nonsense words, that five-year-olds are better able to learn grammatical rules from expansions than from just hearing examples of the rules. He argues that children learn from expansions because they recognize the difference (a 'contrast') between their own speech and the 'correct' adult utterance. Thus, the expansions provide mini-learning sessions for the child.

What implications does this controversy have for interventions with children who have language difficulties? It is quite difficult to consciously repeat or expand speech according to whether or not it contains a grammatical error. As a result, it would not be easy to institute such responses even if we had strong evidence about the benefits of feedback. On the other hand, there seems to be little in the way of argument that should dissuade adults from using expansions and repetitions, and, after all, there is the possibility that they could provide some form of assistance. Our own feelings are that a responsive and encouraging style of interaction which sometimes expands and repeats children's utterances is likely to provide a supportive environment for language learning, but that language is more likely to be acquired when it is part of the 'game' of conversation than a lesson.

CONNECTIONIST NETWORKS AND LANGUAGE ACQUISITION

The parameter setting explanation of language acquisition involves ideas about special cognitive operations which are specific to the processing of speech. A contrasting viewpoint has been put forward by those who have used *connectionist networks, neural networks* and *parallel distributed processes* (the terms are often used interchangeably) to model language acquisition. This research attempts to discover whether general learning processes are sufficient to enable language acquisition to take place (see Plunkett *et al.* 1997). Computer programs are designed to mimic the complexity of information processing in the brain. As a result, there are many inter-connections between an input message and some form of output. In studies of language acquisition computers are usually given speech which concerns a specific aspect of grammar, e.g. they might be given verbs in the present tense and have to learn to produce the past tense form. The computer is given speech which is converted into a numeric form. The speech is processed at the input layer (see Figure 2.1), and the hidden units in Figure 2.1 affect the strength of the connection between the input and output. At first the computer makes what can be thought of as a 'guess' at which response is correct (at this stage the hidden units are usually set so they behave in a random manner). After this guess the computer usually is given information about whether its response was correct or incorrect. Typically, if the response is correct the tendency to produce that response (and related ones) is strengthened by altering the influence of the appropriate hidden units; if the response is incorrect the tendency is weakened. This process is known as back-propagation. Computers are 'trained' by being repeatedly provided with feedback about their responses to the input. Such training has enabled computers to learn various features of language such as the past tense of verbs. It should be noted that few people claim that the computer programs exactly imitate the way children acquire language; rather this work enables people to investigate whether language acquisition can occur by a process of learning and whether the speech to children contains information which would allow this learning to take place. There is also interest in connectionist networks because they can learn to produce elements of the morpho-syntax of a language without being given any rules, and without there being any rules within the network (unlike parameter setting accounts).

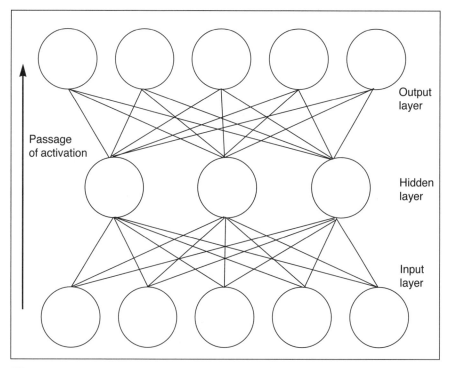

Figure 2.1: A simple connectionist network (many networks have considerably more input, hidden and output units)

One of the first examples of connectionist modelling of language was conducted by Rumelhart and McClelland (1986) in relation to the way children learn the past tense form of verbs. The computer was given a series of examples of the present tense of English verbs, for each verb that was presented the computer selected which of various forms of the past tense was correct. The computer was then given information about whether its choice was indeed correct or incorrect. The computer program did not form a direct association between the present tense of a verb and the past tense of the same verb, as most previous models of learning have supposed. Rather, the computation of the associations was a much more complex process involving a network of associations, so that a number of parallel connections could be modified as the result of feedback. Furthermore, connectionist networks which are trained in this way can produce the correct form of the past tense from verbs which they have not been given before. It is important to emphasize that the connectionist model was able to produce behaviour which is similar to using a grammatical rule, but this was achieved by using a single process which did not involve the use of a rule. The researchers compared the computer's performance with that of children. At the time it was thought that the computer's learning followed the correct and incorrect use of the past tense by children.

This and other work has resulted in a more careful analysis of children's speech (see Plunkett, 1995). It would seem that there is an initial error-free period when children are able to produce regular verbs (e.g. start*ed*, finish*ed*) and irregular verbs (e.g. went, was) with very few errors. This is followed by intermittent errors which involve the *over-regularization* of irregular verbs (e.g. 'go-*ed*'), the verbs which are over-regularized tend to be the low frequency irregular verbs. Subsequent connectionist models of the past tense have been able to mimic this pattern of development and this seems to have been possible because the irregular verbs are much more common than the regular ones (think how often you say 'went' rather than 'started'). In other words, connectionist networks (and possibly children) are able to learn irregular verbs because they are so common in the speech input, and this learning occurs despite the fact that children also abstract a general principle of adding '-ed' to regular verbs. There are strong indications that this abstraction of a general principle occurs when vocabularies reach a critical size.

Connectionist networks also have successfully 'learnt' a number of other grammatical rules. Of particular interest have been connectionist models which have learnt rules involving a grammatical relation between different words which are separate from one another in an utterance (e.g. what is sometimes termed the agreement between a noun and a verb). This research is still at a relatively primitive stage, but the findings hold out the promise of identifying mechanisms that can learn those grammatical structures which have proved to be very difficult to model when using other techniques.

This and other research has challenged the parameter setting explanation in several ways. First, the learning mechanisms are not specialized for language, these are general learning processes that can be used to model linguistic and non-linguistic cognitive processes. Second, the computer does not contain any linguistic rules (all the learning is in terms of mathematical adjustments which govern the choice of output), yet the computer produces behaviour that appears as if it was governed by rules. Third, there is no specific innate knowledge of the rules of grammar supplied to the computer. Thus, it would seem that non-specialized but sophisticated learning systems can acquire linguistic forms in a very different way from that suggested in PPT theory. Interestingly, the more recent connectionist work has emphasized that language emerges as a product of innate capacities to process information which is coupled with particular frequencies of grammatical forms in the child's environment. This has been coupled with arguments that children learn language by matching the form of speech they hear with the function it serves in communication.

However, there are two serious issues which need to be resolved before connectionist accounts can be regarded as providing a convincing general account of language acquisition. The first is the issue of feedback. Most connectionist networks are given feedback about the correctness of every single response that they make; as we have seen, this does not occur with children. One idea that goes some way to overcoming this objection involves children as they listen to speech, making predictions about what will come next. In this way, they would be provided with the correct version of language in relation to their predictions. However, as yet we have no evidence that children actually do this. The other issue is that most connectionist modelling involves a single linguistic form (e.g. past tense) and speech used by the computer is usually selected to only contain these forms. Children on the other hand seem to learn a number of linguistic forms at the same time (e.g. tense, plurals, word order, etc.) from a very complex set of information. It remains to be established whether connectionist systems can be devised to deal with a much higher level of complexity in the input and output.

Connectionist modelling is still in its infancy and so it is unclear what contribution this approach will make to our understanding of children with language difficulties. One argument put forward by its advocates is that we find out more about linguistic processes when we have to clearly specify the type of input that children receive, and have to test whether what the speech computers produce corresponds to the development of language in children. The work has already suggested that the acquisition of regular and irregular forms is possible because of the distribution of these forms in the speech to children. Such work emphasizes that the type of speech input to children will influence which grammatical forms are learnt and at what age. A more direct application has been research which has examined the effects of brain damage. Computer models have been trained to learn certain forms of speech, and then parts of the connectionist system are destroyed to mimic the effect of brain damage. The computer network produced learning curves similar to that of the children with brain damage.

SUMMARY

Although we have reviewed important explanations of language acquisition, for us, none is entirely satisfactory. The strength of the parameter setting approach is that it specifies innate capacities that might enable language acquisition to take place. Further, it is consistent with the idea that there is something special about language which makes it different from many other of our thought processes. However, the setting of parameters seems to be a crude and biologically unlikely process. Furthermore, the theory is very difficult to test and does not provide particularly clear suggestions for intervention. One implication of the theory is that further exposure to the target grammatical expression might help the parameter to be set; another possibility is that the difficulty with the parameter setting process might represent a biological limitation.

The explanations which stress the way that children's social environment can assist language acquisition capture an important aspect of care-giving. This research is able to account for the growth of semantic and pragmatic communication skills, but has difficulty in explaining the way grammar is acquired. In addition, it has been surprisingly difficult to show that adults who more frequently employ particular features of speech help children to acquire language at an earlier age. An added complication to working out the role of environmental input is that language might be acquired by a variety of routes and sources, so that an absence of one type of information does not necessarily result in delays. The connectionist approach provides an interesting alternative to parameter setting. In some ways it can provide a compromise between extreme claims from nature and nurture. The approach provides what is equivalent to an innately specified set of cognitive operations, which process information from the environment. However, it is still unclear how much we can learn from the use of connectionist models; they have shown that computer programs can learn to produce grammar from speech input, but it is going to be difficult to know whether children process information in the same way.

Chapter 3

Specific Speech and Language Disorders

The majority of children acquire language in an effortless fashion. To the joy and amazement of parents, children progress from babbling in the first year to the complex use of grammatical utterances by the time they enter school. However, for a substantial minority the language acquisition process is effortful and often requires additional, specialized help. Difficulties can occur with both acquiring language and using the language system to communicate. As an example, consider the following description of Joe. Joe is an 8-year-old child in a mainstream class explaining to his peers about a visit to the doctor:

Teacher	'Nice to see you back Joe. Where were you yesterday?'
Joe	*No response.*
Teacher	'Where did you go yesterday Joe?'
Joe	'Uhn Doctor mnh mnh doctor.'
Teacher	'Why did you visit the doctor?'
Joe	'I sore tummy.'
Teacher	'Did the doctor give you any medicine?'
Joe	'Yes, I sleep all night.'

At 8 years of age, Joe had failed to develop the language skills that we would expect in an average 4-year-old; acquiring the language system has been a long-drawn-out process for him. His speech is typical of children with language difficulties. He often omits the endings of words such as *ed* and leaves out prepositions, such as 'on'. His vocabulary is small for his age and his speech is slow and often dysfluent. Yet there is no obvious reason for Joe's poor language skills; his hearing is normal, his non-verbal abilities are average and there are no physical impairments that would affect his speech production.

Children such as Joe can seem quite mysterious to teachers and parents. Even when help is requested, clarification of the child's problems can be complex. Speech and language difficulties also raise complex issues for the assessment of a child's special educational needs (see Chapter 7). Most conventional assessment procedures contain large amounts of language and therefore language difficulties compound the assessment procedures. Even supposedly non-verbal assessment procedures can contain subtle linguistic elements. Deciding on the most effective and economical support can raise a range of issues:

- What precise help does the child need?
- How should this help be provided?
- Where should the help be provided?
- Should the curriculum be modified to provide the child with full access?

Each of these questions requires careful analysis and the ultimate decisions will depend on the child and the resources available. Children with specific speech and language difficulties can have a diverse set of problems. They are most often characterized by speech problems, expressive language which is limited in vocabulary and grammatical development, as well as comprehension deficits that may not be obvious. Some children appear to have difficulties confined to a particular component of language, whereas others have difficulties that pervade many aspects of language and communication.

The chapter begins by describing the nature of the children's difficulties and the problems that exist in accurate identification of specific speech and language problems. To support the children's language learning it is important to understand the nature of their language problems. This is followed by an examination of the current state of the research literature in addressing these issues. Language problems do not only affect the language system, and evidence is provided about the ways in which language difficulties affect wider aspects of the children's lives.

A PRIMARY LANGUAGE PROBLEM

A language difficulty is identified when a child has problems in the acquisition and development of oral language. Language and communication difficulties occur for a variety of reasons, including organic causes (such as hearing loss (see Chapter 6) or other physical disabilities), early language experiences or as part of a general difficulty in learning and cognitive functioning (see Chapter 4). This chapter considers the group of children who experience language difficulties without any of these causes. A precise understanding of the children's developmental patterns and the reasons that these difficulties occur have eluded practitioners and researchers for many years. There is growing evidence that language difficulties occur in families, thus establishing a genetic link for some language problems.

The children and their difficulties have been described in a variety of ways. This confusion is reflected in the variety of terms that have been used to describe the children. These include *developmental aphasia, specific language impairment,* and *developmental disorders of language*. This list is not all-inclusive and more recently new terms have been added to describe particular types of problem. New, more specific descriptions have begun to emerge, including *specific grammatical language impairment* or *word-finding difficulties*. Unfortunately, little consensus exists about the appropriate terminology. In this chapter we use the term 'specific speech and language difficulty' to describe children who have *primary* speech and language difficulties.

Identifying a specific speech and language difficulty

The identification of language difficulties, *per se*, is problematic. Conventional classification systems used by doctors and psychiatrists include categories related to specific language problems. The *International Classification of Diseases and Disorders* (ICD 10) (World Health Organization, 1990) describes the category of 'specific developmental disorders of speech and language' while the *Diagnostic and Statistical Manual of Mental Disorders* (DSM-IV) (American Psychiatric Association, 1994) uses the term 'developmental language disorder'. The criteria to make these specific diagnoses centre on three issues:

1. Performance on a language test below the child's chronological age.
2. A discrepancy between the child's language skills and their non-verbal abilities.
3. Language abilities that cannot be attributed to any other cause.

Each of these criteria will be discussed in turn. The basic format of the assessment process is discussed in Chapter 7. The first criterion captures the essential notion that the child's language must be delayed from the norm or present a different pattern from the norm. At one level this should be obvious. However, the norm itself is not easy to characterize. There is considerable diversity in the rate at which children acquire language, especially in the pre-school period. Thus, there is no exact point that divides normal development from that which should cause concern. As we shall see in Chapter 7, whether a child is deemed to be lagging behind their age-matched peers will depend on the assessments used. Having established a delay, this on its own is not sufficient to decide that a child has a *specific* problem with language. It is also necessary to consider the child's developmental profile more generally.

The second point narrows the potential group of children by requiring that a discrepancy exists between the child's language skills and their non-verbal ability. Traditionally, specific speech and language difficulties have been defined by contrasting an average or above-average non-verbal cognitive ability with oral language skills that are significantly lower. This is called a *discrepancy*. Generally discrepancies in either expressive or receptive language are considered, but the precise language skills to be measured are not specified. Table 3.1 presents the guideline criteria suggested by Whitehurst and Fischel (1994). A standard deviation is a statistical term. Any child who scores one standard deviation from the mean (average) is in the lower 16 per cent for their age, while a child who is two standard deviations below the mean is in the bottom 2 per cent for their age.

	Criteria
Most depressed language score	Two standard deviations below the mean of their age
Least depressed language score	At least one and a half standard deviations below the mean of their age
Non-verbal IQ	No more than one standard deviation below the mean

Table 3.1: Proposed criteria for identifying SLI

The notion of a significant discrepancy is problematic. Firstly, it is important to decide how much of a difference is significant. Aram and his colleagues (1992) have shown that variations in the discrepancy criteria that are used can make a 25 per cent difference in the number of children identified as language 'disordered'. Even with the least restrictive criteria they found that 40 per cent of a sample of children who were defined by clinicians as language disordered would not have been identified as having a language disorder using discrepancy criteria alone. Such a large gap between the judgements of experienced clinicians and diagnostic criteria are worrying. Have the clinicians identified subtle patterns that the conventional assessments miss? Do the assessment procedures involve elements that are difficult for children with language difficulties *per se*? These concerns in combination with other assessment problems mean that clinicians rarely rely on discrepancy criteria alone. As shall be seen, the requirements for research studies of these children are different.

It is also important to realize that, on their own, discrepancies often fail to account for the diversity of children's performance in different language and cognitive tasks. This may be particularly problematic when a child is experiencing an additional learning difficulty. Consequently, while the use of discrepancies may be a helpful framework for structuring an understanding of children's development, the complexity of the identification process gives rise to doubts about the reliability and validity of the procedure. Children who may be having major and specific language problems can be missed with these identification processes.

Perhaps the most commonly used core criteria to identify children with a specific speech and language difficulty is that their language problems *cannot* be explained in terms of other cognitive, neurological or perceptual deficits. A common set of exclusionary criteria is presented in Box 3.1. Effectively children are identified by applying the negative criterion that language difficulties occur without any obvious explanatory factors.

The relatively tight criteria that are used to identify language problems in

To be diagnosed as having a specific speech and language difficulty a child must not have:

- Hearing sensitivity less than 25dB across the frequencies.
- Presence of emotional/behavioural problems.
- History of obvious neurological deficits as reported by parent or teacher.
- Performance IQ below 85 (i.e. below average non-verbal test score).
- Presence of speech motor deficits.

Box 3.1: Common exclusionary criteria

conventional categorization systems often do not fit neatly with the problems that are common in classrooms and nurseries. These children often have additional special needs such as middle ear problems or motor difficulties. Research studies suggest that when strict exclusionary and discrepancy criteria are used, many clinically defined language-impaired children are excluded from the sample. Many factors may contribute to this mismatch between clinical and research definitions of specific language difficulties, including variations in professional judgement, measurement problems, and differences in the understanding of the core problems (see Dockrell *et al.*, 1997).

This can cause major problems for practitioners and the children they see. The Code of Practice (DfE, 1994) on the identification and assessment of special education needs pays particular attention to speech and language difficulties. A number of key questions are highlighted to ascertain the child's difficulty and their ensuing special educational needs. Two of the five questions refer to discrepancies between actual and expected performance. The specific measures to make this decision are not specified in the code, although there are suggested criteria such as parental report, observation, teacher assessment and standardized assessments such as Standard Attainment Tests. The code offers a more flexible framework through which to interpret the language-based needs of children.

In an attempt to capture the diversity of children who present with speech and language difficulties it is often helpful to consider the child's performance in terms of primary and secondary needs. Primary difficulties are considered to be the child's main problem whereas secondary difficulties are additional problems which can co-occur with the main problem. It is not necessary to assume that the secondary needs are caused by the primary needs, although they may be. Moreover, primary needs may change throughout the course of development. Considerable advances have been made in charting the problems that co-occur for these children. The medical term to describe co-occurrence is 'co-morbidity'. For example, problems in attention and problems with fine and gross motor skills have been noted to co-occur with specific speech and language difficulties.

HOW MANY CHILDREN HAVE A SPECIFIC SPEECH AND LANGUAGE DISORDER?

It is difficult to determine the number of children with a specific disorder. Children with specific speech and language difficulties are not a rarity. However, the numbers reported in the literature vary tremendously. James Law and his colleagues (1998) have carried out a review of all the research in the area and report prevalence estimates in the literature varying from 0.06 per cent to 33.2 per cent. This means that if the larger estimate was correct, in every group of 100 children, on average 33 would have a language difficulty. Whereas, with the smaller estimate there might not be even one child with a problem in the group. Why do the figures vary so widely? It is likely that the variation is the result of four quite different factors:

1. The criteria used to define the language difficulty.
2. Whether discrepancy criteria are included.
3. The age range under consideration.
4. Whether longitudinal data are considered (i.e. information collected from children as they develop).

Prevalence

Reliable prevalence figures depend on clear-cut criteria for identifying difficulties. Children's language develops at different rates; this alone makes it difficult to pick out differences from the norm. Most prevalence studies have focused on pre-school as opposed to school-aged children and use such criteria as no speech at eighteen months or unintelligible speech at school age. Others have focused on the nature of the child's language. Ingram (1972), for example, suggested that signs should include use of abnormal structures and/or processes. It has also been suggested that discrepancies between abilities in different language components could serve as indicators. This is an interesting suggestion since it forces an exploration of the patterns of language skills within an individual child. So, for example, a child who had a large and accurate vocabulary at age 4 but was only producing two-word utterances would be presenting with an uneven profile within her language systems. Profiling approaches also require that cut-off points for atypical patterns be established. The numbers of children identified could vary quite widely depending on how a language difficulty is defined. By combining a whole range of different studies Law *et al.* (1998) concluded that roughly 5 per cent of children have speech problems alone and 6 per cent of children experience speech and language problems.

Age is also a critical dimension in estimating prevalence. What might be regarded as a problem at 4 would not be viewed as such at eighteen months. So age-independent criteria are inappropriate. Studies that follow the changes in children's language profiles are an important way of clarifying the extent and nature of speech and language difficulties. Evidently some children overcome an initial delay, yet for others the pattern of difficulties changes over time (Aram and Nation, 1975; Scarborough and Dobrich, 1990). This is borne out by Bishop and Edmundson (1987), who found that approximately 40 per cent of children who had language problems at 4 years had resolved these problems by the middle of the fifth year. Yet there is no indication that language problems decline appreciably above the age of 10 years. The consensus is that children who are still experiencing difficulties in the school years will continue to have some form of language-based difficulty.

An important addition to these longitudinal studies is a special project in Cambridge, England. The Cambridge Language and Speech project (CLASP) is addressing the normal variation in development (Burden *et al.*, 1996). It is a longitudinal study into the nature, characteristics and outcome of language and psychiatric difficulties in a community sample of children. The researchers constructed a questionnaire addressed to the parents. Such an approach acknowledges that the parents are the ones who are generally most aware of their child's development achievements. The second major aspect of the CLASP study is that children were not included in the study if their language difficulties could be explained in other ways. So children with a learning disability, chronic illness or profound hearing loss were excluded. Following a first stage of identification, children's language, motor skills and current behaviour were assessed. The results of the screening and subsequent assessment indicated that 6.9 per cent of respondents were identified as having a language problem and, as is generally the case, more boys than girls were having problems.

The controversies around prevalence and identification show how difficult it can be to decide when a child's language is 'truly' of cause for concern, that is, their language is sufficiently different to warrant extra help. To some extent the answer to this question depends on the nature of the child's problem. It is also age-dependent, as shall be seen in the section on prognosis. Some would argue that, given the high percentage of pre-school children reported to have language delays, oral language development should take a higher profile in the normal pre-school curriculum. This certainly happens in some European countries. School-age children with language difficulties pose rather different problems. In general it is advisable that if there is any concern about a child's language progress it should be discussed with a trained professional such as a speech and language therapist or a psychologist.

NATURE OF THE LANGUAGE PROBLEMS THAT THE CHILDREN EXPERIENCE

Recent years have witnessed a tremendous growth in the understanding of the characteristics of children with specific speech and language difficulties. It has been shown that the children form a mixed group in terms of language difficulties (Fletcher, 1991; Conti-Ramsden *et al.*, 1997). The fact that these children have a mixed profile of language difficulties has made it very difficult to arrive at a consensus about what characterizes the children's underlying linguistic skills and to offer a consistent explanation of what causes the problems. An important step in developing an understanding of difficulties with the language system has come from accounts that specify the sub-components that are important for effective language use. These sub-components include grammar, vocabulary, phonology and pragmatics (see Chapter 1). The sub-components of the language system are the tools used to create language. Each of the sub-components of the language system can be studied and assessed independently. However, this does not mean that the components work independently. They interact in the overall process of comprehending and producing language and this issue will be discussed at the end of this section.

Delayed or disordered language?

The distinction between a delayed or deviant language system has been drawn by clinicians for a number of years. A delay suggests that the child is acquiring language in a normal fashion but at a slower pace than their age-matched peers. Thus, a quantitative gap exists between the child's skills compared to children of a similar age. In contrast, deviant or disordered language implies a qualitatively different pattern of development, one that differs in terms of the way in which language processing occurs and/or the order in which the language is acquired. On the surface this seems like a straightforward distinction but it is not easy to determine whether a child's language is qualitatively different or not. To do this a detailed account of the normal pattern of development is needed. As yet good normative data do not exist for all components of the language system. Moreover, it is not easy to identify clear cases of asymmetry between subcomponents. Thus, distinguishing delayed development from disordered development is problematic.

Some researchers have argued that the use of language age controls in studies can tell us whether the children with language problems have delayed development (see Box 3.2). However, isolating one component of the language skills of an 8-year-old and comparing it with the skills of a 3-year-old

Normally we compare a child's performance with children of a similar age. This provides chronological age comparisons. An alternative comparison is to compare a child with others who are functioning at a similar level on a particular skill. For example, if we have a 10-year-old child whose vocabulary is at an age equivalent of 5 years 6 months, a vocabulary age match would be typical children with vocabulary ages of 5 years 6 months. This would provide a language age match. This would be one way of establishing whether a child's language differs from the expected developmental pattern. For example, we could ask whether the child provided similar verbal definitions to the language age comparisons. If the child's language performance was similar to other children of 5–6 we could hypothesize that his language was delayed. However, if the child behaved in a different manner from the language age matches we could conclude there is a difference in performance.

Box 3.2: Language age controls

is confounded by the fact that the 8-year-old will have different linguistic experiences and be trying to convey different messages. This will influence both what the child says and how they say it. Equally, a delay in one aspect of the language system may make overall language appear deviant because of an interaction between the components. As an example, consider a child who has difficulties finding the right word to use. This difficulty is described as a word-finding problem. This may be the only aspect of the child's language system that is impaired but it is likely to have a wider impact on communication. For example, the child might develop some unexpected strategies to cope with situations such as providing descriptions for objects or making up words. A more detailed discussion of practitioners' views of word-finding problems can be found in Dockrell *et al.* (1998).

As another example consider Mary, an 8-year-old with poor articulation, who is occasionally misunderstood. To cope with this she had developed the strategy of repeating what she had to say several times – whether or not the listener had understood. Her communication therefore appeared unusual, even though there was a reasonable explanation for what she was doing. Thus, it is possible for a straightforward delay to result in what appears to be disordered language. It is important when introducing the distinction between delayed and different patterns of development that very clear comparisons are made. In the absence of more precise criteria it is best to describe a child's problems in terms of a specific difficulty without making assumptions about deviance or disorder.

The sub-components of the language system

Analysis of children's language has shown that children can have difficulties with each of the sub-components of the language system. The following sections describe the types of problems that have been identified and highlight some of the explanations that have been offered for the problems that occur. Explanations of language problems are presented in two different ways. There are explanations that are language-specific and often focus on the sub-component under investigation. Explanations are also offered at a more general level, which reflects the way the cognitive system works. It is unlikely that there is a single cause for the difficulties being described. The first step is to provide an accurate description of the difficulties children experience; then the possible explanations of why the difficulties occur can be evaluated. There are often several different explanations for why a particular kind of difficulty might occur. A major limitation of simply describing, as opposed to explaining, a linguistic difficulty is that interventions will lack focus (see Chapter 8). Interventions are a very good test of theoretical explanations. Unfortunately, the majority of explanations presented below have not yet been tested by intervention studies.

Figure 3.1 presents schematically how the key components in the language system can be related to each other. Each of these will be considered, starting with basic perceptual features and moving towards issues of representation and communication. At each level it is possible to have problems with either receptive or expressive language. This is a commonly drawn distinction when considering children with language problems but in most cases it may be too extreme. At its simplest level, expressive language difficulties are always easier to detect. Children who have difficulty pronouncing words accurately are described as having verbal dyspraxia. The children seem clear about what they want to say; there are, however, difficulties in planning the motor output. Mispronunciation is easily detected. Equally, when a child is dysfluent or ungrammatical in their speech this is easily noted. It may be much harder to pick out the subtle nuances of misunderstandings that occur in the comprehension of normal conversation either in terms of sentence constituents or pragmatic meaning.

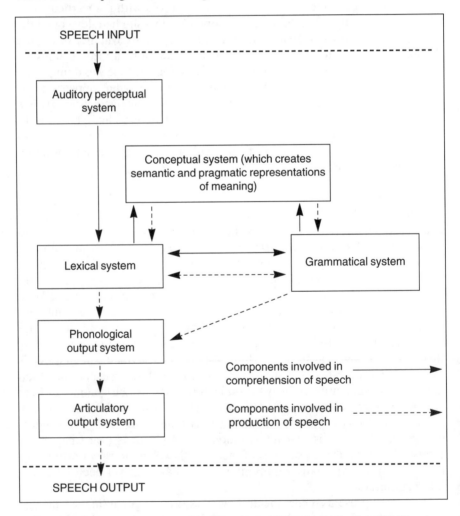

Figure 3.1: Key components in the language system. Source: Dockrell and McShane (1993)

Auditory processing problems

To learn language a child must be able to detect when sounds occur and also discriminate between and categorize sounds. Problems with the early stages of auditory processing are particularly significant for language acquisition. If a child is unable to detect differences between certain speech sounds, such as *t* and *c*, or detect pitch changes, there will be less opportunity to develop accurate speech representations. Difficulties with processing the auditory input can result in a degraded signal being available for phonological representation.

Paula Tallal and her associates (1990, 1996) have spent many years investigating the speech processing patterns of children with language difficulties. Her research team has shown that some children have marked impairments in the ability to perceive rapidly presented verbal material of brief duration. More recently their data suggest that these processing problems can occur with non-verbal material as well.

There is strong evidence to support a processing deficit explanation, yet at present it does not explain all the problems children have with the language system nor does it predict the different patterns of phonological difficulties children can have. For example, it has been established that children with phonological deficits demonstrate auditory processing problems. We also find children with other language difficulties who have normal phonology. This suggests that different types of difficulties contribute to different types of language problems. Moreover, even within the group of children with phonological difficulties, clinical experience suggests that different patterns of problems occur. Nevertheless, these data clearly indicate that even when children can pass hearing tests they may have subtle processing difficulties that will affect language acquisition. The work of Joy Stackhouse and Bill Wells (1997) has provided a range of detailed materials for profiling these subtle speech-based distinctions.

Phonological problems

Children with disordered phonological development continue to face difficulties in producing sounds long after their peers have mastered the sound system. The result of this persistence is a phonological system in which very early processes coexist with later ones. Pam Grunwell (1985) has shown that other patterns also occur: unusual/idiosyncratic processes, variable use of processes and systematic sound preferences. It is possible to identify at least two types of functional articulation disorders where there is no noticeable organic reason for a child's speech to be abnormal. There are those cases in which the child's problem is solely located in the production side – in planning and executing movements involved in producing sound. There are also children who have an inadequate or deviant phonological system. These latter organizational difficulties are referred to as *phonemic difficulties*. As one example, children in this group may not produce a sound correctly in one word yet may use that sound as a substitute for another sound in another word. Thus, they are able to produce the sound but they do not produce it in the appropriate contexts.

If the child's difficulty is only on the output side then there is no reason to assume that the child's syntax should be affected. However, there may be problems with the articulation of particular sounds that have implications for syntax, such as inflections being absent, e.g. *s* and *ed*, or words may be combined in an unusual fashion as in *outside-in* instead of inside-out. The representational problems in cases of phonemic difficulties may create syntactic difficulties because the input received by the grammatical system is likely to be impoverished. For example, many words can have a suffix added to form a new word of a different grammatical class as when *collide* becomes *collision*. Such phonological changes are likely to be hindered among children with phonemic difficulties.

Vocabulary problems
Children with specific speech and language difficulties can have difficulties in both learning new words and producing known words. The children are often delayed in their first use of words. Subsequently, they continue to add new words to their vocabularies at a slower rate than normally developing children. The slow acquisition is mirrored in their reduced understanding of vocabulary items. In addition to general delays in production and comprehension, there is a group of children who have word-finding difficulties. Most people are familiar with the experience of being unable to recall the name of something or someone. This is often described as the 'tip of the tongue' phenomena. For children with word-finding difficulties it is assumed that the word is in their receptive vocabulary but there are significant difficulties in retrieving the word when it is needed.

Since a number of factors are involved in specifying the meaning of a word, difficulties may be caused by more than one determinant. Several explanations of these lexical difficulties exist including:

- *Poor phonological short-term memory*: being unable to remember what has just been said.
- *Under-specified phonological representations*: the sound pattern of the word is not stored fully in memory.
- *A failure to implement word-learning strategies*: failing to use a process to limit the possible options when a new word is encountered.
- *Poorly established semantic representations*: words are not grouped together with other similar words to form concepts.

It is also possible that the precise nature of the difficulties may vary between individual children. One child may have poorly specified phonological representations which makes accessing a word difficult, while another child may have ill-defined concepts. Intervention in each case would be targeted rather differently.

An interesting and important addition to an understanding of children's vocabulary difficulties has been the discovery that greater problems occur with certain word classes. Children with language difficulties tend to use a greater number of uninflected verb forms (i.e. present tense) and have a less diverse verb lexicon than their age-matched peers. It has been argued that while some of the children's other problems may become less significant, their difficulties with verbs are likely to persist. A number of different research teams are attempting to address this problem. It might well be that the children's difficulties with verbs are intricately linked to some of the grammatical difficulties displayed by these children.

Grammatical problems
A large majority of children with specific speech and language difficulties have problems with the syntax of language. Difficulties with the formal aspects of language manifest themselves in a number of ways. Generally there are simplifications in speech output, omissions of function words and short utterances. The production of articles (e.g. *a, the*), prepositions (e.g. *in, on, under*) and pronouns (e.g. *he* and *she*) are omitted, as are the endings of verbs. Careful study of both the child's grammatical constructions and the structures they fail to comprehend is necessary to locate the exact nature of the problem. Again a number of different explanations have been offered to account for the difficulties these children experience, including:

- Perceptual deficits.
- Inability to compute syntactic relations.
- Failure of innate syntactic abilities to mature.

Lawrence Leonard (1989) has suggested that there is some indication that children fail to produce unstressed syllables of shorter duration. This has led to the view that phonological problems could account for the children's difficulties with grammatical morphemes. Others have argued that the children's difficulties in producing grammatically correct language are best explained by difficulties in linking the sentence constituents together. Thus children can manage the plural of a noun because it simply marks the number of an object, i.e. *one apple; two apples*. In contrast, number marking on verbs requires the child to be able to link elements of the sentence together – 'The dog hunts' or 'The dog and cat hunt'. The ending on the verb depends on the subjects of the sentence.

Clarifying the difficulties with comprehension is equally difficult. Heather Van der Lely and her colleagues (1990, 1997) have shown that children with grammatical language difficulties have problems extracting information from sentences that are in a non-standard word order or have complex dependent elements. Identifying these difficulties has required the researchers to develop very precise experimental techniques. In the experiments the child needs to match a sentence with a picture. They need only say 'Yes' or 'No' in relation to the sentences but they can be very complex such as 'Baloo Bear is tickling himself'. Van der Lely argues that the children have specific problems with PPT (see Chapter 2). The syntactic difficulties experienced by these children raise major theoretical issues for researchers. It remains to be seen whether they can be parsimoniously explained by one causal factor.

Pragmatics

More recently practitioners and researchers have considered a range of higher-order linguistic difficulties that can occur. There are several different types of difficulties children experience in producing and understanding language in social situations. Pragmatic difficulties occur when children have problems in engaging in communication, such as taking turns in conversation, using language appropriately or observing the principles of co-operative conversation. Often irrelevant responses to questions are given and the comprehension of connected discourse is impaired. The adults interacting with the children have significant problems in following the conversation and there is a frequent need for clarification. An example from our work will help illustrate the case:

> James was talking with an adult about home. The adult asked James whether he lived in a house or a flat. James replied 'A flat'. The adult then asked 'Which floor do you live on?' James responded with a blank expression. The adult then asked 'Do you live on the ground floor or do you have to walk up stairs?' James replied 'I live in a flat'. The adult again asked 'Yes but which floor? Is there a lift or are there stairs?' James replied 'My floor has lovely carpets in all the rooms.'

There is further evidence that children with specific language impairments have difficulties drawing *inferences*. To make sense of much communication it is necessary to go beyond the information in the words and grammar and draw inferences. A number of studies have shown that children with specific speech and language problems have difficulties making inferences.

This is a topic which has caused practitioners major problems. There are few assessment tools to address these problems and the implications for intervention need to be clearly worked out. Theoretical accounts of these difficulties are still in their infancy. Dorothy Bishop (1997) has provided a clear and incisive review of the area. She identifies three possible theoretical contenders:

- Impairment of information processing.
- Inadequate opportunity for social learning.
- Impairment of social cognition.

Her synthesis of the area is that 'the answer is likely to vary from child to child'. It is important to realize that these children may form a special subgroup of children with speech and language disorders. Some authors have argued that semantic pragmatic disorders are part of the autistic spectrum (see Chapter 4 and Boucher, 1998).

Summary

This section has considered the types of problems children have with the sub-components of the language system. Although the explanations vary they are all tied specifically to the language system and therefore fit with the modular approach to language described in Chapters 1 and 2. Such a modular approach also fits with attempts to identify discrepancies in the child's performance. Describing language as a combination of sub-components offers clarity to aid understanding and precision to devise investigations. On the other hand, it can make language appear piece-meal and fail to provide a complete picture. There may be associated difficulties where particular sub-components or limitations may co-occur. Looking at a single sub-component will fail to show the associated difficulties. By compartmentalizing language in this way there is a danger of failing to consider the functioning of the cognitive system more widely as well as the representational functions that language fulfils.

A WIDER VIEW OF LANGUAGE

Two separate lines of investigation provide an important contrast to the sub-components approach. The first approach attempts to identify subgroups of children with language problems whereas the second searches for explanations outside the language system itself.

Subgroups of children with language difficulties

Painstaking research over the last few decades has helped unpack the multiplicity of difficulties that children can experience and has allowed differentiation of a range of sub-groups. For a long time professionals have tried to deal with the diversity of this group of children by referring to sub-groups. One such example is the work of Rapin and Allen (1987). They proposed six sub-groups based on patterns of clinical presentation:

1. Verbal auditory agnosia, that is problems with comprehension.
2. Verbal dyspraxia, that is limited speech, impaired production of sounds.
3. Phonological programming deficit syndrome, that is speech which is fluent but hard to understand.
4. Phonological-syntactic deficit syndrome, that is mispronunciations and dysfluencies.
5. Lexical-syntactic deficit syndrome, that is word-finding problems and immature syntax.
6. Semantic-pragmatic deficit syndrome, that is understanding and using language.

A brief outline of these subtypes can be found in Bishop (1997). Both DSM-IV (American Psychiatric Association, 1994) and ICD 10 (World Health

Organization, 1990) now identify sub-groups for specific language impairment.

Other researchers have classified children on the basis of their performance on standardized tests. A recent example comes from the work of Gina Conti-Ramsden and her colleagues (1997) in Manchester. They studied 242 7-year-old children attending language units in England. Analysis of the children's test scores revealed six distinct groupings. These sub-groups were similar in nature to those reported by Rapin and Allen. An exciting element of the Manchester study was that the test profiles were complemented by teachers' and speech and language therapists' opinions. The research thereby fulfils both research criteria and practical experience.

Dorothy Bishop (1987) has suggested that a useful way forward is to attempt to describe the children's language in detail through using a linguistic framework. Paul Fletcher (1991) has attempted to do just this. His analysis of already collected data resulted in four different groups:

1. Fluent, few speech errors and adequate clause/phrase structure.
2. Dysfluent and adequate clause/phrase structure.
3. Dysfluent and clause and phrase structure problems.
4. Relatively fluent, few errors, clause and phrase structure problems.

Reliable and valid systems for identifying sub-groups of children are still in their infancy. It is less likely that clear sub-groups will be identified in the pre-school period since there is still difficulty in distinguishing enduring from transient difficulties. In contrast, sub-grouping work with school-age children seems more promising. This is particularly important if it can be demonstrated that specific profiles of language difficulty require specific forms of intervention. Moreover, the development of sound sub-groups should help evaluation of different causal explanations of language difficulties. For example, if particular sub-groups of children had difficulties with phonological representations this could be tied to auditory processing problems.

Explanations not based on language processes

Solving tasks uses *cognitive resources* and language is no exception. One reason why children might have difficulty with language is because they may have access to fewer cognitive resources. Basically, the argument is that the mind functions as a limited capacity system. If resources are used for one task, there are fewer resources to expend on another. When skills or competencies are well learned they become automatic and free up cognitive space for doing other tasks. On the other hand, a difficult task or complex situation places additional demands on the cognitive system and will use up the spare capacity that is available. As a simple example, consider learning to drive a car. The thought of playing music, drinking coffee or talking on the phone and driving would have been impossible, yet many experienced drivers do these things (whether they should or not is another question). The driving skill has become automatic and there is spare capacity in the system.

Similarly, an examination of some aspects of language development shows that the nature of the task directly affects the accuracy of the child's performance. For example, toddlers are more likely to use new inflexions (that is, the endings on words such as *-ing* and *-ed*) when expressing familiar meanings than unfamiliar ones. This indicates that their level of grammatical competence is not always evident when they are dealing with unfamiliar information. Such situations result in decreased performance. Similarly utterances which are more complex (e.g. that contain several clauses) are less likely to include all the underlying elements and young children's errors increase with syllabic complexity. Could it be that children with language difficulties have limitations on the amount of linguistic information they can deal with?

There are cases where children can demonstrate partial mastery of a grammatical structure and that level of mastery varies across situations. Such a result is not consistent with a specific linguistic deficit. Rather it indicates that the ability is not well established. Our own research provides similar information. We found that children with word-finding difficulties were similar in accuracy to their language age peers but slower to respond than both chronological and language age peers. What such a situation means is that whenever a child is required to do a new or complex task in parallel with even a simple language task their performance falls.

Working memory
Susan Gathercole and Alan Baddeley (1990) have suggested that a poor or reduced ability to store information in working memory could be a contributory cause to language difficulties. Working memory is a limited capacity store that supports language processing. They found that the children with language difficulties performed less well than typically developing children on a task that required immediate recall of non-words. The fact that the children with language difficulties were poorer than the younger language age-matched controls is of particular significance. They concluded that the children with language difficulties could retain less material in their immediate memory. This, they argued, could affect the child's ability to form a stable representation of the new word. So a child with poor immediate memory who encounters the new word *tarantula* would have problems keeping the word in memory long enough to create an accurate memory trace that could be used in future situations. Thus, working memory can constrain the development of speech production since it depends heavily on phonological storage capacity.

Cognitive processes
A defining characteristic of children with specific language impairment is that their non-verbal skills are at least within the average range. Arguments about discrepancies and primary problems are based on the understanding that the children experience no specific cognitive difficulties. Yet a common hypothesis

about language difficulties is that they reflect impairments in more general cognitive processes. A large number of hypotheses have been investigated about the relation between cognition and language. Many have resulted in negative rather than positive conclusions about the causal role of cognitive processes. Recent research has, however, established that children can have subtle but significant cognitive problems across visual, auditory and tactile stimuli (Johnston, 1991; Stone and Connel, 1993). As an example, consider a study by Johnston and Smith (1989) where children with language impairments were able to act appropriately in response to verbal instructions specifying the selection to be made from a set of three toys (e.g. take the house, take the tall one). Yet, they performed significantly worse than age-matched controls when required to base their actions on non-verbal models provided by the actions of two experimenters using similar sets of toys.

A difficulty has been identified in the performance of these children in solving tasks which require the child to generate a rule such as 'All black cats need to be fed'. Nelson and colleagues (1987) argue that these problems with hypothesis generation cannot be explained by an inability or qualitatively different process for learning the information. Rather, the data suggest that the children have less capacity for processing verbal and non-verbal information. This is particularly true when they are encoding new information. There is further evidence that directing children with language difficulties to specific cues can improve their performance disproportionately. Here again relevant research focuses on the child's information-processing capacities.

THE WIDER IMPACT OF EXPERIENCING A LANGUAGE DIFFICULTY

Several studies of children with specific language difficulties have reported a high rate of linguistic, educational and social impairment persisting many years after the language difficulty was first diagnosed. A number of retrospective studies have indicated that children with speech and language difficulties often develop academic problems. In retrospective studies, adults or older adolescents are asked to remember the difficulties that they had experienced in the past. Retrospective studies may tend to report more favourable outcomes than studies that are based on direct assessment of the individual. In a concurrent study, Julie Dockrell and Geoff Lindsay (1998) have shown that children with primary language problems have difficulties with literacy, numeracy and attention. They also have lowered self-esteem. It is important to point out that not all children have all problems and there is considerable variation in the severity experienced by individual children.

Literacy development

Reading is language-based. It would not be surprising if children with language difficulties have difficulties learning to read and spell, given the close relationship between language ability and literacy. Silva and his colleagues in New Zealand (Silva, 1987) followed up 937 children at two-year intervals. The data from the children at 9 and 11 years demonstrated that the reading scores of the children with language disorders were increasing at a significantly slower rate than those for the remainder of the sample. Children with receptive and expressive difficulties were more at risk for reading problems than those with either receptive or expressive problems alone. Thus there are clear indications that children with specific speech and language difficulties will experience additional problems.

Many research studies have shown how important the awareness of sounds (phonological awareness) can be in learning to read. The ability to segment words, blend sounds together and be aware of onset and rhyme play a central role in the early stages of reading. Thus, in children who have poor phonological awareness, literacy difficulties are to be expected. Moreover, it appears that the critical factor is a phonological problem, rather than articulation difficulties. Children with developmental verbal dyspraxia are more at risk for specific spelling problems than children who have structural abnormalities with oro-motor musculature.

Thus, there is strong evidence to link disturbances of phonological representations with literacy difficulties. As yet the direct impact of lexical and syntactic difficulties is less clear (but see Catts and Kahmi, 1999). If children are having difficulties comprehending oral language there are strong reasons to suspect that this will be parallelled in an understanding of written text. The studies of Jane Oakhill and her colleagues (Oakhill, 1994) support this view. The children in their studies did not have specific language problems but were less skilled comprehenders, they drew fewer inferences when processing spoken *and* written material. In addition, they were less likely to integrate meaning across utterances. This work is corroborated by the research of Victoria Joffe (1998), who has shown that children with specific speech and language difficulties are not as able as their age-matched controls at using context to imply meaning.

Children with language difficulties may be missing out on a whole range of literacy experiences. For example, much emphasis is placed nowadays on early book reading. Mogford-Bevan and Summersall (1997) have shown that there are difficulties in book reading for parents of children (2;6–3;9) with language comprehension delays. Picture-book reading occurs significantly less often in these dyads. This is despite adequate opportunities. Parents found the experiences unrewarding and there was a gradient of success in picture-book reading depending on the severity of the language problem. One might expect that if children were lacking one-to-one experiences this might have repercussions for nursery contexts. Thus, there is convincing evidence from the early stages of literacy that the development of children with language difficulties will be compromised.

Literacy difficulties are not inevitable. There are reports of some children with language difficulties who do not show this expected difficulty in reading and spelling (Bishop and Adams, 1990; Magnusson and Naucler, 1990). It may be the case that certain aspects of the language system have more powerful influences on literacy skills than others

Number development

There are also interactions between language learning and the learning of mathematics and there is growing evidence that children with speech and language difficulties experience difficulty with numbers (Conti-Ramsden *et al.*, 1992; Donlan, 1993; Fazio, 1994, 1996). Younger children have difficulties in rote counting, have a limited repertoire of number terms and frequently miscount objects. Older children have difficulties in the storage and retrieval of rote sequences, including counting larger numbers and learning multiplication tables. These difficulties appear to be located in the storage and retrieval of the specific phonological forms, although there is also evidence that the children have difficulties in making these tasks automatic. To date the evidence on the number skills of children with specific language difficulties indicates that the children's problems are located in the rote elements rather than the conceptual aspects.

Social interaction

Language and communication are essential components of interpersonal relations. Similar complex factors are involved in interaction with peers. The research on the conversational interaction of children with specific language problems and their peers is mixed. Grove *et al.* (1993) found that when language-impaired children interacted with other children who had language problems, they were as communicative as their typically developing mainstream peers in terms of how talkative they were. In contrast, the research on interaction with regular peers is less positive. Data from Hurtford and Hart (1979) suggest that children in integrated language units tend to work and play with other children with language difficulties and that although the children talk to their typically developing peer group, typical children do not initiate talk with the language-impaired children. There is a high degree of dependence on the teacher. Moreover, there is a strong indication that language-impaired children have difficulties making their views known and influencing their mainstream peers (see Gallagher, 1991).

Self-esteem

Children with learning difficulties face persistent academic failure and their self-concept is particularly at risk. There is no reason to assume that children with specific speech and language difficulties are an exception to this. Yet there has been little work to date examining the self-concept of children with a language difficulty. Our own data clearly indicate that professionals feel that many of the children who were identified as having a specific language problem had poor self-esteem (Dockrell and Lindsay, submitted). Wendy

Rinaldi (1996) has highlighted how language difficulties can create behaviour that is difficult to manage. She refers to these as techniques the child uses to distract attention away from their communication difficulty. A similar strategy is often found with children with other special needs. Consideration is needed of the wider range of factors that influence how children are valued and how they value themselves (Dockrell, 1997). The majority of studies show that there are significant differences between the status of 'disabled' and 'non-disabled' students in mainstream classrooms. Studies of children with general delays, specific learning difficulties, specific language impairments, hearing impairments and physical disabilities have all shown that these students experience peer rejection (Horne, 1985).

PROGNOSIS

Children develop at different rates. Not all children whose language skills are behind at age 3 will have language problems later. In fact, the evidence suggests that roughly 40 per cent catch up with their peers who have not shown any language difficulties. It is as yet unclear whether this 'catch up' should be described as part of the normal variation or 'spontaneous remission'. Spontaneous remission suggests that a problem existed but that it improved of its own accord. Describing the improvement as reflecting normal variation may be more accurate given the limited knowledge of language development across the population at large. It is becoming more evident that children with early language problems that have apparently improved may experience other language-related difficulties, such as in literacy.

Small sample studies of children with expressive delay (Scarborough and Dobrich, 1990) suggest that there are risks of academic learning difficulties for such children, even when their problems are apparently resolved. Other research suggests that the long-term risks for children with slow expressive language development may be small. Bishop and Adams (1990) found that children with delays in language development at age 4 who moved into the normal range by age 5½ did not generally show significant reading problems by age 8½. Whitehurst and Fischel (1994) reported that reading and mathematics scores obtained from school records of children who presented as late talkers were well within the normal range when these children were 7 years old. However, recent data from the original Bishop sample is disconcerting (Stothard *et al.*, 1998). Their results suggest that even in the group of children whose language problems had resolved performed significantly less well on phonological processing and literacy skill at age 15 to 16. It is clear the prognosis for individual children will depend on the nature of the early language problems.

For example, Rhea Paul and her colleagues (1996) have been investigating the implications of expressive delays. They have reported that over 70 per cent of children with a history of language delay had moved within the normal range of expressive language by kindergarten and even those who had not were able to function at the low end of the range on school achievement. By second grade (7 years) over 80 per cent of children with a history of expressive delay had moved within the normal range of expressive language and school achievement; even those who continued to have immature expressive language did not differ significantly from peers with normal language histories in either reading comprehension or reading recognition.

SUMMARY

The criteria to identify children with speech and language difficulties varies. This variation impacts on both prevalence estimates and the kinds of problems that are included in the definition. Children can experience specific problems with sub-components of the language system. To date there is no single cause that can explain the variety of problems that these children experience. It seems likely that more than one causal mechanism may be involved. Many children who have early language problems experience continued difficulties. These can include problems with literacy, numeracy and peer relations. Intervention (see Chapter 8) appears to have significant effects on the children's language development. As such, appropriate identification and assessment of these children, linked to clearly planned interventions, is an important objective.

Chapter 4

Learning Disabilities and Language Difficulties

EXPERIENCING LEARNING DISABILITIES

Some children whose general abilities are appropriate for their age have a specific language impairment (see Chapter 3). It is also the case that there are children whose more general abilities are lower than would be expected for their age. This chapter focuses on the latter group. One might expect that children with learning disabilities will produce speech which is consistent with their other abilities, neither better nor worse than these other abilities. However, often this simple prediction is inaccurate. It is important for parents, teachers and therapists to be aware of any such strengths and weaknesses, as this can affect teaching, perceptions and general social interaction.

There also has been an interest in this issue from a more general theoretical perspective. Psychologists and linguists have for a long time puzzled over whether general abilities affect language or whether language affects other abilities. A related theoretical issue concerns the dispute between those who believe that language is a modular system which is largely independent of other abilities or whether language can be influenced by the level of ability. One might expect that by examining children who have learning disabilities this question could be answered. Unfortunately, the available evidence is not decisive for this argument. Even so, this debate provides a useful context to examine the communication and language of children with learning disabilities.

Types of learning disability

There are many forms of learning disability. A distinction is often made between learning disabilities which are caused by organic factors (genetic characteristics, maternal illness, maternal drug use, prematurity and brain damage) and those caused by what is termed 'psychosocial disadvantage'. The latter occur when children are brought up in deprived circumstances where there is a lack of support for learning basic skills. There have been disputes about whether learning disabilities are more often caused by genetic or socio-cultural factors. The issue is not as straightforward as it might initially seem and we prefer to steer clear of such arguments and instead focus on the fact that both biology and environment play a part in children's language development, with the exact contribution of either biology or environment varying from syndrome to syndrome, and from child to child. For example, it has been known for a long time that children with Down syndrome, a condition which is caused by a person having certain genetic characteristics, make much better progress in a supportive family than in an institution; the environment affects their development. However, it is also known that the large variation in abilities among children with Down syndrome who are brought up in families is not entirely due to the way the families care for them, but due to the biological characteristics of the individuals.

Children with learning disabilities are often identified on the basis of their scores on intelligence tests. Intelligence tests assess a number of abilities such as producing and understanding language, solving problems and memorizing information, as well as reading and mathematics (often intelligence tests have a bias to language skills). The scores on individual items can be put together to give an IQ score (intelligence quotient) which tells us the relation of the child's ability to that of the theoretically 'average' child of the *same* age (see also Chapter 3). Intelligence tests are usually designed so that an average child of any age receives a score of 100, a child who is more intelligent than average will receive a score higher than 100 and one who is less intelligent than average a score below 100. In the UK, children with general learning disabilities are usually considered to have scores below 70. This is a statistical cut-off point, as the tests are usually designed so that 2 per cent of children will have scores less than 70. It is important to realize that intelligence tests only give an approximate idea of a person's ability, so that there will not be much difference between two children of the same age who have scores of 72 and 68 on an IQ test. The following terms are often used to classify children in terms of their IQ score: 'mild or moderate' learning difficulties is used to refer to children with an IQ of between 50 and 70, and the term 'severe' is used for those who have an IQ below 50.

Another statistic is sometimes derived from the scores on individual items on intelligence tests, that of *mental age*. A mental age of 4 years would indicate that a child is scoring on the IQ test in a similar manner to an average 4-year-old, thus this score needs to be interpreted in relation to the child's actual chronological age. Although these scores do provide an overall impression of the level of ability of a child, there are worries that such scores fail to capture the characteristics of children who have strengths in some areas and weaknesses in others.

Not everyone accepts that IQ is the best way of identifying learning disabilities and it is sometimes suggested that it is better to assess individuals on their ability to conduct an autonomous life where they have to adapt to the demands of society. Two aspects are usually assessed, personal independence and social responsibility. However, it is much more difficult to assess such characteristics, especially as what is expected from an individual changes with age. Even so, knowledge of such abilities often plays an important part in making decisions about appropriate support. In general terms, it is accepted that the language profiles of children with learning disabilities are delayed in comparison to the norm, and that delays become more pronounced with age. Thus, the differences between two teenagers, one with intellectual impairments and one without, will be more pronounced than the differences between the two youngsters when they were toddlers. It is also recognized that the majority of children with learning disabilities follow the normal course of language development, but with a later onset, a slower rate and a lower final level of achievement. Language is likely to be more severely affected, the greater the degree of intellectual impairment. Most researchers now conclude that the differences between the language of people with mild, moderate and severe learning difficulties are quantitative rather than qualitative, and also that, on the whole, language patterns are delayed rather than different.

This chapter examines communication and language in relation to particular forms of learning disability. The reason for this is that identified syndromes provide a way of understanding the pattern of communication and language in a particular group of children, and communication and language are not always predictably related to IQ scores. This is because the picture is complicated by other factors, such as aetiology, life experiences and quality of intervention, which affect the impact of a learning disability. The chapter considers the more common forms and better researched learning disabilities: Down syndrome, autism, Fragile X syndrome and Williams' syndrome.

DOWN SYNDROME

Identification and incidence

About one in 600–800 children have Down syndrome, making it the most common genetic cause of learning disabilities. The physical characteristics of children with Down syndrome consist of a larger than typical distance between the eyes and a narrowing of the eyes, as well as a nose of reduced size. The hypotonicity of the muscles (floppiness) provides additional cues as to the existence of the disability. The formal identification of the syndrome is dependent on genetic analysis and in most cases this involves the presence of an extra 21st chromosome. In a small proportion of individuals with Down syndrome, some of the cells contain the usual number of chromosomes and other cells contain an extra chromosome. There is considerable variability in the abilities of children with Down syndrome. It used to be thought that these children would not progress beyond a mental age of 4 to 5 years. However, there is increasing evidence that some individuals can achieve much more than was originally supposed.

The development of communication and expressive language

In the first few months of life infants with Down syndrome often appear to be making reasonable progress; however, there are subtle indications of slightly different patterns of communication. The infants appear to cry less and cry less violently, which often gives an impression that they are less 'demanding'. There are delays in the use of vocalization, smiling and eye contact and there appear to be more vocal 'clashes' at around four months, although by nine months the amount of clashes seems similar to those of typically developing children. Later, communication using gestures and single word utterances is usually appropriate for their level of ability.

Generally, the content of the children's vocabulary and its size in relation to mental age are similar to that in typically developing children; in older children with Down syndrome their vocabulary may be larger than one would expect on the basis of their language ability. In typically developing children, at around eighteen to twenty months there are a number of changes which seem to be associated with a new level of functioning, the use of pretend play, the ability to produce two-word utterances and a rapid expansion of vocabulary (see Chapter 1). It would appear that when children with Down syndrome reach this level, more notable difficulties start to occur. A variety of explanations have been put forward about these delays in productive speech and use of grammar. None is yet accepted as being totally satisfactory, but it is useful to be aware of the possible causes of these delays and the associated research findings (see below).

Children with Down syndrome tend to produce 'formulas' which involve a set of words that are used as a phrase, such as 'Here you are'. These may be followed by two-word speech where each word is on occasions combined with other words. The more advanced multi-words speech of the children is rarely produced before four years of age and not all individuals reach this level of competence. Often multi-word speech does not contain all the appropriate grammatical structures and there are a number of reports of difficulties with the use of personal pronouns (he, she, they). Word order is not always inverted for questions and speech can have a telegraphic character.

There also have been suggestions that the speech and cognitive development of children with Down syndrome may have a plateau where there is little or no advance for several years. However, more detailed work by Robin Chapman and her colleagues (1991; 1995) with a reasonably large sample of adolescents has identified continuing development in the adolescent years, at an age when some researchers thought that language development stopped. They also found that individuals with Down syndrome could communicate surprisingly effectively given their level of grammatical ability. Other studies have suggested that interventions can produce gains in the language of adolescents.

Explanations about language development in children with Down syndrome: social, physical and cognitive processes

Over the last decade it has become increasingly apparent that the speech produced by children with Down syndrome is less sophisticated than would be expected from their other abilities. There is some uncertainty about the degree of delay, but findings from Robin Chapman (1991; 1995) suggest that the grammatical complexity of speech may be about a year behind what would be expected on the basis of their scores on a test of non-verbal memory. A test of non-verbal memory was used to provide a measure of general cognitive ability which would not be directly influenced by verbal ability. However, it was also found that on measures of speech comprehension, in this case the ability to choose the correct picture in relation to a word, tends to be ahead of what might be expected on the basis of non-verbal memory scores. These findings suggest there is an appreciable gap between comprehension and production. This next section explores the reasons for delays in language.

Social interaction and language input

During early non-verbal social interaction, children with Down syndrome are reported to have a lower interest in objects, which seems to be coupled with difficulties in attending to the person who is communicating and to the object which is the topic of communication. They also infrequently request objects by pointing or reaching. The amount of non-verbal requesting has been found to be related to their later progress in the use of speech. This could be caused by a variety of factors, the most obvious one being that these non-verbal skills provide a foundation for later speech.

Social interaction between carers and children who are known to be at risk for developmental delay is often different from that with typically developing children (see Chapter 2). The social interaction tends to be more directive and controlling on the carer's part, and there is usually more questioning of the child. As a result, the language input and associated social interaction are usually different with children who have Down syndrome. What is not certain is whether this has an impact on their language development. The fact that this style of interaction often involves topics of the carer's rather than the child's interest, and often involves the use of questions which require one-word answers rather than conversations, would suggest that such a style is *not* likely to promote the use of productive speech (see Chapter 1 for a discussion of the forms of interaction which promote vocabulary growth in typically developing children). Furthermore, this style of interaction may reduce the opportunities for children to produce speech, which is of course precisely the difficulty shown by children with Down syndrome. However, as already mentioned, it is possible that this style of interaction is helpful and appropriate for children who have less sustained attention and who are less likely to initiate conversations.

A finding that argues against adult speech style being a cause of language delays is that children with Down syndrome generally have better comprehension skills than productive skills. One might expect that if input factors were responsible for the delays then both of these dimensions would be affected equally. Given the uncertainties about the harm or benefit of a particular style of speech input, there can be no clear recommendations about the way one should talk to children with Down syndrome. Our own view is that it is probably best for carers to use their 'natural' responses rather than try to adopt a style of interaction which may seem inappropriate to them. Carers should also experiment with different styles to discover which seems easier and better for their child.

Difficulties in hearing

It has been estimated that three-quarters of children with Down syndrome have problems with hearing. These are due to physical problems, including a susceptibility to otitis media (see Chapter 7). The hearing difficulties often result in problems in detecting conversations which are spoken quietly and in detecting some of the higher frequency sounds. In theory, problems with hearing could result in difficulties in the production of speech. However, there are reasons to doubt whether this is a full explanation for speech difficulties of Down syndrome children.

There have been contradictory research findings from examinations of whether the degree of hearing loss is related to language abilities in children with Down syndrome. The work of Michael Marcell and his colleagues (1992) found that the degree of hearing loss is related to some but not all aspects of speech production abilities. In contrast, research by Robin Chapman (1991) has not found a close relation between hearing loss and speech in older children and adolescents. An argument that goes against the idea that hearing difficulties result in speech difficulties is that both the production and comprehension of speech are not equally affected.

Thus, the limited available evidence suggests that the effect of hearing loss on speech is subtle rather than widespread and powerful. However, it is important to bear in mind that hearing loss when combined with other learning disabilities may result in language delays. In addition, the effects of hearing loss may depend on the timing and its severity. Consequently there should always be a policy of maximizing the learning opportunities of Down syndrome children by assessing and assisting with hearing.

Difficulties in using and remembering auditory information

Children with Down syndrome have been found to have difficulties using information which is presented through the medium of sound and speech. Teenagers typically can only repeat back three or four digits of a list that is spoken to them, while typically developing teenagers can usually repeat back seven digits. It would also seem that they do less well than would be expected in tests where they have to remember and repeat a series of spoken numbers, but not in tests where they have to remember a picture and reconstruct it from parts of the original picture or use visual spatial skills. Furthermore, typically developing children are better at remembering material presented when it is spoken rather than when it is written (e.g. numbers said as words rather than written on cards), but no difference is found for children with Down syndrome. A number of authorities have suggested that children with Down syndrome have a difficulty in the short-term storage of auditory material. However, Robin Chapman and her colleagues (1991) have reported that mental and chronological ages, rather than short-term auditory memory, are the best predictors of the language abilities of children and adolescents with Down syndrome. Thus, both experience of language use and general cognitive abilities may influence the ability to use speech.

Another very interesting perspective about this issue is provided by the findings from Sue Buckley and her colleagues (e.g. Buckley and Bird, 1993). They report that children with Down syndrome can be taught to read even when their language is at a very low level. Furthermore, learning to read appears to have a beneficial effect on language. These findings suggest that the relative strength of visual processing in children with Down syndrome allows them to take a different route into reading and language.

Difficulties in producing sounds

Children with Down syndrome are often observed to mispronounce words and because of this their speech can be difficult to understand. Such observations are backed up by investigations which have identified the production of speech sounds as one of the areas of greatest difficulty. Children with Down syndrome have a large tongue in relation to their mouth cavity and their muscles are hypotonic. Both of these characteristics could cause mechanical difficulties in sound production.

Several pieces of evidence suggest that language delays in children with Down syndrome are not directly caused by mechanical difficulties in the production of sounds. A number of investigations of the development of babbling (see Chapter 1) have shown that babies with Down syndrome produce the same range of sounds as children of similar chronological ages. If there were mechanical problems then one might expect certain sounds to be absent.

Surgery has been used to reduce the size of the tongue in some children with Down syndrome in an effort to assist the production of sounds. However, the effectiveness of such interventions is a matter of dispute, so even if there are benefits from surgery they do not appear to be dramatic. In addition, some people who have mechanical difficulties with their speech production system are able to produce appropriate sounds by using different techniques from those normally employed. In addition, some individuals who are not able to speak because of conditions such as cerebral palsy are able to acquire language. While these lines of evidence are not conclusive they do suggest that mechanical problems are not necessarily the sole cause of speech or language problems in children with Down syndrome.

There is stronger evidence that children with Down syndrome have difficulties in producing target sounds. It seems to be the case that they are able to produce a range of speech sounds, but have difficulty producing the sound when they need to do so. It has been proposed that this could be caused by difficulties in planning and constructing the fine motor movements which are necessary for speech production. There also is evidence that the children have greater difficulties in perceiving speech sounds than might be expected on the basis of their general level of ability. In theory these characteristics would not necessarily cause delays in the development of language; however, the difficulties of being understood and the frustrations of not producing appropriate sounds, when coupled with the other characteristics of these children, might result in such delays.

Summary

The message coming from the research on the communication and language of children with Down syndrome is that they have particular difficulties with the accurate production of sounds and with the rules of grammar. As yet it is not clear why children with Down syndrome should have these problems with language, and it may well be that the language problems are a result of several interacting factors. Thus, the findings indicate a need to target these aspects of language by carers and professionals, but as yet there is uncertainty about the causes and the best form of intervention.

AUTISM

Identification and incidence

Autism was identified in 1943 by Leo Kanner, and a closely related syndrome was independently identified in 1944 by Hans Asperger. Later work by Lorna Wing (1988) suggested that autism consists of a triad of impairments involving social relationships, language and rigidity of thought. Table 4.1 outlines a set of features that are used to identify children with autism. It should be emphasized in relation to such definitions that there is a great range of behaviours; degrees of severity and behaviour is not always consistent.

Autism is a rare condition, with recent estimates that it affects 0.01 per cent of the population, although it is possible that conditions related to autism (i.e. much less severe conditions) make up nearly 1 per cent of the population. The latter have begun to be known as autistic spectrum disorders. Some individuals with autism occasionally have abilities which are quite unexpected given the level of their other skills. Examples of this are the drawing ability of individuals such as Steven Wiltshire, and success in performing instant and seemingly impossible calculations (such as identifying the day of the week when given a date such as 3/11/52). Such individuals are sometimes referred to as 'autistic savants' and it should be stressed that they are an exception within this already exceptional population.

Characteristic	Criteria
Social interaction	1. Marked impairment in the use of non-verbal behaviours.
	2. Failure to develop peer relationships appropriate to mental level.
	3. Lack of spontaneous seeking to share enjoyment, interests or achievements with other people.
	4. Lack of social or emotional reciprocity.
Communication	1. Delay in or total lack of development of spoken language.
	2. In those individuals with adequate speech, a marked impairment in the ability to initiate or sustain conversation.
	3. Stereotypes and repetitive use of language or idiosyncratic language.
	4. Lack of varied, spontaneous make-believe play or social initiative play relative to developmental level.
Restricted repetitive and stereotyped behaviours, interests and activities	1. Encompassing preoccupation with stereotypes and restricted patterns of interest that is abnormal in either intensity or focus.
	2. Inflexible adherence to specific, non-functional routines or rituals.
	3. Stereotypes and repetitive motor mechanisms.
	4. Persistent preoccupation with parts of objects.

Table 4.1: Criteria used to identify autism. Source: American Psychiatric Association (1994)

The nature and development of communication in autism

The most prominent feature of the communication of children with autism is that it is so very different from that of other individuals. In relation to children with Down syndrome a major concern is the way language is less sophisticated than their other abilities. In autism however, development is deviant (in the technical sense of the word) rather than simply delayed. Consequently, our focus concerns why their communication is so different.

Children with autism appear to be poor at using the direction of another person's gaze to help them work out the referent of a novel word and this may hamper vocabulary growth (Baron-Cohen *et al.*, 1997). Autistic communication is often described as mechanical, with an absence of commenting about aspects of their environment (e.g. by pointing at objects), a lack of eye contact with other people and little following of another's eye gaze. It has been estimated that about half of the individuals with autism are not able to speak or use language. In some cases, this appears to be because of a lack of motivation to engage in social processes rather than a lack of capacity to produce words. Furthermore, there are indications of different patterns of interaction. Some individuals with autism seem aloof, avoiding eye contact and other social interaction. Others are passive and, although they may respond, they rarely initiate interaction. A further group initiate interaction, but do not seem to be interested in the replies that people give them.

Autism is usually, but not always, accompanied by a low IQ. There is a tendency for individuals with a low level of general ability to have little in the way of productive language and to have difficulties in engaging in communication. There are claims that children who do not produce single-word speech by 6 years are unlikely to develop the use of multi-word speech. About one-fifth of children with autism have IQ scores in the normal range. There is great variability in the characteristics of these individuals, but even those who make the most progress experience difficulties relating to and communicating with other people. A closely-related condition is Asperger's syndrome. Some think this is similar but not as severe as autism and involves similar difficulties in communication. There is debate as to whether or not Asperger's syndrome is part of the spectrum (i.e. range) of autistic disorders.

Individuals who are able to speak are sometimes echolalic (i.e. they echo what has been said and often this is delayed and at inappropriate times) and may use pronouns inappropriately, such as saying 'I' when they mean 'You' and vice versa. Children with autism also use words in idiosyncratic ways and have unusual intonation patterns, although the words are mostly spoken clearly. Speech may involve only a very limited range of conversational topics (such as what type of car a person owns) with a set of questions which do not appear to involve any real interest in the answers that are provided. Some of the other characteristics of the communication of children with autism will become apparent in the following discussion of the syndrome (see also Powell, 1999).

Autism has attracted considerable research interest, with much of the effort being directed towards explaining the characteristics of the syndrome. Issues related to communication have been central to this research. At present there are a number of explanations about autism which can account for some, if not all the characteristics of the children. We outline current explanations about autism which are concerned with the way that cognitive processes can influence the pattern of communication and speech.

Theory of mind and mindblindness

One of the most influential explanations is that children with autism suffer from 'mindblindness'. This refers to the lack of an ability to understand that other people can have different ideas, beliefs, or thoughts from one's own. This is such a fundamental part of our own thinking that often it is difficult to appreciate how the absence of this capacity would radically alter our lives. Claims about mindblindness can be traced back to work concerning what has been termed 'children's theory of mind'. A study by Hans Wimmer and Josef Perner (1983) investigated whether young children believe that another person has the same ideas as themselves, and whether the children could appreciate that another person can have a different perspective. They found that children under about 4 years of age were not able to appreciate that someone might have different knowledge from themselves.

Shortly afterwards, Simon Baron-Cohen, Alan Leslie and Uta Frith (1985) found that children with autism usually gave the incorrect answer in these

The following is acted out with puppets and some toys. Sally, one of the puppets, is made to put a marble in a particular place so that it can no longer be seen. Sally leaves the room, Anne (another puppet) enters and puts the marble somewhere else out of view. Sally then returns and the child is asked 'Where will Sally look for the marble?' Children below about 4 years of age usually indicate where the marble really is; in other words they fail to distinguish between their own (true) belief and the (false) belief of Sally. Children over 4 years of age are usually able to appreciate that Sally will look in the place where she left the marble.

Box 4.1: A false-belief task: the Sally-Anne Task

tasks (for an example of a theory-of-mind task see Box 4.1). This suggests that children with autism do not have a theory of mind and could explain why the children have a mechanistic view of the world and a lack of interest in other people's thoughts or emotions. Further work provided additional supporting evidence. For example, individuals with autism were found to be able to order pictures according to a sequence of activities, but not according to what people might be thinking. They could understand a process of sabotage, but not one of deception. They would point to obtain an object they wanted, but not to show something to someone, and had difficulty with metaphorical expressions. Clearly an inability to understand other people's minds would affect many aspects of communication (see Box 4.2, page 72 for a discussion of why children with autism do not develop a theory of mind).

However, there are problems with this explanation. For one thing, it fails to account for some characteristics of autism, such as the restricted range of interests, the desire for sameness and routines, as well as the preoccupation with detail. In addition, about one-fifth of children with autism are able to pass the theory-of-mind task and consequently they seem to have some ability to understand thoughts which are different from their own (although when tests of more advanced theory-of-mind abilities are given most children with autism fail these). Furthermore, mindblindness does not fully explain the children's difficulty with language. Typically developing children below 4 years do not have a theory of mind yet they are able to use language, so it does not follow that mindblindness should directly interfere with early language development. Having said this, it is interesting that many of the speech difficulties (e.g. pronoun reversal, echolalia, obsessive speech) and other characteristics of children with autism can be explained by a lack of appreciation of what others are thinking and a lack of understanding about the purpose of communication.

Another feature of the cognitive development of children with autism can be more directly related to language difficulties. Children with autism do not seem to engage in pretend play in the same way as other children. In typically developing children, pretend play is often seen at about eighteen months. It is widely thought that pretend play involves the ability to form a second mental representation of an object, for example pretending a banana is a telephone.

Several explanations have been put forward about mindblindness; these contain interesting ideas about the development of non-verbal communication and its relation to the development of other skills. Peter Hobson (1991; 1993) has suggested that children with autism are unable to perceive the emotions of other people. Most of us have no trouble in recognizing when someone is surprised at an event, we do not even have to consciously work out what the person is thinking, we seem to automatically perceive this emotion much as we automatically perceive that a vase is blue, or that a person's face is male. This seems to be a process of direct perception which involves little or no conscious effort (see Chapter 1). Peter Hobson suggests that babies with autism lack this ability to read another person's emotions.

He also uses a feature of social interaction that occurs at around nine months to explain why children with autism do not develop a theory of mind. At this age, typically developing children take part in triadic relationships between themselves, an adult and an object or event, the triadic relationship occurs when both infant and adult are attending to the same thing. Peter Hobson believes that triadic relationships provide the opportunity for children to learn that adults can have different reactions and thoughts from themselves. For example, an adult may laugh at a jack-in-the-box popping up and surprising them, while the infant might be fearful.

Interestingly, at about this age children begin to show social referencing when they look at an adult to check his or her reaction to something. Thus, it is proposed that because children with autism are unable to understand the emotions of others, they fail to develop an understanding that other people can have different perspectives from themselves, and this has consequences for later development. Most authorities agree that pretend play involves being able to have thoughts which are no longer tied to the obvious characteristics of an object or situation, for example, as when a child treats a banana as a telephone. Hobson links the early absence of understanding others' minds and emotions, to the failure to develop pretend play. He suggests that understanding different perspectives to one's own lays the foundation for developing alternative secondary representations that occur in pretend play.

A different explanation has concentrated on the cognitive basis of the deficit. Simon Baron-Cohen (1997) has argued that during the first year of life infants are primed to attend to the direction of people's eye gaze and use this to identify the focus of the person's interest. He believes that from this can grow an understanding of their emotions. He supposes, like Peter Hobson, that the perception of interest and emotions together with the experience of triadic relationships allow a child to begin to work out that their reactions to an event can be different from that of another person.

A prediction from this account is that children who are blind should show similar characteristics to children with autism, as children who are blind would not be able to make use of eye gaze in working out the interest and attention of other people. Children who are blind sometimes show similar behaviours to children with autism (e.g. echolalia and pronoun reversal), but this is not as severe, persistent or as widespread as might be expected from Simon Baron-Cohen's explanation.

Box 4.2: Why do children with autism have 'mindblindness'?

It is also thought that this ability to form a second way of representing the world is necessary to be able to use words to stand for things in the world. Thus, speech problems in some children with autism might partly be attributable to the difficulties of forming secondary representations. Interestingly, it has been suggested that the inability to form a second representation of something (such as what another person is thinking) may be a reason why children with autism do not develop a theory of mind.

Central coherence and executive functioning

It is known that children with autism are better than children of the same age at memorizing a series of unrelated items, but are worse at remembering related items (e.g. the names of furniture) – they do not seem to make use of the extra thematic information. Uta Frith (1989) has argued that these and other findings indicate that children with autism have difficulty in abstracting a common feature from a diverse set of information and this can explain their problems on theory of mind and similar tasks as they fail to relate different bits of information to arrive at the correct solution. The idea of central coherence can be applied to the communication problems of children with autism. The lack of central coherence may have the effect of making their world disjointed and incoherent. For example, a child with autism may be attending to the sound of speech, but fail to integrate the sounds they hear with ongoing activities; to be able to communicate effectively information from a variety of sources needs to be processed, such as sound, actions, facial expression, context and past history. As a result, a lack of central coherence may make it both difficult to work out the structure of communication that other people use, and difficult to communicate about the world in a flexible and adaptable manner.

Another recent explanation involves the idea of executive functioning. This is defined as the ability to maintain appropriate problem-solving intentions in order to reach a future goal and involves being able to inhibit a usual response. The frontal lobes of the brain are believed to be involved in such responses. Ozonoff and her colleagues (1991) noticed that there was similarity between some of the characteristics of individuals with autism and patients who had deficits in executive functioning because of damage to their frontal lobes. Furthermore, it also became apparent that a number of the characteristics of autism could be explained in terms of deficits in executive functioning. For example, individuals with autism typically will insist on following routines and can become very distressed when some aspect of their life is organized in a different way – showing forms of perseveration. In addition, some individuals with autism seem unable to stop repetitive behaviours such as hand-flapping, or the spinning of objects, while others engage in self-injurious behaviours such as self-mutilation or head-banging. It also can be argued that the problems in executing flexible action plans is responsible for their patterns of communication, where they have problems in inhibiting inappropriate behaviours.

Summary: the relation of cognitive and language abilities in autism

The communication and speech of children with autism is different from other children. The idea that children with autism have difficulty understanding what other people think accounts for many of their difficulties with communication and possibly language. If children with autism cannot imagine that people have different ideas and thoughts from themselves, then the motivation for communication is considerably reduced. It should also be remembered that the difficulties that children with autism have in creating secondary representations (e.g. engaging in pretend play) may be a more fundamental reason for language difficulties. Words are arbitrary symbols which stand for something else and they are the building bricks of language. Thus, one of the primary difficulties in autism is with communication and this results in difficulties with language. Their development is in sharp contrast to, for example, a child with hearing impairment who is motivated to communicate and requires the means to accomplish this by the use of hearing aids or sign language. The individual with autism can fail to understand communication and therefore has subsequent difficulties with the language system.

FRAGILE X SYNDROME

The X chromosome is one of the two chromosomes which determine the sex of an individual: females have two X chromosomes, males have an X and a Y chromosome. Fragile X syndrome is a form of learning disability which is caused by the genes on part of the X chromosome. The long arm of this chromosome looks pinched and liable to break and this has given rise to the name of the syndrome. It is thought that about 1 in 750–1,000 males are affected by the syndrome and that about 1 in 500–750 females are carriers; it is believed to be the most common inherited cause of learning disabilities. However, the expression of the syndrome does not seem to follow a straightforward genetic path and it would appear that the condition can become increasingly severe across several generations until the syndrome is fully present in a particular generation. Nor does the syndrome seem to follow the typical pattern of recessive genes like haemophilia in which females carry a recessive gene, which does not affect them. Somewhere between one-third to one-half of females who carry Fragile X have learning disabilities and/or emotional difficulties. Furthermore, although one might expect that all males with a fragile X chromosome would have learning disabilities, this is not the case; some may not show any learning disabilities. Genetic counselling is usually vital to help potential parents to understand the complex nature of this syndrome and to come to terms with the diagnosis.

Fragile X syndrome in males is associated with facial characteristics such as a longer than typical face, prominent and thick ears, and possibly a prominent forehead and jaw. These features may become more apparent with increasing age. Many post-pubertal males also have larger testes than normal and there are other physical characteristics which are less closely associated with the syndrome. However, it should be noted that there is variability so that a number of individuals do not show any of these characteristics. Some of the facial characteristics are also present in females with fragile X, but there is a much lower incidence of the associated physical characteristics.

Males with Fragile X syndrome appear to have a relative strength in the processing of simultaneous information, but a weakness in the processing of sequential information (e.g. short-term memory or sentence construction). In addition, with increasing age there appears to be decline in IQ scores. Females who are affected by the syndrome also have difficulties with spatial tasks and with executive functioning.

The speech of males with Fragile X syndrome has often been described as unusual as it has a sing-song quality, may sound jocular, and may occur in short bursts. These seem to be due to difficulties related to impulsivity and the rate at which speech is produced. In addition, parts of words or whole words may be repeated more than usual, and there can be difficulties in the pronunciation of sounds. These language difficulties have been attributed to problems in co-ordinating the mechanisms involved in speaking. Comprehension abilities are often more advanced than one would expect on the basis of vocabulary size or mental age. The individuals seem better able to engage in conversation and ask for responses than children with Down syndrome or autism. However, there can be repetitions of phrases which obviously is detrimental to conversation, and in this respect the speech has some similarities with that of children with autism. There has been controversy about whether Fragile X syndrome and autism are overlapping and related syndromes, and as yet there is no conclusive answer. Nonetheless it does seem to be the case that individuals with Fragile X have a number of similar characteristics to individuals with autism, although these are less severe in form.

WILLIAMS' SYNDROME

Williams' syndrome is quite rare, with an incidence of 1 in 20,000–50,000 live births (the condition is also known by other names such as infantile hypercalemia and supravalvular aortic stenosis; Williams *et al.* 1961). The condition involves problems in the metabolism of calcium and calcitonin, learning disabilities, failure to thrive, hyperacusis (increased sensitivity to sound) and a characteristic facial pattern which has been described as elfin. The condition appears to be caused by abnormalities in chromosome 7. The IQ of individuals with Williams' syndrome is usually in the 50s and 60s though there can be a considerable range with some individuals having IQs of around 90. The children are able to identify faces at a level expected by their chronological age, but appear to have worse than expected problem-solving, number and spatial abilities.

Much of the research on children with Williams' syndrome has been concerned with the possibility that language is more advanced than their other abilities. A detailed study of this asymmetry has been provided by Ursula

Bellugi and her colleagues (Bellugi *et al.*, 1988; 1994). Bellugi (1988) described the abilities of three adolescents with Williams' syndrome. The individuals were unable to lead independent lives as they had difficulty dressing themselves, remembering routines and dealing with money. The three adolescents were assessed on cognitive tasks and it was found that they were not capable of accomplishing problems which are typically solved at 7–8 years. They were also found to have difficulties with tasks involving visual–spatial abilities, such as drawing, but performed at adult levels on a task involving the identification of familiar and unfamiliar faces. Their mental ages were between 5 to 9 years. In contrast, the productive and receptive vocabularies were about two years in advance of their mental ages. In addition, the children were reported to use uncommon words (not only was the conversation of these young people fluent, but they also showed advanced grammar). An assessment of comprehension of sentence structure (from the TROG, Test for Reception of Grammar) revealed age-equivalent scores that were appropriate for their mental age.

There also have been reports of a marked difference in narrative skills, with these children giving interesting and attention worthy stories in comparison with children of matched cognitive abilities (Reilly *et al.*, 1990). However, the fluency may mask a lack of comprehension and understanding of the subject matter. In addition, the children have problems with irregular verbs and plurals (e.g. they say 'mouses' rather than 'mice').

Bellugi and her colleagues (1994) obtained parental reports about the language of children with Williams' and Down syndrome who were between 1 and 6 years of age. Both groups showed delayed speech development until they reached the language level equivalent to typical children of between sixteen and thirty months. After this level the linguistic abilities of children with Williams' syndrome increased in relation to their vocabulary size. This suggests that there may need to be a set of cognitive abilities which are necessary (but not sufficient) for language to proceed. These findings have been used to argue against a modularity account of language acquisition as certain basic cognitive abilities may need to be in place for language acquisition to take place.

More recently a number of reports have started to question whether the language of individuals with Williams' syndrome is markedly more advanced than their other abilities and that the appearance of advanced language does not involve all parts of the language system (Karmiloff-Smith *et al.*, 1997). It has also been suggested that there might be considerable variation within the syndrome (Greer *et al.*, 1997). Jarrold *et al.* (1998) have put forward the idea that verbal and non-verbal skills develop at different rates and it is only in more able individuals that language is relatively more advanced. In addition, there is evidence that the process of language development may be different from that in typically developing children (Karmiloff-Smith *et al.*, 1997; Stevens and Karmiloff-Smith, 1997). Thus, there are still many uncertainties about the development of communication in children with Williams' syndrome – something that may partly be due to the small samples who are involved in research studies.

ACCESSING THE CURRICULUM

An important message from the research on children with Down syndrome is that their relative weakness in the production of speech can easily result in an underestimation of their other abilities. Where tasks are difficult for these children it may be better to use visual aids when this is possible, rather than relying on verbal explanations. However, such attempts should not result in a neglect of the use of speech, as a supportive speech environment is likely to assist the development of language. The support may involve giving children more time to provide replies and to try to structure speech around their interests. In addition, hearing checks need to be made and speech directed to them should be spoken clearly and audibly. Not only are there difficulties in producing language, but there are recent findings about difficulties with arithmetic. There also is evidence that children with Down syndrome may be particularly good at avoiding tasks which they find difficult by the use of social diversions and other devices, therefore special efforts may be required in teaching and assessment.

For children with Down syndrome or with autism, sign languages such as Makaton and BSL (British Sign Language, see Chapter 7) have been used as an alternative form of communication. It is argued that the use of signs may be easier for children to process as it corresponds to their input preferences and it is less transitory in nature than speech. Signing appears to be especially suitable for children with Down syndrome who have a strength in their ability to remember visual–spatial relations and to produce sequences of hand movements. Signing also builds on existing gestural abilities, it is quick, and it is inherently generative. For example, one boy created novel compounds in sign for words which he did not have in his spoken vocabulary: RED-APPLE for 'tomato' and DOCTOR-SHOP for 'hospital'. The disadvantages of signing are that care-givers need to be taught signs in order to recognize them, the signs have to be recalled from memory, and some care-givers sign quite inaccurately. There are reports of children who appear to benefit from signing; however, there is a lack of research evidence about gains relative to other forms of intervention and the long-term effects of using signs. In the case of children with autism, the available evidence suggests that the usefulness of signing is variable and that the same type of communication problems occur as with speech. As we have already noted, for children with autism, language delays usually arise from their communication difficulties, and therefore they need to be assisted in developing these primary communicative abilities.

Another technique that is sometimes used employs pictures to help with communication. This can provide a child with the rudimentary tools to express their needs. Often the child carries the pictures around with them. Graphic representations include pictures, photographs or line drawings, symbols or written words. A selection is made to reflect the needs and interests of the individual, and these are then displayed in books, charts or communication aids with speech output. The child finds the symbol on the display, and points to it to indicate the topic of conversation. Studies show that graphic symbols are easier for children to understand than written words because of their pictorial qualities.

The availability of augmentative and alternative communication systems means that individuals need not be debarred from communication because of speech production problems. Although previously these systems were considered as alternatives to speech and to each other, current approaches are more flexible, and promote the combination of all modes of communication that are useful to the person. When people can use speech, sign and books with symbols and pictures, the possibility of a successful interaction may be increased, if not guaranteed

The communication problems of children with autism mean that it is difficult to gain their attention, especially as they are much less likely to follow the interests of another person, such as a care-giver or teacher. Furthermore, the lack of responsiveness makes skill and thought necessary to sustain interaction and teaching. The children often exhibit challenging behaviour, especially when routines are changed or the child is put in a situation of uncertainty. Patricia Howlin (1998) has suggested that such behaviour may partly be a result of an inability to communicate wishes and uncertainties to others. In children who can use speech it needs to be remembered that the children tend to treat speech literally and do not understand the pragmatics of the communication ('Have you lost your tongue?' can provoke a search). In addition, some recent research suggests that the children may have problems in remembering events that happened to themselves, so they will sometimes answer questions about what has happened by relying on their general knowledge. The dislike of changes to routines also makes it necessary to be careful when new approaches to teaching are introduced. The fact that the children may respond to changes or difficulties with tantrums calls for patience and thought about the best policy to deal with these outbursts. It is worth remembering that praise and social-based rewards or encouragements may be a less powerful reward to children with autism; however, they often enjoy activities with which they are familiar, and food or even music can sometimes act as a reward. Unfortunately, although there are many ideas about intervention with these children, success is often limited.

One issue which is not easy to resolve is the extent to which programmes need to adapt to the ways of thinking of individuals with autism or to challenge some of their dispositions, such as impersonal social interaction. TEACCH is specifically designed to assist the development of communication of children with autism. It is a highly structured programme which may help children to understand what is expected of them and to communicate within clearly defined parameters. However, despite the progress that children show in these highly structured situations there are worries that this form of intervention does not help the children to generalize their communication skills to other situations.

In the case of individuals with Fragile X syndrome there is evidence that it may be more difficult to acquire skills and abilities after the adolescent period. In addition, attentional problems and hyperactivity make teaching difficult. It is sometimes pointed out that the benefits of breaking tasks down into small sub-components will not be particularly effective because of the difficulties these children have with the processing of sequential information. Instead, greater gains may be obtained from the presentation of the overall idea, and visual illustrations are reported to be particularly helpful.

PEER RELATIONS

Children with Down syndrome are often perceived as being sociable and friendly, and children with autism are often perceived as being unsociable and unfriendly. Some research has indicated that the stereotype of children with Down syndrome may not be completely accurate; however, it is certainly true that they have few problems with social relations in contrast with children with autism. Children with Down syndrome develop friendships and relations with others. However, children with autism find it difficult to relate to others and may sometimes find this threatening and confusing. They show attachment to care-givers but this often seems to be based on gratification rather than a relationship. Social difficulties are often greater during peer interaction with other children, who may not be as sensitive as adults to the needs of a child with autism. There are suggestions that peer interaction is best facilitated with other non-autistic children who have been given explanations and suggestions about the way to interact with the child who has autism, but it needs to be recognized that the whole situation has to be dealt with carefully and sensitively. Less is known about peer interaction with children who have Williams' syndrome. These children have been reported to have poor relations with peers, but can have good relationships with adults, especially if the adults are prepared to engage in extensive conversations. They also appear to be sensitive to the emotions and emotional states of others.

SUMMARY

One message to take away from this chapter is that the communication and speech of children with learning disabilities is not necessarily at a level that might be expected from their other abilities. Children with Down syndrome have problems with language relative to their other abilities, but their use of speech and communication is not markedly different from children who have similar language abilities. In contrast, the communication and speech of children with autism can be very different from a child with a similar vocabulary size or mean length of utterance. Investigations are now beginning to provide ideas about why autistic communication and speech are so different, but as yet no one theory provides a completely satisfactory explanation. Less is known about the communication and speech of children with Fragile X. These individuals have some characteristics which are similar to those of children with autism, although it is still uncertain whether explanations about autism can help us understand this condition. Children with Williams' syndrome are reported to have speech which is more advanced than would be expected on the basis of their other abilities.

Chapter 5

Sensory Isolation and Visual Impairments

What happens to language development when one or more of the usual channels of communication are absent? Three important forms of sensory deprivation are: isolation, visual impairment, and hearing loss. Studies of children who experience sensory difficulties allow evaluation of the ways in which language processes are robust and independent of modality. They also provide opportunities to examine first hand the differential impact of different language learning environments. Isolation is by far the rarest deprivation to affect children and because of this, studies of the impact of isolation are usually single case studies (see Skuse, 1988 for a review).

A simple model about the effects of environmental input predicts that these forms of deprivation might disrupt and delay language acquisition. The research findings generally fail to support such a straightforward prediction. Instead, in many ways, language acquisition appears to be remarkably resilient. Yet how do children manage when information is minimized or degraded in one modality? In what ways, if any, does the pattern of language development differ? Are the language sub-systems differentially affected? What compensatory mechanisms are put into place? These are important questions to answer so that language learning may be supported appropriately and more precise models of language acquisition may be developed.

This chapter first considers some cases of children who have been isolated from speech input and discusses the way that this has affected their language development. Research shows that there can be remarkable advances once a child is placed in a suitable environment. This is followed by a discussion of the nature of visual impairment and its effect on the development of communication. The next chapter considers hearing loss in relation to the development of communication.

ISOLATION

Over the centuries there have been a number of reports of children who have been raised in isolation, either by wild animals, as a deliberate experiment, or as the result of severe neglect. An Egyptian pharaoh is supposed to have raised children in isolation to discover what language they would naturally use. There are accounts of children being raised by wild animals, for instance Kaspar Hauser in the nineteenth century, and more recent reports about children who have been kept away from speaking individuals.

We already know that young children can often recover from early and extreme deprivation if subsequently they are given a more stimulating and enriched environment. The same appears to be true of language even if there are several years with little or no language input. Such findings suggest that the language acquisition process is relatively robust in the sense that it can still operate once the appropriate conditions are present. However, recovery does not always occur, and in such cases it is difficult to know whether there was some feature of the isolation which prevented recovery (e.g. age of isolation, age of detection, type of isolation) or whether the child had learning disabilities when he or she was isolated. Consequently, when no recovery occurs there is usually a large degree of uncertainty about the precise reason for this.

Two cases illustrate the remarkable advances that can occur after a child has not heard speech for several years. In the 1940s a child, called Isabelle, was identified who had been kept in isolation in a darkened room with her mother who was deaf and without speech (Mason, 1942; Davis, 1947). Isabelle had been given an inadequate diet, was severely malnourished and had severe rickets. During her isolation she communicated with her mother with gestures. The mother and Isabelle escaped from the isolation when Isabelle was about 6 years old. On her admission to hospital Isabelle behaved like a wild animal and only made croaking sounds. After one week in the hospital she started to make speech sounds and seemed to rapidly pass through the normal stages of speech. After eighteen months she had a vocabulary of over 2,000 words, could read and write, and could compose imaginative stories.

The second case involves two male Czechoslovakian twins whose mother died after giving birth (Koluchova, 1972; 1976). The children then were in a children's home for eleven months, spent six months with their aunt, and next went to stay with their father and stepmother. The father was of low intelligence and the stepmother was exceptionally cruel. The boys were never allowed out of the house and were kept in a small unheated closet or in a cellar. When discovered at 7 years the children could hardly walk, had acute rickets, were very fearful, and their spontaneous speech was very poor. After placement in a hospital and then a foster home, excellent gains were made in social adjustment and speech. The children are now adults and appear well adjusted and cognitively able.

Genie, the third case, was found when she was 13 years old (Curtiss, 1977). Her history was one of isolation, severe neglect and physical restraint; she was kept strapped to a child's potty in an attic. Her father punished her if she made any sound. On discovery her appearance was of a 6- to 7-year-old child. She was described by Curtiss as 'unsocialized, primitive, and hardly human', making virtually no sounds and being hardly able to walk. Genie has not achieved good social adjustment or language despite intervention and being placed with a foster family.

These cases have relevance to the claim that there is a critical period for language acquisition so that it is difficult to acquire language after puberty (Lennenberg, 1967). The studies provide some support for this idea in that all the children who were discovered before puberty acquired language, whereas Genie, who has failed to acquire language, was discovered during her adolescent years. However, some caution is needed before accepting this conclusion, as Genie may have had a learning disability before her isolation. Another interpretation of the difference between Genie and the other cases is that Isobelle and the twins had some minimal social interaction which may have helped to develop rudimentary social skills, and these provided a template for their later, rapid linguistic progress. The cases also fit in with some recent ideas that language development might be 'put on hold' if children do not possess a sufficiently large vocabulary, and can resume when the vocabulary reaches an appropriate size. In contrast, the data do not easily fit with John Locke's (1997) view that there are critical periods for language development determined by neurological factors.

There also have been investigations of hearing children of deaf parents. These children usually receive virtually no intelligible speech from their parents. However, various studies have indicated that these children do not necessarily have delayed language development. It has even been claimed that if there are at least five hours of contact with speaking individuals the children's speech will develop at a more or less normal rate. Again these findings emphasize that language development can occur even when the language learning environment is very different from that of the typical child.

Taken together these two sets of findings point to the robustness of language learning processes. Children can, after profound deprivation, make remarkable recovery in general and with linguistic abilities specifically. Needless to say, the recovery depends on placing the child in a supportive and stimulating environment. In addition, language learning appears to take place even when there is much more limited speech than is typical.

EXPERIENCING A VISUAL IMPAIRMENT

The seminal work of Fraiberg (1977) alerted investigators to the experience of blind children and the ways in which these might have an impact on development. Views about language acquisition in blind children are contradictory. Some researchers have argued that blind children acquire language in a similar way to sighted children, while others suggest quite different developmental paths.

In some ways it is surprising to think that children with visual impairments might be at risk of experiencing a language problem. Why should visual information and language development be related? Yet visual impairments deprive the child of a rich input that provides a context for understanding words and interpreting utterances. As shown in Chapter 1, vision plays a critical role in early pre-verbal communication. Many of the communicative exchanges that happen between caretakers and infants occur through the context of a visual collaboration such as pointing and sharing. Vision enables infants and children to acquire information from different locations and provides a framework to organize the information received from the auditory modality. It is precisely because vision offers continuity and detailed information about the child's surroundings that it can be seen as a potent source in early learning.

Types of visual impairments

The visual system can be impaired in a range of different ways. Problems with vision can be subdivided into two categories: first, serious defects likely to cause a disabling impairment of vision, ranging from partial sight to complete blindness; and second, more common and usually less incapacitating defects including squint, colour blindness and so forth. This section is concerned with the first of these two categories. Generally the term 'blind' is used for children who have no vision or limited light perception, whereas the term 'severely visually impaired' is used when the child has a minimal amount of form vision.

Visual impairments are measured along two dimensions – acuity and field defects. Acuity involves both the sharpness and clarity of vision. Effectively it is a measure of how well a person is able to separate adjacent visual stimuli. There are specific measures for assessing visual functioning. Visual impairments bear a number of similarities with hearing impairments. Firstly, they lie on a continuum and no sharp delineation can be drawn between a visual impairment which is disabling and a visual loss which is not. Secondly, age of onset varies – even a few months of visual experience can make a difference for a child. There is evidence that even small amounts of residual vision can provide additional information which enables the child to gain greater information from the environment.

The size of the field of vision represents the area that a child can see when looking straight ahead. Severely reduced fields of vision result in tunnel vision. Box 5.1 describes some common visual problems and their implications for the child's perception.

Visual problem	Impact
Myopia – shortsightedness	Problems with distance vision
Hypermetropia – longsightedness	Blurred near vision
Astigmatism	Blurred vision, possible confusion of letters and numbers

Box 5.1: Impacts of visual impairment

Both within-child and situational factors will influence a child's use of their sight. These factors include the child's experiences, motivations, needs and the expectations that are placed upon them (see Barraga, 1976). Thus, children with comparable levels of visual acuity may use their sight differently. The child's current level of visual functioning is an important factor in how they respond to their environment and the ways in which intervention and support can be managed.

Identifying a visual impairment

Primary cases of visual impairment are frequently detected by the child's carers, although a number will be discovered by neonatal examination. Special examinations of the visual system should occur if there are known risk factors. Otherwise screening during the pre-school years should identify non-disabling problems. Problems identified at screening should be followed up by more detailed testing. Box 5.2 presents some warning signs for carers.

- Abnormal appearance of the eyes.
- Wandering eye movements.
- Poor fixation and visual following.
- Avoidance of light.

Box 5.2: Warning signs of severe visual impairment

Associated factors

There is a wide range of problems that can affect a child's visual status. Many of these causes are associated with other difficulties. In an RNIB survey (RNIB, 1994) more than half of the children were found to have one or more additional disabilities including impaired hearing, specific language problems, physical disabilities and learning difficulties. The survey also suggested that those children with poorer sight were more likely to have additional impairments, especially in the areas of communication and cognitive functioning. These additional problems make it difficult to draw conclusions from research where children's profiles are not clearly specified (see Lewis and Collis, 1997). Recently concern has been raised about a possible link between blindness and autism (see Chapter 4 and later in this chapter). More recent studies have attempted to control for this factor by grouping blind children according to ratings on the Childhood Autistic Rating Scale.

The child's language learning environment

The visually impaired child potentially misses out on two important levels of environmental stimulation. The first, and most obvious, is the constant visual stimulation that surrounds us as we live our lives. The second is more subtle and is governed by the interactions children have with their carers and peers on a daily basis. Blind children may be particularly sensitive to the language input they receive since they are so reliant on it. For a sighted child, oral input is only one of several sources of information they receive.

Chapter 1 described how carers monitor their infants' visual behaviour and line of regard to scaffold the language learning environment. A number of studies have documented how the signals provided by the severely visually impaired child to their carer can differ from those provided by sighted children. The children are described as having a limited repertoire of communicative behaviours and bland facial expressions with an absence of expressive behaviours. In addition, a behaviour described as 'stilling' is reported. 'Stilling' refers to cases where a child actually stops what he or she is doing completely. Stilling can be interpreted by carers as disinterest; however, an infant's stilling may signal interest rather than disinterest and be a strategy to increase attention to auditory stimuli. Such behaviours are believed to have implications for carers' responsivity. Research by Baird and colleagues (1997) confirms this conclusion. The visually impaired infants in their study displayed few behaviours that mothers considered meaningful. Furthermore, their results indicated that even those behaviours that were displayed by the blind infants provided the mothers with fewer messages. So not only were the babies emitting fewer signals, but those signals they were emitting appeared to be interpreted in a narrow fashion. These data stress the role of the context in which the child is developing. To help support the child's learning, carers need to be aware of their impact. This, of course, implies that the possible negative outcomes of visual impairment on interactional patterns can be modulated.

There is increasing evidence that while carers provide more labels of objects to blind children, unlike the parents of sighted children this labelling is not followed up with comments and questions which introduces new information. In many cases the utterances are not supported by a context that is perceivable by the child so the child has no non-visual ways to contextualize the interaction. Interactional patterns with severely visually impaired children are frequently not sustained or continued by carers. Ultimately fewer interactions will result in limited opportunities to engage in conversation and thereby limit the children's opportunities to develop the necessary discourse skills. In support of this line of argument a study by Kekelis and Prinz (1996) demonstrated that there were significant differences in the conversational patterns and responses of blind and sighted children. Specifically they found that:

- Blind children contributed fewer utterances to the overall conversational exchanges.
- Parents tended to ask children questions that were less likely to promote conversation, instead testing the children's knowledge or understanding.
- Parents were less likely to respond contingently to the child's utterances.

Only two blind and two sighted children participated in the study, so caution should be taken about generalizing. Overall, there is a picture emerging of a different interactional pattern that is set up between the blind and severely visually impaired child and their carers. However, it should not be assumed that simply because the patterns of interaction are different, they are deficient. Parents may be responding appropriately to the specific needs of their child. Parents usually do establish a successful framework for language development by combining sound, touch, rhythm and movement to support verbal interactions (Fraiberg, 1977). Further, some researchers have argued that mothers actually predict the children's language levels and respond to these in terms of the pace of the language input they provide by their repetitions and rephrasings. Thus the mothers could be behaving in an exemplary fashion by matching the children's needs. Again, care must be taken about generalizing since the conclusions come from studies with small numbers of children. These data do, however, highlight the importance of a careful analysis of the input provided in the verbal channel by the parents and the match that exists with the child's needs.

HOW MANY CHILDREN EXPERIENCE A VISUAL IMPAIRMENT?

Visual impairment has an incidence of been two and five per 10,000 (DHSS, 1988). It is therefore a rare impairment. It is estimated that 25 per cent of school-children will have a sight problem that needs attention. Many of these problems will not impede the child's development and learning in any way. Given the rarity of visual impairment, studies with these children are often compromised by small samples, differing levels of visual acuity, other confounding disabilities and the complicating factor of prematurity. This has led some researchers to argue that the sensible way forward is to do detailed investigations of single cases. Yet as McConachie and Moore (1994) have suggested, children who take part in single case studies may not be representative of the wider population of blind children. Complementary data needs to be collected from larger samples to substantiate and refine the conclusions from single cases.

NATURE OF THE LANGUAGE PROBLEMS THAT THE CHILDREN EXPERIENCE

As previously noted, blind children have been described as having normal patterns of language development, delayed patterns of language development or different patterns of language development. The conflict between the results of the various studies can be explained by a variety of factors:

- Early studies frequently included children who had other associated learning difficulties which could result in reduced language scores.
- Methods which rely on single standardized measures may fail to capture subtle differences in language development, creating the impression that language is similar to that of typically developing children.

- Lack of distinction between initial stages of language learning and later stages may result in different conclusions about the children's linguistic skills.

Studies have noted the use of routine phrases, echolalia, pronominal reversals, flat intonation, articulation difficulties and a limited range of prepositions and questions (see Chapter 4). Interpreting what these differences mean when they are demonstrated to exist is more complex. Some have argued for a relative robustness of the language system independent of visual information, while others have highlighted subtle differences which are dependent on visual experiences and early patterns of interaction.

Expressive language and phonology

Since blind children can hear everything that is said to them, it is not immediately apparent why they should have difficulties in developing spoken language. However, there are a number of studies that suggest that subtle differences and delays do occur, particularly early in development. For example, Preisler (1977) discusses a longitudinal study of the development of ten congenitally blind children, the majority of which were delayed in their acquisition of first words, word combinations and conversational language. For the majority of children with visual impairments, these early language difficulties have resolved themselves by around the age of 5 (Webster and Roe, 1998), but some difficulties may persist and it is not clear what the long-term implications are for learning and social interaction.

Ann Mills (1988) carried out a detailed study of the development of phonological skills of a number of visually impaired youngsters. Counter-intuitively, she concludes that the children's phonological development is slower and follows a slightly different pattern than that of sighted children. This is surprising because there is no obvious reason to suspect that visually impaired children should have phonological difficulties. Her careful analysis suggests that the children make more errors in production of sounds that have a visible articulation. Further inappropriate substitutions occur for sounds with visible articulation, such as 'm' and 'p'. This developmental difference is transitory, rather than lasting, and does not appear to interfere with the visually impaired child's ability to communicate. Mills' data are important for two reasons. In terms of our understanding of visually impaired children it emphasizes the importance of specific information on the developmental trajectory. From a more general view it accentuates how studies of normal development can easily miss additional information that the child might use in the language learning enterprise.

Vocabulary

Several researchers have investigated the vocabulary development of visually impaired children. In early language blind children are likely to develop a large number of labels for their own actions and for specific objects such as household objects. Again there are a number of contradictory reports. Data from a comparatively large sample (McConachie and Moore, 1994) provide evidence of a delay in the initial use of vocabulary, but once started the children on the whole make rapid progress.

Vocabulary is a good example of a case for examining the subtler aspects of development. The content of the children's vocabulary is different. Blind children seem to use more terms for social interaction ('Sorry', 'Excuse me') and words referring to their own actions, and fewer adjectives than typically developing children. Moreover, words may be used in idiosyncratic ways, such as only referring to their own actions. Further, there is less use of general nominals, such as dog, but many more specific nominals, such as a particular dog's name. Sighted children tend to go through processes of overextension (words used too generally, such as *daddy* for all male adults) and under-extension (*bear* used only for the child's teddy bear). Blind children tend not to overextend their vocabulary, and to underextend words for a longer time. A number of authors have argued that increased use of specific nominals reflects a failure to generalize names to other objects. Andersen and her colleagues (1993) suggest that this indicates that the process of word learning is different. They concluded that the meanings of 65 to 75 per cent of the blind children's first 100 words remained tied to the original context of use throughout the single-word period. This is different from the initial overextensions and generalizations of typically developing sighted children.

Why this underextension occurs is presently unclear. One possibility is that the children do not possess the conceptual framework to attach to these new terms; that is, for example, they do not use the word 'dog' because they do not have a concept of 'dogness' but they recognize their own dog (for which they have a name). Alternatively, it may be that the children are not constructing hypotheses about word meanings to the same extent as sighted children. This might be explained by the children's hypotheses being constrained by their experience of touch, that is that the children's opportunities to test out their ideas will be limited by their visual experience. As an example consider the learning of the word 'dog'; because a blind child will not see different dogs the child will not be in a position to work out the notion of 'dogness'. Thus the information that the child has available would not support the use of more general hypothesis testing. An important step to clarify these issues would be to compare patterns across word classes where children have different types of experiences.

Other researchers have taken a different approach to the problem. Sarah Norgate and colleagues (1998) argue that focusing on the development of object terms in blind children is to seriously underestimate their skills. Over-extensions will be underestimated because children will have limited opportunity to over-extend object names because they have less immediate access to other objects. Moreover, children have fewer words in their vocabularies which can be over-extended. Norgate proposes that the focus of vocabulary investigations should be on action terms, where the visually impaired child is more competent.

This view of lexical development as different and possibly delayed has not gone unchallenged. Barbara Landau (1997) argues that there is not enough evidence to suggest that the children have different conceptual structures and naming practices. Rather she suggests that blind children's access to the world and their ability to establish joint reference occurs through their finger-tips. Their ability to learn a vocabulary is grounded in their ability to use the grammar of the language to guide and constrain their hypotheses. The reasons why a child might not extend a word are more to do with their not receiving information that 'invites additional usage' than a problem with categorization skills. These studies of visual impairment provide a rich data base to test current models of vocabulary acquisition (see Chapter 1). Furthermore, they emphasize the need to carefully consider interpretations of language differences; differences are not necessarily delays.

Grammatical skills

The acquisition of syntax in children who are visually impaired does not seem to be very different from that in typical children. The onset of some syntactic constructions can be slightly delayed, but rapid advances are made by the time the child is 3 years of age (Landau and Gleitman, 1985). Yet again specific differences in the pattern of language use have been noted. Visually impaired children tend to omit auxiliaries in their sentences. One possible explanation of the failure to use auxiliaries is the high use of imperatives in the speech directed to them. Imperatives do not contain auxiliaries and thus the child's input is deficient in this respect. Visually impaired children will, of course, hear auxiliaries being used in the speech of the adults around them and a careful model would need to be constructed to explain their own specific failure to use the auxiliary. To date such a model is missing.

Delays have also been noted in the children's appropriate use of pronouns and spatial deictic terms such as 'this' and 'that'. In both cases these language differences have been explained in terms of the children's difficulties to recognize shifting roles and thereby changing perspective. In contrast to these difficulties with deixis there is evidence that children are precocious in their grammaticalization of time. Severely visually impaired children tend to refer to past events in contrast to the sighted child's preference to refer to the here and now. Sighted children tend to develop spatial reference before time reference, whereas the visually impaired children follow the opposite pattern. The children's focus on the sequential nature of events may sensitize them to the time dimension as opposed to spatial dimensions. Thus the different pattern of development reflects their experience with language and the world. The data from blind children appear to support the view that there is not one single route to language acquisition.

Pragmatics

The earlier discussion about carer-infant interactions suggests that blind and visually impaired infants have fewer opportunities to learn and understand the rules of interpersonal communication. This is further corroborated by evidence that blind and visually impaired children can have difficulty using language appropriately in communicative contexts. Their language can be perceived as self-centred and irrelevant to ongoing conversations. This is related to difficulties in deixis previously discussed. An example from Andersen *et al.* (1993) illustrates this point (see Box 5.3).

Teddy is a totally blind two year old. In this excerpt he has just wakened from a nap and a researcher goes in to greet him:

Teddy	Researcher
	Can you say 'Hi'?
	Hm
Did you go see Nicole?	
	Nicole? What did you say?
Did you?	
	Did I what?
Did you?	
Exaggerated intonation	Did I what?
Did you () -h- ()?	
	Did Teddy go see Nicole?
Hm?	
	Did Teddy go see Nicole?
Hm?	
	Huh? I bet Teddy saw Nicole
Did you saw Nicole?	
I did it	

Box 5.3: Talking with a visually impaired child. Source: Andersen et al. (1993), p. 28

As Andersen *et al.* (1993) explain, Teddy uses the wrong pronoun – you – which confuses the researcher. Starting the exchange with a question in response to a statement further adds to the confusion. The development of an appropriate set of pragmatic skills is important for later social interaction with peers and other adults. It would appear that this is an area where visually impaired children are particularly vulnerable.

ASSOCIATED FACTORS

Working memory

In previous chapters the role of verbal memory processes in the child's language learning has been highlighted. In general we have been concerned with how limitations in verbal memory processes may have an impact on the child's language learning skills. Interestingly the opposite can occur for blind children. On average children who are blind perform at the same level or lower than do their sighted peers on most sub-scales of intelligence tests apart from digit span. Digit span is a verbal memory task where children are required to recite back a list of numbers that is presented. It appears that congenitally blind children develop better memory spans, though even a small amount of sight removes the advantage. This advantage may well be associated with the children's enhanced skills at dealing with sequential information. Further studies could elucidate whether the verbal memory span confers any additional advantage on language-related tasks.

Cognitive processes

The absence of vision does not dramatically reduce the capabilities of the cognitive system. When children with associated difficulties are excluded, children with visual impairments reflect the general range of intellectual abilities and as such there are no specific reasons to assume that these will impact on linguistic skills. There is some indication that the symbolic play of blind children may be delayed. Play has been described as repetitive and manipulative with less inclination for children to assign symbolic roles to objects of play. However, the children's play patterns may be due to the lack of appropriately designed and organized play environments, rather than to any inherent problem with the ability to develop symbolic representations. Thus, analysis of children's cognitive skills needs to consider the role of the environment in affording particular opportunities.

Children's abilities to classify and form concepts is another area of cognitive development that has been isolated for specific investigation. Some observational studies have shown that visually impaired children demonstrate a lack of sorting behaviour. This lack of sorting objects into groups could affect their language development by restricting the categories that are set up for naming. Vision can be thought of as a motor for exploration. Reduced opportunities to explore result in a reduced knowledge base on which to hang further language development. In the case of nominal reference the children do not have an extended set of exemplars from which to develop their own linguistic hypotheses. As Landau (1983) states 'where relevant experience is lacking, concepts cannot develop; and where concepts are lacking, word meanings cannot be learnt' (Landau, 1983: 63). However, as we have just seen in the discussion about vocabulary acquisition, these data have not gone unchallenged. Further information is required to assess the adequacy of the different positions on visually impaired children's sorting skills.

Blindness and autism

Some of the behaviours that have been described as typical of the blind child, such as echolalia and difficulties with pronouns, are reminiscent of autistic features (see Chapter 4). Moreover, some blind children engage in repetitive, stereotyped body movements which can become quite persistent. To what extent do the behaviours of the congenitally blind child differ from autistic children? Certainly there has been a higher incidence of autism recorded in the blind population than would normally be expected. Recent work by Rachel Brown and her colleagues (1997) suggests that there are autistic-like features in the children's language and behaviour. However, in their sample clinically defined cases of autism were associated with cognitive impairment. It is possible that congenital blindness predisposes a child to autism. But unlike autism, the child's difficulties with collaboration (co-reference) may be more amenable to change with appropriate social experience.

ACCESSING THE CURRICULUM

In general, the language of blind children is not impeded but the experience language encodes can appear to differ. There is little evidence that the language skills of blind and visually impaired children *per se* will impact on access to the curriculum through the oral modality. The commonly reported literacy delays may occur for quite different reasons. For example, a number of studies have found that pre-school recognition of the written alphabet is an important predictor of reading ability. This has led researchers to conclude that exposure to environmental print and letter learning prior to formal reading instruction has important consequences in the pre-school development of reading skills. This type of exposure is compromised for the blind child and appears to directly impact on their reading skills (see Connelly and Barlow-Brown, forthcoming, for a discussion of the acquisition of Braille). There is, therefore, a need to present information in alternative ways that build on the sophisticated language skills that the children have developed by the time they enter school.

CONCLUSIONS

The lack of visual stimulation makes a child's task of making sense of the world around them different and potentially harder. Greater load on the child's memory system may result in tasks that require additional information processing to be acquired at a slower rate. These differences in developmental experience are reflected in language by:

- What is talked about.
- Certain generalizations that are made about the language system.
- The way the system works.

The robustness of the language system, in spite of the loss of visual information, is impressive. Some have concluded that this reflects the minimal role that knowledge of perceptual features plays in the development of the language system. Barbara Landau (1983) argues that the intact grammar system provides enough information for the child to develop a semantic system. Alternatively the child's adaptation to visual impairments illustrates the conditions under which, with the right support and social sensitivity, the language system can accommodate variation in input. This approach emphasizes the different routes that acquiring a language may take. Moreover, it emphasizes the flexibility of the cognitive system, providing the child receives the appropriate support. Recent work by Norgate (1998) adds further weight to this argument. Her research highlights the role of routines and rhymes (both occurring through the auditory modality) as a basis for practising lexical and pragmatic skills. Thus, studies from visually impaired children suggest that in learning language social processes can compensate to some extent for a lack of visual information, and in many cases the problems which occur can be transitory in nature.

Chapter 6

Hearing Impairments

EXPERIENCING A HEARING LOSS

Children who have a hearing loss experience reduced oral language input through being unable to hear the speech that is directed at them and the speech that occurs around them. Although children have access to visual cues, no single speech sound can be identified with certainty using purely visual information. Consequently, children with hearing impairments experience a different form of language input than their hearing peers. This does not mean they are lacking the cognitive or linguistic skills required to learn a language; rather the experience of a hearing loss denies them full access to spoken language. This has been clearly expressed by David Wood *et al.* (1986): 'Hearing impaired children have problems learning spoken language and written representations of such language, because they hear little (or nothing) of what people say.'

Alternative ways of supporting oral language, such as lip-reading and hearing aids, can be helpful but they do not compensate for the loss of auditory information. For example, the use of lip-reading is slowly mastered, has information missing and uses up the visual channel. Thus there are high attention demands involved in lip-reading and the visual attention directed at the speaker means that the child has a reduced opportunity for seeing things that are happening in the surrounding area. Hearing aids present different problems. Difficulties in boosting the threshold for certain sounds or slight increases in sound can result in a much greater sensation of loudness for the child (recruitment). Recruitment can be quite disturbing and interfere with the processing of other sounds. Cochlear implants provide limited but potentially useful information about sound. Electrodes are inserted in the cochlea, which stimulate the nerve ending directly. Preliminary data suggest that for profoundly congenitally deaf children such implants can have positive effects on oral language, vocabulary and reading (Dawson, 1991), but the procedure is very controversial. It is rarely possible to completely compensate for losses by enhancing oral input.

Children with hearing impairments can communicate in a number of different ways. Some communicate orally by attempting to use oral language in the same way as typically developing children. Others will use particular techniques to support their use of oral language, such as cued speech. At the other extreme some children acquire and use only sign language. Many children will use a combination of oral language and signing to communicate their ideas and understand the language of others. As such, studies of the children can enhance our understanding of the language system in two ways. First, they provide an assessment of the role that spoken language plays in the development of oral language skills. For example:

- How necessary is clearly specified auditory information for the successful development of language?
- Are certain auditory inputs more important than others?
- Can children compensate for lack of clarity in the speech information they receive?

Second, they investigate the ways in which differences across modality – oral and sign – demonstrate similar developmental processes. Conventional analyses of language acquisition tend to focus on oral language. Comparisons of children's acquisitions of sign and oral language allow identification of modality-specific processes. By corollary a comprehensive analysis of the strengths and needs of children with hearing difficulties will lead to the development of more appropriate interventions and support. The aim of this chapter is twofold: first, to describe the types of difficulties that children can experience as a result of different kinds of hearing loss; and second, where data are available to contrast the acquisition processes in the visual and auditory modality.

Children who experience a hearing loss are not a unitary group. The children vary on a range of different dimensions that are critical to the language acquisition process. Moreover, we cannot predict the language or psychoeducational performance of hearing-impaired children on the basis of hearing levels alone. There are four key dimensions that need to be considered when considering the impact of a hearing loss:

1. The type of hearing loss and the degree of loss.
2. Any associated factors such as learning difficulties, visual impairments.
3. The time of onset and identification of the hearing loss.
4. The child's language learning environment, e.g. hearing parents, parents who sign.

Types of hearing loss

Figure 6.1 shows the different parts of the hearing system. How the child's hearing is affected depends on which part of the auditory system is working ineffectively or has been damaged. Hearing varies both in terms of the extent

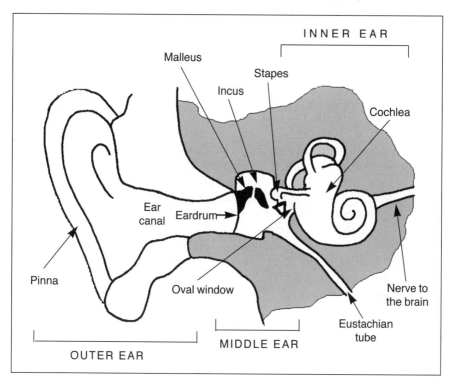

Figure 6.1: Cross-section of the ear

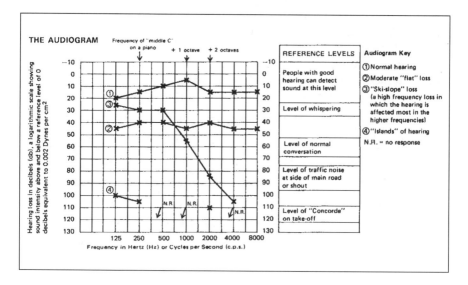

Figure 6.2: An audiogram. Source: Somerset Education Authority (1981)

of loss a child experiences and in the nature of the loss the child experiences. Four types of loss need to be distinguished:

1. *Conductive* hearing loss is caused by diseases or obstructions in the outer or middle ear. The passage of sound is impeded, with the result being similar to putting damp cotton wool in your ears. Many kinds of conductive losses are amenable to medical or surgical treatment to improve or restore the hearing. Otitis media (often known as glue ear) is a common form of conductive loss. In otitis media the transmission of sound across the middle ear is impeded because the eardrum and ossicles are prevented from vibrating freely. One of the complicating factors about middle-ear problems is that they can be fluctuating, so at one point a child appears to hear perfectly normally and at another does not respond.
2. *Sensorineural* losses are caused by damage of the hair cells in the inner ear or nerves. In these cases, sounds are distorted rather than dampened.
3. *Mixed* hearing losses occur when a child experiences a combination of a sensorineural loss and a conductive loss.
4. *Central* losses are a result of damage to the central nervous system.

Regardless of the type of hearing loss, a child's hearing test results are plotted on an audiogram which measures both the *intensity* and *frequency* of the loss.

The extent of a loss refers to the intensity of sound required to elicit a response from a child. This varies from mild to profound and is measured in decibels. Intervals in a decibel scale are not equal. Rather, they are logarithmic. This means that the actual difference between 100 and 120 is much greater than the difference between 20 and 40. Table 6.1 indicates the potential impacts of different kinds of losses. There is considerable controversy over the correct term(s) to use when describing individuals who experience a hearing loss. Some favour the use of the term 'deaf' for severe and profound losses while others accept the term 'hearing impairment'. In this chapter we have opted to use 'hearing impaired' unless the literature we refer to uses the term 'deaf'. In such cases the use of 'deaf' is retained.

It is important to realize that even when speech discrimination is near

Category	Decibel loss	Impact
Normal	up to 25	Minimal in adults
Mild	26–40	Difficulties listening in noisy situations such as classrooms
Moderate	41–55	Difficulties with normal conversation in quiet environments
Severe	56–90	Need for amplification to process speech
Profound	greater than 90	Limited and distorted speech sounds even with hearing aids

Table 6.1: Categories of hearing loss and their impact on listening

normal in quiet situations, it can be significantly reduced in noisy environments such as classrooms, playgrounds, cars and busy streets. In these situations the child is in danger of missing auditory information and can appear to behave differently from other children.

Speech sounds contain a range of different frequencies, and sounds differ in their frequencies. Vowels are commonly low-frequency sounds while consonants are commonly high-frequency sounds. Since children can have different levels of loss across the frequencies, this means they can miss parts of words as well as whole words. Figure 6.2 provides examples of different hearing losses across frequencies and intensity. Conductive losses tend to affect all frequencies or may be worse in low frequencies, whereas sensorineural losses can vary across the frequency range. A child with a high-frequency loss would have difficulties hearing the beginnings and endings of words. These are mainly the consonants such as 't' and 'f'. Vowels, in contrast, have mostly low-frequency components. A low-frequency loss would affect the processing of the sounds in the middle of words. As an example, consider how different losses could affect the child's ability to hear the word *fat*. A child with a high-frequency loss might get *a*, whereas a child with a low-frequency loss might hear *f-t*. Consequently, children with hearing losses can lose key words or parts of words and thereby make mistakes on tasks that they are capable of completing.

An important first step is to decide what constitutes a significant hearing loss. Many would argue that the 25-decibel loss that normally defines the beginning of a hearing loss in adults is too strict a criterion for children. Some researchers have argued that losses as small as 15 decibels can influence school achievement. Any degree of hearing loss that interferes with a child's ability to understand the language that they hear and understand the demands that are placed upon them is of concern (see Northern and Downs, 1984). This is a more flexible approach to defining hearing loss, but one that requires a careful analysis of the research literature to identify when and how hearing losses affect learning.

Associated factors

Hearing impairment is often associated with and caused by other problems, especially neurological problems. The main causes include rubella, cytomegalovirus, cerebral palsy, anoxia at birth, prematurity and meningitis. The presence of such additional problems makes assessment more complicated and calls into question research conclusions made about hearing loss that have not excluded children with additional disabilities. Generalizations about the effect of a hearing loss alone cannot be made if the child also has a learning difficulty or a visual impairment.

The time of onset and identification of the hearing loss

The time at which a child experiences a hearing loss is critical for the development of later oral language. Children who are born with severe or profound hearing losses (described as congenital deafness or prelingually deaf) never experience full oral language experiences, which has a major effect on later language learning. In contrast, children whose hearing loss occurs after they have started to master the oral language system (postlingually deaf) will possess linguistic representations that can support their later language learning.

Early identification can help parents and carers understand the child's communicative needs. Early exchanges between the primary care-giver are highly dependent on a subtle interweaving of communication. The sooner parents or carers realize that a child requires a different pattern of interaction, the better the likely communicative outcome for the child. In a large study by Levitt *et al.* (1988) the age at which intervention was begun was one of the best predictors of later language skills. This was most marked for deaf children of hearing parents

Learning to sign early has an important effect on later signing fluency and competency. The age children start to sign has a lasting effect even in individuals who have been signing for a long time. Mayberry and Eichen (1991) studied a group of individuals who had been signing for over 20 years. The group was subdivided into three: some participants had learned signing early, a further group had learned as teenagers and the final group had learned as adults. The group who had been signing since early childhood were more competent in syntax, semantics and morphology than the other two groups.

The child's language learning environment

Previous chapters of the book have highlighted the continuing debate about the role of early experience in later language learning. There is evidence from the hearing population that early language experiences are important. The communication exchanges of many hearing-impaired children are different from that of their hearing peers. These children tend to receive less linguistic information due to being unable to hear all the speech directed to themselves and other people. Mothers also speak less frequently to their hearing-impaired children and use atypical intonation patterns so that the quality of these children's language experience is lower than that of their hearing peers. For example, in the early years mothers may talk through or ignore early babbling (Gregory and Mogford, 1981). This contrasts with the finely tuned interactions which were described in Chapter 1. Some researchers have described these different interactional styles as dominant and controlling. The alternative view is that some strategies are constructive adaptations to the child's impairment.

In general, studies of input have focused on children with sensorineural losses. Variations in communication style have also been documented in children with conductive losses (Wallace *et al.*, 1996). They demonstrate that children with histories of chronic otitis media who experienced more directives and fewer enquiries from their parents scored more poorly on measures of expressive language than similar children whose parents used more interactive styles of communication. The study generally supports the position that all language input is not equal. The data suggest that children specifically need language experiences that involve interaction (see Chapter 1).

Being a 'deaf' child of a 'deaf' parent carries significant advantages. Most children of 'deaf' parents learn to sign with their parents. The parents provide linguistic and communicative role models for their children and engage with their children. This differs markedly from the general experience of hearing-impaired children with hearing parents and has many positive effects.

HOW MANY CHILDREN EXPERIENCE HEARING LOSSES?

Difficulties in definition and sampling mean that there is variation in the numbers of recorded cases of hearing impairment. David Hall (1996) suggests that 1.3 children per 1,000 experience a congenital sensorineural or mixed hearing impairment averaged over frequencies of greater than 40 decibels in the better ear. About 90 per cent of children with congenital or early onset deafness are born into families in which both parents are hearing. A further 7 per cent of such children have one 'deaf' parent and about 3 per cent have two 'deaf' parents.

Conductive problems are more common than sensorineural losses. Approximately one in five children will have a mild hearing impairment at some point in their school career. It has been estimated that at least 30 per cent will suffer from some conductive loss in the first few years of life with a peak occurrence between six and eighteen months. Children with other difficulties such as Down syndrome and cleft palate are more prone to such problems.

Identifying a hearing loss

Children's hearing is screened at various points in development. On the whole, the screening is rather crude, picking up only clear cases of loss, and the assessments are highly likely to miss intermittent losses. There are various signs that should alert a parent or a teacher to the possibility that a child may be having difficulty in hearing. These are presented in Box 6.1. There are some cases where it would be hard to distinguish a hearing loss from other types of

1. Lack of attention.
2. Looks at speaker's face.
3. Response to sounds is inconsistent.
4. Speech is difficult to understand.
5. Speaks loudly or quietly.
6. Understanding is limited.

Box 6.1: Indications of a hearing loss

developmental problems. In these cases other professions, such as speech and language therapists and psychologists, should become involved to help clarify the situation.

MANUAL COMMUNICATION AND SIGN LANGUAGE

Manual communication refers to all forms of interpersonal communication that depend on visuo-spatial use of the body, head and hands. Sign language is different from manual communication, as Jim Kyle and Bencie Woll (1985) argue, it is a language. It is the natural medium of language for 'deaf' people, but until the 1970s was viewed as essentially gestural and pictorial, and hence not an appropriate medium for education. Since then research has established that sign languages are linguistically structured, with a vocabulary and a distinctive grammar, organized on visuo-spatial rather than auditory-vocal principles. Different forms of sign language exist, such as British Sign Language and American Sign Language. In sign language space is used to indicate such things as tenses, subject and object. Facial expression and body movement are used in conjunction with hand gestures to modify meaning. Words are not signed, meanings are, so there is not a separate sign for every word in English. One sign may convey the meaning of a whole phrase in English such as 'it slowly came to a close'. Alternatively, there may be several different signs for the same word that expresses different concepts. There is increasing recognition that pupils with hearing impairments need to develop their skills in the modalities of both sign and speech and that sign language is best learnt from adults who are fluent signers.

Sign language is the principal means of communication for many prelingually 'deaf' individuals and for those who become 'deaf' early in their lives. There is now widespread agreement among researchers that the general course of language development is quite similar across modalities. There is more controversy about the extent to which modality-specific differences exist. Even for children with hearing impairment who are using oral language to communicate, there needs to be an awareness that the children will be much more reliant on other sources of information. Visual cues are an obvious one, but easily forgotten in the communicative act. The children will also use tactile and kinaesthetic feedback.

There has been a long-standing debate about how deaf children ought to be taught. At one extreme there are those who believe they ought to be instructed in an oral only mode, e.g. using lip-reading and being taught to use speech. In contrast there are those who believe that effective communication is so important that children ought to be taught in a fashion that allows them to develop the most competent mode of communication. This, it is argued, entails total communication (sign and oral). In comparing the development of sign and oral language skills, it is evident that for children who sign, their sign skills are significantly more advanced than their oral skills. Moreover, their sign language skills are generally on a par with the oral language levels of their hearing peers. Further, to date the evidence indicates that the early use of signing does not hamper the development of oral language skills. In addition, there may be strong educational and social reasons to enhance a child's language capacity irrespective of modality. Of course this raises major issues about which children should be encouraged to learn sign language and how this will affect the child's wider school community. An important research tool for studying patterns of language development is to compare the acquisition of signing with the acquisition of oral language.

NATURE OF THE LANGUAGE PROBLEMS THAT THE CHILDREN EXPERIENCE

The information presented so far should make it clear that it is not possible to make blanket statements about the language skills of all hearing-impaired children. The extent of the hearing loss, the quality of speech with amplification, the age of onset, the age of diagnosis and the extent to which amplification is used will all impact on a child's language development. However, the comparison between the auditory and the visual modality should provide interesting insights about patterns of development. In general, children learning to sign and those learning to speak acquire many aspects of language in the same way and over a similar time period (Bonvillian, 1999).

Unfortunately, interpreting the results of research studies is further complicated by a number of methodological problems. Many studies are of only one or two children. Other studies are confounded by the inclusion of children whose hearing impairments are accompanied by other neurological, physical or emotional difficulties. Moreover, large differences in results can occur, depending on whether children are receiving oral or manual education. However, the large differences do not always go in the same direction.

Many studies of the language skills of severely and profoundly hearing-impaired children rely on analyses of written language since their oral skills can be so poor. This is not a straightforward procedure because it cannot be assumed that children's written language skills reflect their oral competences. Written language requires a range of additional cognitive skills and information-processing resources. Consider the ability to put pen to paper. It is often much easier and more fluent to speak. The errors made when writing may reflect the act of writing rather than a conceptual gap in the understanding of the language system. Children are generally much more advanced in their oral use of language than the written form. Thus, when discussing children's language skills, caution must be used in drawing fixed conclusions from written data.

Language acquisition for prelingually deaf children may happen in three ways:

1. Explicit instruction in spoken language.
2. Instruction in signed and spoken language.
3. Natural learning of sign from parents.

For children whose losses occur postlingually, or who experience conductive losses, spoken language is the major medium through which they learn.

Conductive and sensorineural losses of hearing are generally treated as different both conceptually and in terms of research approaches. The first section below documents the research about the effect of conductive losses on language development, while the second section considers the development of language skills in children experiencing sensorineural losses. It highlights the differences between oral and manual acquisition for children with sensorineural losses.

Conductive losses and language development

There has been a continuing debate surrounding the impact (or not) of conductive hearing losses on language acquisition and school performance. For example, the short- and long-term effects of otitis media are not well specified. Some studies suggest that language is compromised whereas others are more equivocal. Conductive losses are associated with other measures of disadvantage, such as poor housing, which are in turn associated with slower development of language skills and poorer academic achievement. This makes the interpretation of some of the studies difficult. Recent studies have addressed this issue by being selective about the children included and more precise with the data analysis.

In cases where otitis media occurs early, for long periods of time, and where occurrences are marked, the impact is clearer. Thus, for example, hearing losses of more than 20 decibels are associated with poor articulation. Frequent occurrences of otitis media are associated with delays in spontaneous speech. Children tend to display a reduced number of consonants and a predominance of vowels. The pattern of development is complex and may contribute to developmental language disorders (Friel-Patti, 1992).

Nonetheless current evidence suggests that when a child experiences continuous middle-ear problems there will be an effect on language development. Long-term studies need to assess the permanence of the effect. A study by Friel-Patti and Finitzo (1990) of children who were *not* disadvantaged makes this point clearly. They looked at a group of children over the first two years of life. Children with otitis media fared less well on language measures. The influence may not be severe and children's language scores may still fall within the average range, but they will be depressed in comparison with the norm.

Sensorineural losses and language development

Children with severely impaired hearing have a delay in onset and are slow in the rate at which they learn auditory-vocal (spoken) language. The language of orally trained pre-schoolers can be two to three years behind that of typically developing children (Gregory and Mogford, 1981; Meadow-Orlans, 1987). In tandem with the lower overall language age, hearing-impaired children have smaller vocabularies than their hearing peers. There is some association between speech skills and hearing loss but on the whole language skills do not correlate with the degree of loss except when losses are greater than 115. In the Levitt *et al.* (1988) study mentioned previously there was a slight reduction in language skills as the loss increased from 40 to 80 decibels, but no change was noted between 80 and 115 decibels.

Expressive language and phonology

The onset of vocalization in hearing-impaired children is quite delayed in comparison to hearing infants. In the early babbling stages the vocalizations appear similar, but by the age of ten months there is clear evidence of the impact of auditory deprivation. Children of parents who are deaf have been observed to babble manually at about the same age. In contrast to a gradual reduction in oral vocalizations signing continues with these children.

The speech intelligibility of congenitally deaf children can vary. As a group they are difficult to understand and they may have a distinctive voice quality with flat intonation. Profoundly deaf children often produce speech sounds that are markedly atypical, such as silent articulations, voicing on in-breath rather than out-breath, and abnormal pitch for vowels. Kay Mogford (1988) argues that in other children with hearing impairments, the processes of phonological development appear to be broadly similar to those of typical development, except for specific delays in distinguishing consonants, which are also the sounds that hearing children find most difficult. However, the pattern of phonological development is not predicted by the nature and extent of the child's loss.

Forty-eight per cent of profoundly deaf children are hard to understand orally. 'Deaf' children of hearing parents can have better speech production skills than 'deaf' children of 'deaf' parents but 'deaf' children of 'deaf' parents are seen to use more complex language. The significant difficulties hearing-impaired children have with speech intelligibility and in reading appears to reflect the late acquisition of the phonological representations rather than a total absence of such representations. Careful studies have shown that phonological representations are developed and used by some severely and profoundly hearing-impaired children but the acquisition process is slow.

Vocabulary

On the whole the receptive *oral* vocabulary scores for severely and profoundly hearing-impaired children are significantly reduced in comparison to their hearing peers. Even children with the mildest delays can experience a one- to three-year gap in comparison to their age-matched peers (Davis *et al.*, 1986). Hearing-impaired children use fewer words across all different form classes, such as verbs, nouns, prepositions and so forth. This distinction is even more marked when abstract or infrequent words are considered or when school-aged children are required to select one meaning from several. There is some evidence that the children's vocabulary is not simply delayed but seems to differ in certain key features. So for example, time and quantity terms appear to pose specific problems. There are four possible explanations of the children's vocabulary limitations:

1. Children may simply not have enough experience with the full range of vocabulary items because of their reduced hearing.
2. Interaction with carers may provide a different environment for learning a lexicon.
3. Children's phonological skills may not be sufficiently developed to form adequate phonological representations.
4. The children may have difficulties grasping the relationship between word and referent.

Two sources of enquiry question this last hypothesis. Firstly, Gilbertson and Kahmi (1995) examined the novel word-learning skills of 20 hearing-impaired youngsters. They found that the degree of hearing loss was not related to word-learning ability. In contrast, their results indicated that the population of children with mild to moderate hearing loss can be divided into two groups. The first group develop normally despite their hearing loss, whereas the second group have an associated specific language difficulty (see also Chapter 3).

The second challenge to the word-referent hypothesis comes from the ease of the acquisition of signs in severely and profoundly hearing-impaired youngsters who have signing parents. In these cases there is an early development of first signs and sign combinations. Moreover, age of attainment of early language milestones in sign is highly predictive of the age of attainment of subsequent milestones, but, similar to oral language, there is wide variation between children. However, in contrast to the purported vocabulary spurt in oral language (see Chapter 1) sign vocabulary is acquired in a slow and steady fashion. The content of children's early sign vocabulary is similar to oral vocabulary although there is some suggestion that this may diverge later. Further research is required to clarify the effect of the different factors in vocabulary acquisition.

Grammatical problems

As already mentioned, early studies of grammatical development have frequently relied on assessing the children's written language. Later studies have considered spoken language. Although performance varies considerably, the general conclusion has been that children develop similar syntactic structures but at a greatly reduced rate, that is morphology appears to be in line with MLU (see Chapter 1 for a discussion of Mean Length of Utterance). Although differences in syntactic structures have been recorded, these do not appear to be common to all hearing-impaired students. Children have difficulties in the use of grammatical morphemes such as the use (or lack) of auxiliary (e.g. can, should, will) and past tense markings – so children will say 'park' instead of 'parked'. Similarly, tense markings will also be omitted in written text. Children also fail to respond to negatives. These difficulties may be related to a failure to perceive words. For example, the statement 'Matthew is not happy' may be perceived as 'Matthew is happy'. The evidence from the signing skills of 'deaf' youngsters supports the view that the children can develop a grammatical system in other circumstances and other modalities. Over the pre-school years signing development follows a similar pattern to oral language development in the acquisition of verb agreement, semantic relations and inflectional or derivational morphology. Thus, children who have the opportunity to develop a manual form of communication have access to a rich syntactic structure that they can use appropriately.

Dorothy Bishop (1983a) has argued that the situation may be more complex for oral language than a simple failure to perceive sound. She analysed the performance of prelingually profoundly deaf children's performance on the Test of Reception of Grammar (Bishop, 1983b) and found that the children were generally delayed. However, they adopted systematic strategies for decoding sentences not found in hearing children. For example, some children attended only to the content words and there were significant difficulties with word order. This could well be an adaptive way of dealing with imprecise speech information. Of course, it might be efficient and lead to accurate responses in some cases, but as Bishop's data clearly show, it can also cause the children to make significant errors. Irrespective of the cause of the children's problems such difficulties will affect the conversations the children have and the situations that are effective learning opportunities.

An illuminating comparison can be drawn with the written skills of children with specific speech and language difficulties. Richard Cromer (1978) compared the written language output of a group of 'deaf' children and a group of children with specific speech and language difficulties. The 'deaf' children made more errors but they used more complex sentences and more different categories such as noun phrases, and so forth, per sentence – even when the sentence lengths were comparable. At first glance this appears to support the view that the children have problems with auditory processing rather than with specific aspects of the grammatical system. Such straightforward interpretations require careful consideration. Firstly, there is the problem of inferring syntactic competence from written language. As already discussed, the processes may not be identical. Secondly, there is the issue that initial slow progress in learning to use language may later result in different patterns of performance.

OTHER CONTRIBUTING FACTORS

Working memory

'Deaf' individuals have been shown to have shorter memory spans than hearing individuals (Belmont and Krachmer, 1978). The greater the hearing loss a child experiences the shorter the child's memory span for a range of different materials. Moreover, oral ability for orally trained children is positively related to memory span. Thus, oral skills are positively associated with larger working memory spans. It is likely that the children's reduced working memory span complicates their language acquisition. This does not necessarily mean that the reduced memory span causes the language difficulties. This is particularly important when assessing non-verbal memory. Even purported non-verbal studies may include hidden language-related elements. An example of the interference of verbal elements in non-verbal tasks is presented in Box 6.2. A complex relationship between memory, language and hearing is the most parsimonious interpretation of the children's performance.

> Consider, for example, a task that requires a child to look at a single picture in a book for five seconds, the page is turned and the child then is required to point to the object they saw from a set of three. No language is necessary to succeed at the task. However, what you often find is that children commonly label the first object, possibly in an attempt to recall it. Thus, a simple visual recognition task can be translated into a verbally mediated task.

Box 6.2: The possible impact of verbal factors on non-verbal tasks

Two possible explanations for children's poor memory skills exist. Firstly, it may be that they are simply less efficient at using speech-based codes for memory purposes. The second explanation is based on the suggestion that the children are using qualitatively different memory codes, such as visuo-spatial ones. It may be that both explanations are correct to a certain extent. The use of speech-based codes has been reported by some individuals who communicate orally. Moreover, their use is associated with larger memory spans and higher reading scores. The situation for individuals who communicate with signs is inconsistent, but suggests that some signers may use speech-based codes for memory purposes as well. Of course, other memory codes are available, including visual ones, so it is difficult to create studies that clearly do not involve non-verbal memory.

Cognitive processes

Early studies on hearing-impaired youngsters made the incorrect assumption that thought was dependent on language. Such simple statements are not made today, but researchers do ask questions about different patterns of cognitive development and how this affects the child's language acquisition processes. The cognitive skills of hearing-impaired children are, on the whole, similar to their age-matched peers. Dodd *et al.* (1992) tested children aged 2½ to 4¾ years with severe to profound hearing losses and found that while their language scores were delayed, their cognitive skills were age appropriate. Studies with older children suggest patterns of cognitive differences, not cognitive deficiencies. The very fact of missing out on oral information may force children to use different strategies to solve problems.

ACCESSING THE CURRICULUM

Hearing-impaired schoolchildren typically perform more poorly than hearing children in most scholastic domains. In many ways this is hardly surprising given the curriculum's reliance on language. This is unfortunate because reading *could* serve as an important source of linguistic information for the children. (An important factor to consider is the extent to which they are taught in an oral language-related way.)

Literacy development

When hearing children approach the task of learning to read, the vast majority are competent speakers and listeners. They have a breadth of syntactic and semantic knowledge to bring to literacy learning. Many severely and profoundly hearing-impaired children, especially those who have little exposure to sign in the early years, have very impoverished language when they arrive at school. A large proportion of these youngsters never read well enough to obtain information from newspapers, simple textbooks or instruction manuals. Children whose first language is sign language face the task of reading a language which has different words and grammar.

Most researchers agree that the reading difficulties of congenitally hearing-impaired children bear some relation to their different mode of language acquisition, yet there is little consensus about which aspect of language interferes with which aspect of reading acquisition. Vocabulary level, syntactic ability, knowledge of discourse rules, phonological processing skills and memorial skills have all been considered to play a role (Marschark and Harris, 1996). Reading achievement does not appear to be related to the degree of hearing loss or to intelligence. It is, however, significantly associated with better language scores, be they oral or signed (Waters and Doehring, 1990).

One of the key factors that has been addressed in the research literature is the children's use of phonological skills in reading and spelling. There is some evidence that lip-reading can provide phonological information since articulation movements can provide information about the patterns of the English language. Studies of older severe and profoundly hearing-impaired children suggest that they code information in a sound-based (phonological) form, albeit to a lesser extent than their hearing peers (Dodd, 1980; Hanson *et al.*, 1983). Unsurprisingly, the children are more reliant on visual coding.

In contrast, there is evidence that younger profoundly pre-lingually 'deaf' children do not make use of phonological coding in reading. So unlike the typically developing child, there is no evidence that these children use the sounds of words to support their initial attempts to read. Harris and Beech (forthcoming) have examined this issue and suggest that the early stages of learning to read are problematic for the children because of their poor implicit phonological awareness. Those children who later go on to develop phonemic awareness might do so because they have more intelligible speech. Besides experiencing a lack of phonological awareness, the limited size of the children's vocabulary will mean that they will come across words in print that they have not yet acquired. The children are in effect doubly disadvantaged. In contrast to the negative impact of poor oral skills, exposure to early sign language is beneficial to later reading (Andrews and Mason, 1986; Hirsch-Pasek, 1987).

Number development

Hearing-impaired children lag behind their hearing peers in mathematics. On average hearing-impaired children are 2½ years behind their hearing peers. Much of mathematics is verbally mediated, particularly word problems, thereby disadvantaging the hearing-impaired child. However, hearing impaired children also do poorly on mathematics tests that involve relatively little language. Some researchers have argued that hearing impairment is the cause of children's difficulties with mathematics. Such a model has difficulty in explaining that some children perform at an age-appropriate level or better. Wood *et al.* (1983) found that 15 per cent of their 'deaf' sample performed at average or above average levels in mathematics achievements.

Terezinha Nunes and Constanza Moreno (forthcoming) offer a different perspective on hearing-impaired children's mathematics achievements. They argue that a hearing impairment is not the cause of mathematics difficulties but it is a risk factor. Thus, mathematical development is not seen as different in the hearing-impaired children, but it can be compromised. Their data, collected through a series of videotaped studies, suggests that children with hearing impairments seem to learn numerical concepts in the same way as their hearing peers. However, they experience obstacles with certain mathematical tasks, for example learning to count and the ability to use this knowledge to solve mathematical problems. Interestingly, the children who were signing did not perform significantly better than their non-signing peers. In addition, Nunes and Moreno highlighted the specific difficulties for children who sign. It is difficult to sign and use concrete counting aids, such as fingers, simultaneously. If Nunes and Moreno are correct, there is every reason to assume that with the right teaching environment, hearing-impaired children's mathematical skills should increase substantially.

Social interaction

Hearing-impaired children may experience reduced social experiences because of the restrictions in their ability to interact with their hearing peers. Although supportive patterns of interaction can be developed at home, these do not always generalize to other situations nor are they necessarily appropriate patterns for relations with peers and teachers. Hearing-impaired children may, for example, appear rude or uninterested and this may reduce their interactions with their peers. For those children who are totally reliant on sign, the range of people with whom they can interact will be further restricted. To minimize the potential negative effects of hearing impairments on peer interaction it is important to make sure that the individuals with whom the child comes into contact are aware of the difficulties of experiencing a hearing impairment. In corollary, providing the hearing-impaired child with strategies to negotiate social situations will minimize the unexpected and possibly negative interactions that can occur.

SUMMARY

Language development in children with hearing impairments highlights the central role of oral language information for the child's development. Children can experience a range of different kinds of hearing loss, yet even minor losses of hearing can affect the language acquisition process. The consequence is felt at all levels of the oral language system and for communication more generally. In contrast, for those children provided with the opportunity to acquire sign language, development follows a rather different pattern. The data indicate that the course of acquisition in sign language is similar to that of spoken language but difficulties can arise with mathematics and reading. The major challenge for educators is to provide the child with the best language learning environment, while acknowledging that most hearing-impaired children live in an oral world. Some preliminary work suggests that teaching severely and profoundly hearing-impaired children sign language as a first language and oral language as a second language may have some promising results.

Chapter 7

Identifying and Assessing Language Problems

This chapter considers the key roles of identification and assessment in understanding a child's language difficulties. Identification is the process of noting a problem. Assessments, in contrast, are attempts to answer questions about the nature of a problem in a systematic and reliable way. The tools used depend on the questions that are asked and the population that is studied. Some of the terminology and concepts may be unfamiliar but by the end of the chapter an understanding of the key factors involved in carrying out a competent assessment of a child's language skills should be gained, as well as an awareness of the problems that exist in identifying and assessing language skills. The chapter concludes by considering some elements that need to be addressed in the assessment process.

INTRODUCTION

When was the last time you made a judgement about a person's skills or personality? The likelihood is that you have made such a judgement or assessment at least once in the last 24 hours. Assessing and evaluating people and situations is something people do every day. Many teachers, students and parents consider the topic of assessment tedious; something that has to be done but is not important. The reality is just the opposite. Assessment is something that is done all the time. Assessing situations correctly is a critical step in drawing accurate conclusions about a child's difficulty or the pattern of difficulties across particular groups of children. It is the basis for accurately describing a child's special needs. Moreover it is through the use of appropriate assessment procedures that we have acquired the rich knowledge we possess about children's language and language difficulties. Thus assessment is a fundamental element of developing a better understanding of individual children's needs and understanding the types of difficulties that occur in the development of language and communication

Attempting to understand a child's communicative competence

necessarily involves making judgements. The mother who compares her toddler's explanations with a peer's is carrying out a form of assessment. She is judging her child's performance in comparison with another. The teacher who notes that a child is not able to understand the intentions of others is also assessing; she is judging the child's performance in comparison with a set of skills that need to be mastered. Sometimes assessments are based on extensive evidence. Other times the basis for the judgement can be suspect. Consider a young child's report that states:

> Patrick is unable to attend in lessons. He spends most of his time wandering around the room. He will need extra support in class to stay on task.

Or another that says:

> Helen is an ideal pupil. She is quiet and attentive, working on her own.

A number of factors would influence acceptance of these statements including:

- how long the teacher has known the child;
- the teacher's level of experience;
- whether there were any other factors influencing the child's performance;
- what the teacher means by 'unable to attend' or 'attentive';
- whether this behaviour is typical of the child or unusual;
- the demands of the particular classroom.

Acceptance of the teacher's statement is bound by the nature of the assessment procedure. One would want to know how the teacher drew her conclusions. Similarly, when using research it is necessary to know how accurate the research findings are. As we have seen in previous chapters, research findings vary in their acceptance and generalizability. When assessing a child with a language or communication problem, it is necessary to know how reliable the results of the assessment are (that is whether we would get the same results at a different time on the same measure) and whether the results will generalize to other situations (that is whether the results will apply in different situations). Yet, trying to identify developmental difficulties is a complicated enterprise. Assessments need to:

- be based on sound judgements;
- reflect the essential components of language;
- offer fair comparisons with peers.

Children with communication difficulties

There is little doubt that many children experience difficulties with some aspect of communication, although it is unclear exactly how many children have such difficulties. For the majority of children with special educational needs their language and communication skills occupy a key position in educational planning. As we have seen in the previous chapters, children with language and communication difficulties form a heterogeneous group.

Firstly, the nature of their language difficulties varies. Children have difficulties that vary in severity and kind. At one point on the spectrum are children who have specific difficulties in articulation alone. Another point finds children who are totally reliant on alternative means of communication to express all their views and wishes (see Chapter 4). Box 7.1 lists the types of language problems that children may experience. The problems may occur only as expressive problems (production), but in other cases children will have difficulties with both expression and reception (comprehension).

A major division is drawn between difficulties of expressive language and receptive language. Difficulties can be further identified with:

- Speech processing.
- Phonology.
- Vocabulary (lexicon).
- Grammar (syntax).
- Pragmatics.
- Articulation.

Difficulties frequently co-occur, so a child can have grammatical, pragmatic and lexical difficulties, for example.

Box 7.1: Subcomponents of the language system that can be compromised in development

Secondly, language difficulties are associated with a range of different problems, including sensory (see Chapters 5 and 6), cognitive (see Chapter 4) or physical difficulties. In an inclusive survey of more than 7,000 children, Maurice Chazan and his colleagues (1980) reported that more than 8 per cent of the sample had a severe language problem and 18 per cent had a mild problem. It is important to realize that how language and communication difficulties are defined will determine the prevalence figures presented. Yet whatever cut-off point is used, it is clear that many children experience such difficulties.

The first step in the process is to identify whether a child is experiencing a communication or language problem. A child who has difficulties with communication and language may need extra or different educational experiences to have full access to social and educational opportunities. To meet the child's needs we need to understand the child's skills. In such circumstances language assessment is often part of a wider problem-based strategy to identify the needs of a child. Research studies are needed to understand language difficulties and to identify effective interventions (see

Chapter 8). This involves both studies of the developing language system and an investigation of which aspects of the language system are affected when development does not follow a normal pattern. In many cases we will also be trying to specify the mechanisms that might account for the child's difficulties.

ASKING THE QUESTIONS

There are many different questions which might be asked about a child's language skills. Yet the ways we ask the questions and the processes we engage in to describe the children's problems will be determined by a number of different factors. Three specific factors that influence assessments are:

- theoretical frameworks;
- research;
- individual needs.

Theoretical frameworks

Any assessment will be based on a model of the language system – what language is, how language works and how development proceeds. The model provides what is called a theoretical framework. As seen in earlier chapters, language and communication can be viewed from a number of different theoretical perspectives. When investigating children's language skills, we need to consider both what factors may be responsible for the difficulties that are experienced and which elements of the language system are affected.

Many early studies of language reflected theoretical trends at the time, such as Skinner's work in the early 1950s. Current conceptualizations of language and language learning are heavily influenced by information processing approaches. Two separate elements are typically considered: domain-specific skills and domain-general skills. Domain-specific skills are those which are special to language and would include such factors as phonological memory or forms of grammatical knowledge. Domain-general factors, in contrast, refer to factors that cross a range of different tasks and domains such as memory and attention. Focusing on domain-specific and domain-general skills forces a description of *what* is developing. Within such an investigative framework it is possible to be very detailed about the aspects of the language system under investigation. The ways in which the acquisition process is conceptualized by the investigator will direct which language processes are assessed.

Research

Research about children with atypical patterns of language and communication have a long history. These studies are concerned with describing and explaining patterns of language development in exceptional circumstances. Researchers hope to isolate critical factors involved in development for the group of children under investigation. The data are important both for confirming theories that exist and for developing new theories. How the population under investigation is defined is critical. As we have seen, it is not always easy to draw rigid boundaries to define a population. Consider how we might investigate the language skills of children with chromosomal abnormalities. The inclusion of a child in the study would be governed by very clear entry criteria and the symptom patterns would tend to be similar (see Chapter 4). This is not to say there will be no individual differences.

In contrast, there are other situations where the boundaries are less clear, such as specific speech and language difficulties (see Chapter 3). The goal for the researcher must be to find a clearly definable group where the members of that group have relatively pure versions of the problem under investigation. Assuming acceptable measures for specifying the population, the researcher will then investigate language performance. This assessment may involve conventional tests that compare children with a normative group. There is good evidence that test data are the single most frequent source of information used in the research identification process. Alternatively, researchers may design their own measures and compare children's performance with other groups who are matched either by chronological age, language age or mental age (see Box 7.2 and Chapter 4). In all these situations some form of assessment is carried out.

An age equivalent score is a test score expressed in terms of the age at which that score would normally be achieved. A language age equivalent score of 4:6 would indicate that a child, irrespective of their actual age, was performing in an equivalent fashion to an average child of 4½.

Box 7.2: What is an age equivalent score?

Individual needs

The central goal for practitioners is different. Here the aim is to gain an understanding of the child that is of value to the planning, execution and evaluation of an intervention. Multidisciplinary assessments are often essential with language problems. Such assessments allow the professionals to provide a detailed profile of the child's strengths and needs. For the professional, the primary focus is the child and the family. Different professionals will have different foci. Our own research on practitioners' understanding of specific speech and language difficulties has shown that speech and language therapists and educational psychologists have different views about the nature of the problems and the ways to assess them (Dockrell *et al.*, 1997). Equally, Armstrong and his colleagues (1993) have shown that parents and children approach the assessment process from a different perspective from that of the professionals involved. How such differences ultimately impact on the assessment of individuals is less clear. Assessing a child's special educational needs should be a balanced integration of the views of the various professionals, the parents and the child, where appropriate.

There is much prescriptive literature on how professionals should carry out the assessment process but little research on the actual assessment process itself. Jannett Wright (1993) argues that the aims of any speech and language assessment should be to identify any difficulties with communication; measure the degree of difficulty and the individual's strengths and weaknesses; plan goals of an intervention strategy; plan procedures for intervention and negotiate with other professionals as well as the family; and evaluate progress. Wright's analysis separates identification of the communication difficulty from the more detailed assessment of strengths and needs. In addition, this process is directly linked with intervention (Chapter 8). For the practitioner, profiling the child's special needs is of primary concern.

Summary

This introductory section has discussed issues surrounding the assessment process. It has emphasized the point that informal assessments are part of everyday activity. The range and diversity of children who experience language difficulties has been noted. It has been argued that the questions asked and the way assessments are carried out is determined by theoretical orientation, and whether the focus of the enquiry is theoretical or practical. Although the activities of the researcher and the practitioner both involve assessment, and in many cases may involve the same tools, it is important not to confuse their aims. However, it is important to note that they have much to learn from each other. Research-based studies provide practitioners with pertinent information to inform their assessment process. Practitioner data can serve to challenge the appropriateness of narrow criteria for population identification, highlight inconsistencies within groups and challenge expected patterns of development.

IDENTIFICATION AND ASSESSMENT

Assessment and identification are two complementary concepts. When searching to identify language problems, we ask the question: 'Is there a problem?' Assessment may be very simple and indirect, such as asking a parent a single question, or it may be more detailed and direct by completing a checklist of a child's language behaviours. When professionals use the term 'assessment' they are generally concerned with a more detailed and systematic set of investigations that attempt to specify the nature of the child's language difficulties and possibly identify factors that may have caused the problems. These more formal assessments usually involve the use of some set of tests. Often assessments have the aim of classifying a child's difficulties to allow for a more precise description and analysis. Of course, the value of such an enterprise is entirely dependent on how good the classification system is. Many prominent psychologists in the learning difficulties field have argued that present classification systems are unsatisfactory because they do not adequately describe differences between groups of children.

Margaret Lahey (1990) is keen that identification and assessment are seen as separate processes and we agree. She believes that when trying to identify a problem, judgement should be based on the child's language performance at the point that the judgement is being made. Furthermore, the child's performance should be compared with children of a similar age. In such situations both expectations of normal development and patterns of atypical development need to be explicit. Identification should target children that are actually having demonstrable difficulties, rather than considering potential risk factors such as otitis media (see Chapter 6) or low socio-economic status.

The assessment tools a professional chooses will be determined by their knowledge of language problems and the way they understand child development. Interpretation of the results of any assessment will be constrained by how solid the measures are, the expertise in their administration and the assessor's skills of interpretation. The fact that the criteria and procedures for identifying language problems vary widely among clinicians and researchers creates confusion. It interferes with clear communication between professionals and impedes understanding of language disorders. This will have direct (and negative) effects on service provision and children's eligibility for these services.

Identifying a language problem

The purpose of identification is to distinguish between children who do and those who do not have a language or communication problem. Identification can address two separate issues. Firstly, it can compare a child's performance with the norm (see section on normative assessment) or secondly it can evaluate the types of skills the child has mastered (see section on criterion-based assessment). Asking questions about identification involves searching for differences in patterns of development or skill level. Asking 'What causes a child's language and communication problems?' means searching for the precursors to the problems. Identification does not address the latter issue.

Understanding typical patterns of development is necessary to answer these questions. In the first place we know what skills and competences are part of the language system. In the second place we have information for comparative purposes. We know at what age children typically develop particular linguistic skills. We can also describe the ways in which skills are related to one another (see example in Chapter 1 on pointing). For some elements of the language system we know the extent of variation in normal development. These parameters can often be surprisingly wide (see the findings in Chapter 1 from Elizabeth Bates and her colleagues (1995)). To verify whether children have mastered certain aspects of the language system and whether their performance is similar to that of their peers requires both knowledge of the language system and an understanding of typical patterns of development. These two elements form the key components of a measurable definition of a language difficulty. The initial step for identification is to establish whether language is deviating from the norm. More detailed procedures can aim to discover in what ways language development is differing from the expected pattern. Box 7.3 considers some issues surrounding discrepancy approaches.

Problems with language and communication may present in different ways. Parents are often the first to notice these. Health visitors can also play a key role since they are the professional with whom all young children come into contact immediately after birth and at intervals over the pre-school period. Some children will be identified because they fail to reach early milestones, such as producing their first words or putting two words together. Yet others will bring themselves to the attention of professionals because of misbehaviour, social isolation or problems in learning. Informal observations which highlight a child's 'inability to attend', 'immaturity', or 'failure to listen to instructions' may well be indicators that a child is experiencing a language difficulty. It is, of course, essential to consider the particular behaviour in relation to the context in which it occurs.

Some people have argued that a good approach to identifying language problems is to target groups of children who are known to have a poor prognosis in the area of language. From this perspective, evidence is collected about specific clinical populations, such as children with hearing impairments, learning disabilities, cerebral palsy and so forth. As a means of defining the population of children with language difficulties such an approach has a number of limitations. Firstly, it is dependent on the existence of clearly defined conditions with similar behavioural outcomes. However, distinguishing the range of normal variation from variation which ought to be seen as 'clinically' significant, is a matter for debate. For example, what level of hearing loss should be regarded as critical for defining the relevant population (see Chapter 6)? Alternatively, why should significant delays be defined as being below the 15 percentile (see Chapter 4)? Secondly, there is little information about the normal course of language development in these populations. So, for example, delays in vocabulary development of blind children compared with their sighted peers have been reported. Should these be viewed as inevitable (see Chapter 5)? Are the delays specific to the children in the studies? Can they be explained by other cognitive deficits? The answers to these questions are still unknown. There is no reason to assume that development in such exceptional circumstances will be any less variable than normal development. However, the pattern may be skewed, that is more children in these groups may experience problems and these may be more severe than a typically developing population. Finally, there are children for whom language is their primary problem, with no other associated difficulties. A clinical approach alone would fail to identify these children. In sum, investigation of special populations is an important element in any attempt to conceptualize language problems and describe developmental differences.

A discrepancy occurs when a significant difference occurs between the scores a child achieves in one skill area compared with the scores a child achieves in another skill area. This difference is greater than what would be expected from normal variation. Discrepancy criteria have frequently been used in attempts to identify children with specific language impairment, where a contrast is drawn between language skills and non-verbal ability (see Chapter 4). It is also commonly used as a definition of dyslexia, where a contrast is drawn between the child's literacy skills and general level of ability. However, allusions to discrepancies are problematic. Problems include the methods for measuring the discrepancy, the meaningfulness of the distinction and the accuracy of the normative data being used to conclude that a discrepancy exists.

Box 7.3: What is a discrepancy?

Yet even within these groups we would wish to establish where the difficulties lie with the language system and how they compare with their typically developing peers and their peers with similar problems (their reference group).

Screening

Problems are not always immediately identified at home or in the clinic. It is often difficult to decide when a child's language is sufficiently different from the norm to warrant further assessment. Moreover, there is variability in both the sensitivity of parents and health practitioners to problems and the extent to which they will accept problems. Yet early detection of the presence of language difficulties has long been an important goal of researchers and practitioners alike. In an attempt to circumvent differences among individuals in recognizing developmental difficulties, screening procedures have been introduced in many areas.

Screening is a widely used procedure in medicine. Large populations are surveyed to identify individuals who are showing specific health problems or who may experience difficulties in the future. Screening is important when problems can be reliably identified, such as in cases of hearing or visual impairments. The identification of a specific language problem through a screening procedure is more problematic. The use of such procedures solely to identify language problems may be inappropriate. This is because there is insufficient agreement on what constitutes a language delay and it is difficult to differentiate between children who will go on to have difficulties and those who will improve spontaneously.

There are basically three types of screening – checklists (completed either by a professional or a parent), observation and formal testing. James Law (1992) has provided a description of a range of screening tests that can be used. Such tests need to be evaluated on two dimensions. The first dimension relates to the accuracy in identifying children with language and communication problems. Issues related to accuracy and screening are outlined in Box 7.4.

There are two measures: the hit rate or sensitivity, which is the measure of accurate identification, and the specificity, which means that children without problems are not identified. Identification could be critical in targeting resources for intervention or monitoring and for longitudinal research. There is not much use in having a measure that identifies 100 per cent of the children with language problems but also includes 50 per cent of children without language problems. Equally, there is not much point in having a measure that never falsely identifies a child without problems but fails to identify 30 per cent of the children with language problems. There is always a trade-off between specificity and sensitivity and where one draws the line will depend on the reasons for screening.

Box 7.4: Accurate identification in screening

The second dimension is concerned with the time frame of the screening process. Are we concerned about a present problem of predicting a future difficulty? Some tests are designed to identify the presence or absence of the language problem at the time of testing, that is, they are concerned with *concurrent* difficulties. Whether or not these difficulties improve over time is another issue. Other tests are designed to *predict* the likelihood of a child experiencing language difficulties in the future. In such cases children are thought to be 'at risk'. If a child is deemed to be at risk it is believed that there is a high probability that a language difficulty will occur. Once identified, children can be monitored or targeted for immediate intervention and support.

There are many problems with predicting future needs on the basis of screening procedures. As an example, consider the study carried out in Canada by Linda Siegel (1992). She has had some success in identifying predictive factors for cognitive and language difficulties but her data highlight the complexity of such an endeavour. She studied 104 children who were part of a longitudinal sample; half the children were pre-term and the other half full-term. By considering a range of reproductive variables (including birth order, maternal smoking, previous spontaneous abortions), socio-economic status and perinatal variables such as gestational age and measurement of the home environment, she was able to predict children's scores on the outcome measures which included the Reynell Language Development Scales (Reynell, 1977) and the Stanford Binet Test of Intelligence (Terman and Merrill, 1960). However, there was no simple index to predict these scores, rather there was a need to consider a variety of environmental and biological factors. Thus prediction was by no means straightforward. Moreover, while Siegel's conclusions apply to the group of children with low scores, *as a group*, they do not necessarily apply to every individual case. Prediction is hampered in individual children by dissociations in development, organic impairment and major life events (Largo *et al.*, 1990). Nonetheless, if screening identifies a potential problem the appropriate action is a more detailed assessment of the child's development.

The quest to identify children's educational needs has taken two rather different paths. The first is an attempt to screen for specific complex developmental disorders. An example of this is the checklist for autism in toddlers – *CHAT* (Baron-Cohen *et al.*, 1992). This is a simple checklist to be used by health visitors which focuses on key issues which could predict autism, such as lack of pretend play, lack of protodeclarative pointing (see Chapters 1 and 4), lack of social interest, lack of social play and lack of joint attention. To date there is positive evidence that the checklist can predict autistic behaviour and that the behaviour can be differentiated from more general cases of developmental delay.

The second line of development is more general and targeted at the whole population of a school year group. The British government has resolved to implement baseline assessment at school entry for all children (Education Act 1997). Baseline assessments vary in the skills they cover and how they are managed but several contain elements that assess oral language skills. One of the purposes of this activity is the early identification of children with special educational needs. In principle this move should be regarded favourably and could, in theory, have positive effects for children whose language difficulties would otherwise go unnoticed. However, no specific procedures are specified and, as Lindsay and Desforges (1998) argue, the process is not straightforward. Useful processes tend not to be one-off procedures. Rather, they argue that what is required is a process, over time, using high quality instruments but integrated into a continuous system of monitoring children's development.

In the domain of language, screening procedures should be accurate at identifying problems that actually exist at the time of screening. As an example, consider the Hackney early language screening test. This is a very simple test to administer using pictures and toys to assess the child's language skills. The test identifies language problems well but in some cases may overestimate the likelihood of a child having a problem. So some children who are identified will not actually have language delays as measured by the Reynell Developmental Language Scales or similar standardized assessment tool.

Parent checklists have grown in use and acceptability over the last ten years. They are good indices of expressive vocabulary size in toddlers. Moreover, Fischel and colleagues (1989) have demonstrated that parent report of expressive vocabulary size is an excellent index of language status. Thus, despite the problems with screening procedures there is evidence that some measures provide useful information about the present status of the child's functioning. However, we believe that the general points made about screening by Lindsay and Desforges (1998) are relevant to language. That is, the process should use high quality measures and be integrated into the continuing monitoring of a child's progress. Given the developmental pattern of language, there is an argument that the process should be implemented prior to school entry.

Assessment

Identifying the existence of a language problem is the first step in the assessment process. Researchers will then want to carry out further assessments to investigate their hypotheses about the nature and cause of the problem. Practitioners, in contrast, will want to carry out further assessments to investigate the child's difficulties and plan interventions. Broad ranges of information-gathering activities are available to meet these goals, including observation and testing. A wide variety of assessment devices can be used for the evaluation and diagnosis of school-age children (Sattler, 1992). The situation with younger children is different with fewer valid instruments available from birth to three years (Cicchetti and Wagner, 1990). Box 7.5 provides a list of commonly used assessment tools. Many of these measures have limitations. The choice of the measure must depend on the question for which an answer is sought and the children under investigation.

There are certain features of the language system that make it complicated for any assessment process. It is important to bear these in mind when considering what measures to use. Firstly, language is multidimensional and as such does not easily lend itself to single unitary measures. It is important to consider comprehension and production as well as the more subtle aspects of the language system, such as pragmatics. Secondly, there is much variation in

Pre-school:
British Picture Vocabulary Scales (Dunn et al., 1997);
Reynell Language Development Scales (Reynell, 1985);
Clinical Evaluation of Language Function (Semel et al., 1987);
Language subscales of the BASII (Elliot et al., 1997);
TROG (Bishop, 1983);
Edinburgh Articulation Test (Anthony et al., 1971);
The Bus Story (Renfrew, 1972).

Primary years:
British Picture Vocabulary Scales (Dunn et al., 1997);
Reynell Language Development Scales (Reynell, 1985);
Clinical Evaluation of Language Function (Semel et al., 1987);
Wechsler Objective Language Dimension (Rust, 1995);
Phonological Assessment Battery (Fredrickson et al., 1997);
TROG (Bishop, 1983);
Pragmatic and Early Communication Profile (Dewart and Summers, 1988)

Box 7.5: Commonly used assessment tools

normal patterns of development and this makes it difficult to draw precise boundaries between typical and atypical development.

As evidence to support these two important caveats, consider the work that Pat Howlin has been carrying out in London. Howlin and Cross (1994) have shown that even with children developing apparently normally, there is much variation on their scores on different language measures. They tested 35 children on six language measures and found that while on some measures the children's results appeared normal, on other measures they showed a marked discrepancy from their chronological age (see Box 7.6). Not all of the children completed all tests. They conclude, 'No test, however well designed, can ever be a substitute for careful observations and practical assessments of the child's communicative functioning.' Such results do not mean that assessing children's language should be stopped, rather it is necessary to consider a range of language skills and the child's profile overall.

18/32	British Picture Vocabulary Scales
9/33	Action picture test
7/32	Bus story
4/33	Action picture information
4/30	Test of reception of grammar
1/27	Reynell

Box 7.6: Distribution of numbers of children with low scores (a one-year or more gap between their language age and chronological age) on the tests administered by Howlin and Cross (1994)

While the primary focus of this chapter is the assessment of the child's language performance, satisfactory assessments will include other aspects of the child's functioning. Assessment must be developmentally and culturally appropriate, taking into account the cognitive and social aspects of development. This section considers a range of issues relating to assessing language competence, highlighting the benefits and disadvantages of the approaches. Two issues are discussed: types of comparisons, and limitations of the tools.

Types of comparisons

Assessment involves evaluating a child's performance and comparing it either with their own performance on different types of tasks or with the performance of other children. Frequently these comparisons can involve standard tools. Four types of comparisons can be made, these may be used either alone or in combination:

- standardized norm-referenced tests;
- criterion-referenced tests, developmental profiles or checklists;
- assessments of the processes of learning – dynamic assessments;
- experimental tasks.

Norm-referenced tests

Norm-referenced tests provide information about where an individual lies with a particular ability (e.g. naming vocabulary) or attainment (reading) in comparison with peers of the same age. The measurements are of varying degrees of sophistication: ranks, percentiles, standardized scores or age equivalents. Whatever the measure, the basic principle of norm-referenced tests is to define a continuum of performance from lowest to highest and the measure assigned to a particular individual locates his or her position on that continuum. The test results measure the product of learning and serve as indicators of the differences that exist between a child and his or her peers on a particular task or set of tasks.

An important consideration with norm-referenced tests is their retest reliability and validity. Retest reliability refers to the extent to which the test will produce the same results when the same child is measured at another point in time. For example, retest reliability over a one-month period for intelligence tests is high. The basic definition of validity is the extent to which a test measures what it is supposed to measure. There are a number of different kinds of test validity. Validity can be assessed by comparing a test with a similar test designed to measure the same functions (concurrent validity), so one reading test might be compared with another.

Reliability and validity are not always considered before a test is used. When Plante and Vance (1994) examined 21 tests which purported to identify language difficulties in pre-school children (aged 3 to 4) their findings were disconcerting. Only 38 per cent of the tests met half the necessary criteria for test use and of the four acceptable tests administered to the children only one test (SPELT-II) discriminated in an acceptable way between the language-impaired and non-language-impaired children. Moreover, giving the children more language tests did not make the situation better. These problems are not specific to language measures. In a survey of learning disability programmes, Thurlow and Ysseldyke (1979) found that of the tools used by three or more programmes only 25 per cent were considered to be technically adequate in terms of reliability, validity and standardization sample.

Clearly the use of unreliable measures renders the identification of a specific difficulty problematic:

> Norm-referenced tests provide evidence regarding the existence of a problem. Properly used they can suggest a need for further assessment or help document a need for the initiation or continuation of therapy. Misused they can lead to mistaken understanding of a client's problem, to inappropriate and fruitless therapy programs or to inaccurate conclusions regarding the efficacy of therapy. (McCauley and Swisher, 1984: 338)

There is no logical or empirical reason to assume that language delays and difficulties will only occur for children who are following typical developmental courses. Yet virtually none of the normative language measures that exist are standardized on children from different groups. The assumption is that English is the child's first language and that the child is experiencing no additional disability. Imagine how much harder it becomes to assess a child's language skills when Bengali, not English, is their first language. The problem becomes more acute when the primary language is not spoken by the professionals involved in the assessment process. Similar problems arise when the child has sensory impairments (see Chapters 5 and 6). In such cases the child is prevented from accessing the full range of communicative experiences available. Identifying general language problems and specific language problems becomes a very complex endeavour and in many cases the existence of language problems can be missed. Box 7.7 identifies some general considerations for assessing children with sensory impairments.

Criterion-referenced tests
The discussion about norm-referenced tests has highlighted the fact that sometimes it is inappropriate to draw comparisons among children. Criterion-referenced tests offer an alternative base for comparison. These tests are concerned with the skills a child needs to complete a task or produce an utterance. A previously specified set of criteria are used to assess children, such as appropriate use of the past tense, e.g. *drove* rather than *drived*. In this way the child's success in mastering certain linguistic features can be

Hearing impaired:
Review the extent and nature of the hearing loss.
Establish the preferred communication mode by prior observation.
Establish how the test should be presented – manual sign, gesture, oral or some combination.
Check the test norms – is there an appropriate standardization sample?
Establish the appropriateness of the testing situation, e.g. adequate lighting for lip-reading and lighting in appropriate condition.
Use multiple measures to get a more accurate reflection of the child's skills.

(derived from Vess and Gregory, 1985)

Visually impaired:
Review the extent and nature of the visual impairment.
Check the test norms – where appropriate use a blind neutral assessment.
Establish a clearly defined space for carrying out the assessment.
Simplify the factors involved in localizing the test objects.
Use verbal and tactile guidance to explain tasks with objects.
Use multiple measures to get a more accurate reflection of the child's skills.

(see Brambring and Troster, 1994 for further discussion of these issues)

Box 7.7: Key factors in assessing children with sensory impairments evaluated without making assumptions about their peers' progress. The tests help to identify whether or not an individual possesses some particular skill or competence and may allow for the analysis of error patterns. They are designed to provide a clear indication of what a child can and cannot do. In this way they give guidelines for which skills should next be taught.

The first step in developing a criterion-referenced test is a clear definition of the skills under investigation. If we were interested in children's naming ability we would need to know what skills were involved in accurate naming. These might include recognizing the object, being able to retrieve the word from memory and finally uttering the word. A well-described domain is necessary to identify potential test items. However, the tool might focus on different dimensions and this would result in the construction of quite different scales. For example, the level of competence (how many objects the child can name) could be considered, or speed (how quickly the child names) or the influence of context on naming (whether the child is provided with extra information about the to-be-named object).

Identification of what needs to be measured in a criterion-referenced test is not a simple matter. Equally, as for norm-referenced tests, they must be reliable and valid. Many of the early language checklists serve as a form of criterion-referenced assessment. These appear to offer a good index of early expressive vocabulary. It is less clear that the criterion-based measures of more complex language skills, such as pragmatics, are as valid.

Formal tests provide us with quantitative measures of language performance. It is often necessary and generally informative to supplement such measures with qualitative analysis. Standardized measures typically fail to address the nature of poor scores and individual problems. Researchers often design studies specifically to include measures that are derived from other data sources. Practitioners also extend their assessments by including less formal measures. One systematic attempt to include such factors is the use of dynamic assessment.

Processes of learning

Assessments of cognitive skills have been criticized because they focus solely on learning products – what a child can or cannot do. Similar criticism can be levelled at tests of language ability. An overall score tells us neither about how a child approaches the task nor about which elements of the task they find difficult. In an attempt to counteract this static approach to assessment, process-based procedures have been developed. In such cases the focus is on the process of thinking (e.g. approach to task, strategy use and so forth) rather than the products of learning. Significance comes from what the child has learned during and after interaction with the assessor, who also provides pedagogical input. These assessments are designed to systematically manipulate the context to support learning.

The first of these approaches is best described as a *teaching experiment* and is commonly used by psychologists. Teaching experiments focus on the individual child and the interplay of the child's skills in a particular situation.

Using learning as an assessment technique, one can use a test-teach-test model as a means of gauging an individual's ability to retain the content of the material and to transfer the principles learnt to new tasks. If a criterion-referenced test exists it can serve as an indicator of where to pitch initial teaching. This approach forces the practitioner to be precise about the task components and can make the assessment both relevant and meaningful. Moreover, such an approach allows the assessor to incorporate wider features into the conceptualization of the learning difficulty. However, since there is no external standard interpretation of the child's difficulties, interpretation will be dependent entirely on the evaluator's skills and experiences. Such assessments will need to be supported by additional information if the conclusions are to be generalized to other tasks and other contexts.

The second, and more widely researched, approach is called dynamic assessment or tests of learning potential. Ingrid Lunt describes dynamic assessment as the 'interactional exploration of a learner's learning and thinking processes, and aims to investigate strategies for learning, and ways these may be extended/enhanced' (Lunt, 1993: 152). These assessments examine a child's modifiability in their responses when confronted with a difficult, unmastered task and when provided with adult prompts designed to improve performance. There is growing support for this approach with children who may have difficulty processing various kinds of external stimuli. One of the advantages of such methods is that they could predict the children who are going to show greatest change when offered intervention; that is, their skills and knowledge are likely to be modified. A further advantage occurs in cases where children show great variability in testing, such as the hearing impaired. In these cases it should be possible to describe clearly the types of support that are needed for the child to demonstrate the range of skills they possess.

One non-verbal intelligence test (Snidjers Oomen-R) has been specifically designed to incorporate some of these features. Peter Tellegen and his colleagues in Holland have spent many years developing the present test format. They argue that the SON-R maintains the rigour of standard assessment procedures, while sharing some important procedures and content areas with 'learning potential tasks'. Firstly, it provides feedback to the children. This is generally prohibited in other standard tests. Secondly, it provides several examples so that the child understands the nature of the assessment procedure. Thirdly, it is adaptive so that easier items can be administered after some failures (Tellegen and Laros, 1993a, b).

Olswang and Bain (1996) and Bain and Olswang (1995) have investigated the usefulness of using dynamic assessment procedures with children who have specific expressive language delay. They measured children's per-formance on both conventional and dynamic assessment procedures and then evaluated which measure predicted future change in language production. The dynamic assessment involved providing children with a range of cues, which supported children in increasing the complexity of the sentences they uttered. The dynamic measures were very good predictors of change. In contrast, the more conventional tests (e.g. norm-referenced) did not predict change. They argued that dynamic assessment measures provide more informed information to make decisions about which children are ready to change. In general, language difficulties have not been the focus of dynamic assessment researchers. The Olswang and Bain studies suggest that this could well be a fruitful avenue of enquiry for research. Moreover, for individual children, the practitioner could be provided with valuable advice for intervention about the procedures that were effective.

Experimental tasks

Devising specific tasks to investigate a developmental question has been a popular way to develop a greater understanding of language difficulties. This is a frequently used approach by researchers, which is considered to have several advantages over other methods:

- A task can be designed to tap a specific problem, such as use of questions.
- The method of presentation can be standardized across children.
- Minor alterations can be made in the task to see whether that affects the children's performance.

The task designed by Heather Van der Lely (1990) to test young children's grammatical comprehension is a good example. Here children were presented with carefully constructed questions that varied in the accuracy with which they described a picture. So the children heard questions such as 'Is Baloo tickling Mowgli?' and they were required to say 'Yes' if the answer was correct and 'No' if it was not. Tasks such as this have allowed researchers to develop sophisticated analyses of children's linguistic problems (see Chapter 3 for examples). However, children's performance of these tasks is not simply influenced by their language skills and in such situations it is essential to have comparative data from children of the same age and possibly with the same language skills.

Limitations of the tools

The limitations of existing tools for assessing children's language and cognitive skills need to be considered from two perspectives: their reliability and validity and their ability to discriminate atypical patterns of development. There is now strong evidence to show that:

- There are psychometric inadequacies in almost all commonly used language measures.
- The measures lack concurrent validity (McCauley and Demetras, 1990).
- Standard tests are poor at predicting outcome for young language-impaired children (see Chapters 3 and 8; Schery, 1985; Stark *et al.*, 1983).
- Reliance on single measures to assess language difficulties is unreliable and invalid (Bishop and Edmundson, 1987).

- Even tests that pass relatively high numbers of psychometric criteria may not be precise discriminators of 4- and 5-year-old children.

Such limitations should not mean that we stop using such measures altogether and use less reliable and poorly understood measures instead. However it is important to be aware that it is always possible to test a child and record some sort of numerical result. The critical issue is the interpretation of that result in an informed manner. A culture of critical approaches to assessment should raise the standard of the assessment process. Further, it argues for a strong culture of evaluating the assessment being carried out. The limitations identified mean that researchers and practitioners alike must have:

- An awareness of the psychometric inadequacies of commonly used language measures.
- An understanding that tests can vary with the language component assessed.
- Caution in interpretation of results from children on which a test has not been standardized, e.g. hearing impaired, visually impaired.
- A realization that language skills should be measured across different areas and qualitative information about level of communicative functioning considered.

These limitations have implications for measuring and understanding discrepancies across linguistic and non-linguistic processes (see Box 7.3). Attempts to identify discrepancies between age and achievement, ability and achievement and reference group and achievement have been a major concern of psychologists and special needs researchers for much of this century. Given the limitations of tests, a flexible and informed approach to examining a child's profile of skills should always be used by the practitioner.

THE WAY FORWARD

Reliable and valid assessments of a child's language development and communicative competence are of central importance for studying typical and atypical development. Trying to decide whether a child has a significant language problem or not can be daunting, even for experienced practitioners. The child, the particular tasks under investigation and the context of learning will govern choice of the appropriate measures. However, with a clear understanding of the assessment dilemmas and the processes of normal development, a balanced analysis of problems is attainable. In Table 7.1 (page 132) we provide a framework to organize the assessment and intervention process.

Two key issues need to be considered as identification is attempted and assessment carried out. There is a need to consider a wide range of factors that might impinge on the child's performance. This is particularly critical for clinical work and also has implications for research. These factors include appropriateness of materials, cultural factors, attention and motivation. Assessment occurs in a context of relationships between the child and the task material, the setting in which the assessment occurs and what has been termed the 'social surround' (Messick, 1983) which includes the examiner, other children, and social expectancies such as sense of task orientation, apprehension at being evaluated, and the atmosphere of the testing session. Children's previous success or failure can exert a powerful influence on the child's approach to the tasks. When making inferences about the child's characteristics and competencies the child's opportunities for learning in the school, home and community and the culture of which the youngster is a member should be considered.

Secondly, when we consider the detailed assessment of language, the child's performance should be profiled across a range of language and cognitive dimensions. Sampling language skills in situations that stress the language system can provide valuable insights about the child's difficulties. This may well entail assessment in more complex situations, such as classrooms. Underlying weaknesses in language may only emerge when a mismatch is provoked between the child's skills and strategies and demands of the learning environment. For example, a number of researchers have shown that children may have difficulties in accessing, organizing and co-ordinating multiple mental activities simultaneously or in close succession. It is important not to dismiss clinical judgement or other potential sources of information. Concern about a child's language development should be followed up by a detailed assessment by a trained professional.

Process	Examples	Focus	Checks	Tools	Action	Important considerations
Identification	Limited verbal communication Flat intonation Lack of interest in story books	a) Parents or health visitors aware of unexpected communication patterns b) Identification on a screening test c) Poor performance on baseline language or literacy measures	1. Check hearing, vision and motor skills 2. Check comprehension/production of lexicon, grammar and interaction	A number of screening measures exist which professionals can use Parents also have access to checklists which can help support the identification of communication difficulties. These are often available through relevant charities	If concern not substantiated, monitor development If further evidence of concern refer for more detailed assessment	Corroborate findings with initial referral agent, provide appropriate avenues for further assessment or support if required
Assessment	Failure to combine words to make two-word utterances Unable to follow commands	Developmental level of language performance	1. Norm-based comparisons to establish extent of language problems 2. Check behaviour/social skills 3. Check literacy and numeracy	Professionals have access to a wide range of standardized tests which will establish a child's level of performance in comparison to peers. Ensure the tests are well-standardized and appropriate for the specific task	Target key areas for intervention (see Chapter 8) Intervention will not necessarily be directed at the child's most delayed area of development	1. Never use a single test score to arrive at a decision 2. Ensure that tests are appropriate for the children being assessed, that is be aware of motor, visual and hearing factors 3. Be aware of cultural differences. Do not assume that norms generalize from one population to the next
Assessment leading to intervention		Nature of language problem	1. Criterion referenced assessment to establish target for intervention 2. Use of zone of proximal distance to support scaffolding	Assessments of tasks specifically designed for intervention and profiling subcomponents of language and communication	Information should contribute directly to devising the child's individual educational plan	1. Use flexible means of assessing progress 2. Assume there may be little change on standardized tests 3. Monitor progress in the areas targeted for intervention

Table 7.1: A framework for organizing identification and assessment

Chapter 8

Intervention

The previous chapters have outlined patterns of typical and atypical language development. It has been seen that a child's communicative behaviour is related to a number of different factors and that the understanding of language acquisition involves:

- A recognition of the sub-components of the language system.
- A wider understanding of language as a communicative system.
- An understanding of the impact of other perceptual and cognitive skills.
- An awareness of children's experiences and the context in which a child's language system develops.

In devising interventions, the interplay between these dimensions needs to be considered. This is true whether the aim is to influence the anticipated course of language development or improve the child's ability to use the relevant linguistic skills. The emphasis of the interventions will vary according to the types of difficulties a child experiences. Thus, sensory impairments and cognitive impairments involve different considerations. This is further complicated by the fact that the dimensions outlined do not map neatly on to specific populations. Difficulties can vary between different populations of children and variation also can be found within groups of children developing in typical and atypical situations. The co-occurrence of other developmental problems complicates the picture for many children. This variation alone makes it unlikely that there will be a single intervention which can address the needs of all language problems. Moreover, since groups of children can vary in their individual needs, it is unlikely that there will be one intervention that will meet the needs of all the children within a particular group. For some children interventions will aim to eliminate specific problems but for many the practical goal of an intervention will be to reduce the impact of the child's difficulties. To devise successful interventions we need a clear understanding of both the child's problems and the ways in which these problems impact on the child's life and learning. These factors have been considered in the previous chapters. In addition it is essential to have a framework or checklist of the general issues that need to be considered in planning interventions. This chapter begins by considering this framework. Having constructed a framework it is then necessary to address issues related to setting up interventions and considering particular intervention techniques. Finally we consider the efficacy of language interventions.

This chapter discusses an approach to intervention which is useful in cases where a) specific problems reduce the child's ability to take advantage of conventional developmental experiences, and b) cases where conventional support has failed to maximize the conditions necessary for language learning. Conventional support varies markedly across schools, districts and countries.

Equally it can be the case that two children in the same school with a similar language problem do not both receive language interventions. For example, if one child is disruptive and the other withdrawn, the disruptive child will interfere more with the daily workings of the class. Thus, an understanding of a child's special needs must be evaluated in terms of the group with which they are being contrasted and the effect that they have on the group.

It is essential to consider the whole child in the context in which he or she is struggling to communicate successfully. As a result, interventions need to be matched to context of a child's needs. This means that it is not appropriate to construct a shopping list of interventions. Any list of this type would need to be regarded with a healthy degree of scepticism. Instead our objective is to provide a *framework* that will help in asking the appropriate questions about a child or specific group of children.

WHAT IS AN INTERVENTION?

An intervention is any planned action designed to modify or prevent an unwanted outcome. The purposes of interventions will include the acquisition of new skills and knowledge but will also include supporting the child to use and maintain skills and knowledge they have acquired. The basic assumption is that when a child receives an intervention, their language will improve more rapidly than if they received no intervention.

Governments often develop new educational interventions to prevent children failing at school. Parents develop interventions to improve their child's behaviour. So the construction and implementation of interventions are not tied to specific individuals or professions. One does not need to be a therapist to intervene. However, if interventions are to be successful, the expectation is that the person who is devising and planning them will have expertise in the area(s). Historically the needs of children with communication problems have been addressed from a clinical and medical perspective. Children received help in a one-to-one situation, or in small groups, from speech and language therapists who were often based in a clinic. More recently the understanding of speech and language difficulties has led to a broader approach. Now three complementary professional disciplines are commonly involved in the management of language and communication difficulties: speech and language science, psychology and education. Each of these perspectives contributes a special understanding of the developmental processes involved in learning and language. However, the additional expertise of the child's parents is always necessary when considering the progress of an individual child.

The intervention process can be conceived of as an equation with three elements (see Figure 8.1). The first component involves devising the intervention. Interventions are constructed to meet specific needs, and to do this a hypothesis must be constructed about the nature and the causes of a child's problems. In Chapter 7 we argued that careful and detailed assessments should lead to establishing specific hypotheses about the nature of the child's problem and thereby establish clear goals for intervention.

The second part of the equation is executing the intervention as it was formulated. There is no reason to assume that the intervention needs to be carried out directly by the specialist who devised it. Interventions for many areas of language may be more appropriately carried out by the individuals that a child interacts with on a daily basis, such as carers and teachers, as opposed to a speech and language therapist. However, whoever carries it out must understand its purpose. All too often teachers and parents are asked to carry out tasks without proper guidance.

The final component in any intervention must be an evaluation of its effectiveness *in comparison with* the aims that were set for the child or group of children involved. Most people would not consider altering their behaviour or lifestyle unless they expected a positive change, which was tangible in some way. The same is true of interventions – one needs to know if they are working or not. Unfortunately, evaluating the efficacy of an intervention is not as straightforward as evaluating the impact of some other changes. Children are

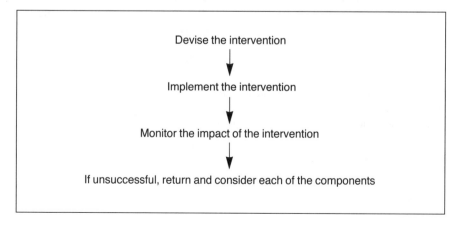

Figure 8.1: The intervention equation

continually changing and changes that occur when no intervention takes place need to be compared with changes that occur because of a specific intervention.

Therefore the intervention process should be viewed as cyclical and requiring constant evaluation. The implementation of the intervention is crucial. Attempting to teach a child new knowledge and skills serves as a test of initial hypotheses about the cause of the child's difficulty. If the intervention proves successful, then this provides support for the initial assessment. If the child's performance does not improve, the intervention will not have served its purpose. Thus, if initial intervention techniques do not lead to success, a return to the assessment of the child's difficulties is required. Either the initial target of the intervention was not the cause of the problem or the target is not amenable to current attempts to intervene, and alternative approaches will need to be considered. It is important that both the content of the intervention and its implementation are evaluated. Children may fail to learn because a programme is misconceived or because it is badly implemented.

One of the most important aspects of interventions is that they are devised in a principled way. The next section draws on present understandings of patterns of development to construct a set of principles that should guide interventions. Subsequent sections consider how interventions can be targeted (setting aims and objectives) and the current evidence about the efficacy of interventions. Finally, two issues are addressed that are important factors in any intervention.

A FRAMEWORK FOR INTERVENTIONS

The need to individualize intervention approaches is a common theme throughout the special needs literature. Our view is that it is important to consider children's individual needs in conjunction with the primary difficulties that are being experienced. This must be done by drawing on a wider understanding of typical and atypical development. There must also be an awareness that identifying the needs of individual children or groups of children does not necessarily mean that interventions need to be carried out on an individual basis. The target of the intervention (*what* is changed) needs to be separated from the ways in which the intervention is implemented (*how* it is changed).

The relationship between these factors can be understood in terms of Klaus Wedell's (1995) model of compensatory interaction. In this model it is not simply what the environment affords or what the child brings that is critical but the match between the environment and the strengths and needs of the particular child. This is shown particularly powerfully when considering the achievements of profoundly deaf children when their parents are also deaf (see Chapter 6). Wedell argues that the factors can compensate (or not) at three levels: the child, the environment and over time. Thus our framework for intervention must consider three factors:

1. Task-based factors.
2. The context of development.
3. Child-based factors.

The key features of the framework are highlighted in Box 8.1.

Factors	Key features
Task factors	1. Identification of key language-based components of the task. 2. Identification of key cognitive-based components of the task. 3. Identification of key pragmatic-based components of the task.
Context factors	1. What are the important dimensions in the child's life – home, school, peers etc.? 2. Is there a match between demands/support in the key dimensions? 3. To what extent is the wider socio-cultural and political situation impacting on the child's needs?
Child-based factors	1. Child's language skills. 2. Child's cognitive skills. 3. Child's motivation and interest. 4. Child's approach to tasks. 5. Interaction between 1 and 4?

Box 8.1: Key features of intervention framework

Task-based factors

The first step in any intervention is to understand the nature of the task that is causing the child problems. Previous chapters have outlined the various components involved in learning language. It has also been shown that some children can have difficulties with different sub-components of the language system. Other children may experience difficulties with non-language components that affect their ability to efficiently produce and comprehend oral language.

One of the major problems in attempting to intervene in cases of language difficulty is the fact that children do not normally have to be taught to talk in the way that they are taught to read and write, so the processes that drive language acquisition are still of considerable debate. The emphasis must be on language and language-related skills. The sub-tasks involved in the task which is causing the child difficulty need to be established and the relevant knowledge base identified that the child must possess in order to master the task. The knowledge base includes facts, concepts and terms associated with particular tasks or domains. It is also necessary to identify strategies that the child needs to use to succeed in the task. These strategies may be either language-specific task strategies or more general executive strategies to do with planning or focusing attention.

Identification of the relevant task components tells us what the child has to

Task factors:

1. Analysis of sub-components of the language system.
2. Analysis of cognitive demands of the task.
3. Analysis of pragmatic demands of the task.

Such a task analysis could be used in analysing a child's performance when required to buy a packet of crisps:

1. Are the questions directed to the shopkeeper?
2. Does the child respond to questions?
3. Can the child comprehend and produce the required vocabulary and syntax?

Box 8.2: Key factors in framing an intervention

do. How the child actually performs the tasks requires an analysis of the requirements of each sub-task. An example of a possible task analysis for a difficulty in responding to questions is presented in Box 8.2. Moreover, each one of the sub-tasks could be broken down further if necessary.

This form of task analysis implies that interventions should be targeted at particular problems, and if a child has a range of problems these will each need to be considered separately in the initial planning phase. Thus, intervention should focus on the child's needs in relation to their current level of performance on a particular set of tasks.

The context of interventions

Interventions should not be implemented or evaluated in isolation from the wider context in which a child develops. Considering the context of development is important for two reasons. Firstly the ways in which a child's language skills develop can be significantly influenced by the experiences which they receive. Secondly, the ways in which a child's problems are interpreted can vary significantly across contexts. All too often consideration of a child's language difficulties has focused only on factors within the child, without due consideration of the child's experiences.

Bronfenbrenner (1979) has tried to specify more precisely what the nature of environmental influences on development might be. In Bronfenbrenner's theory of the *Ecology of human development* the environment is envisioned as a series of nested structures that extend beyond the immediate setting. Each level is thought to greatly affect the child. These levels are called the microsystem, the mesosystem, the exosystem and the macrosystem. They are illustrated in Figure 8.2.

The microsystem for children includes the places they inhabit, the people who live with them, the things they do together and their direct experiences. This means, of course, that the children find themselves in many different microsystems – classrooms, friendships, playgrounds and so forth. Microsystem factors and their effects can be subtle. It has already been noted

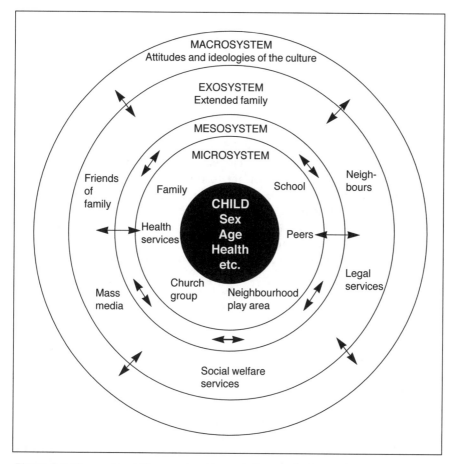

Figure 8.2: The ecology of human development. Source: Garbarino (1982)

how parents of atypical learners are more directive, but the simplification of linguistic level in many cases appears to be related to expressive level, not cognitive skills. Therefore the process of simplification has both advantages and disadvantages. Interventions are generally targeted on the individual child working within a particular microsystems.

Ideally, special provision should be designed as mesosystem (links between microsystems) models, so that for example, clear links are set up between what the child experiences at home and what is occurring in school or a link is established between what is occurring in therapy and what is occurring in the classroom. There is, for example, clear evidence that some of the most successful interventions involve some element of parental participation.

The last level of Bronfenbrenner's model is the *macrosystem*. It is not a specific environmental context but refers to the ideology and values of a culture, which affect decisions made at other levels of the model. The issue of whether children with learning difficulties should be educated in mainstream schools is determined by a complex set of educational and economic factors, which reflect the values of a particular culture at a particular time (Wolfendale, 1987). Clarifying these issues is not always straightforward and depends on an understanding of the system in which the child is based and the wider cultural beliefs that are held by the community in which the child is developing.

To help us consider these different factors a useful analogy can be drawn from the field of genetics. Geneticists talk of a 'reaction range'. This is the extent to which a behaviour, trait or ability can be influenced by the environment. Thus the child's environment can offer different kinds of opportunities to develop (or not) language and communication skills. As Bronfenbrenner shows it is important to remember that a child's learning takes place in a wide range of settings. This means that the reaction range can be influenced by the behaviour not only of carers, but also by classroom language demands and expectations, as well as the attitudes and belief systems of the teachers. An understanding of these contextual factors also helps interpret variation in a child's performance and should create a sensitivity to the facts that:

1. It is possible to be misled if children's language is not examined in a variety of contexts, and
2. Intervention in isolation from real-life situations and functions can be seen as counter-productive.

To be effective, interventions need to take into account the different contexts in which the child is functioning and the ways in which the difficulties the child is experiencing impact on that context. Language interventionists need to know how best to maximize the positive effects of significant others on language learning to help each child achieve their potential. In some cases managing change in the child's learning environment will go a significant way in tempering the child's problems.

Child-based factors

Finally we turn to the child's contribution to the intervention process. By dealing with the child last we in no way want to minimize the importance of the child's characteristics in the intervention process. Rather we wish to highlight the background knowledge that is a necessary prerequisite to interpreting the child's needs. Assessing a child's needs for intervention is rather different from assessment for identification. As seen in the previous chapters, identification involves some specific assessment to clarify the types of problems experienced by a child. Once a specific language problem, cognitive delay or sensory impairment is identified, the much more complex task of profiling a child's linguistic skills and matching them to the child's needs and that of their educational environment must be undertaken.

Having outlined the cognitive prerequisites for accomplishing the task, one must then consider the cognitive skills of the child and identify the mismatch between the two. The task decomposition makes it clear that the profiles of performance need to be considered in a range of different contexts rather than by global categorization of the child's language skills or cognitive ability. Here the concern is with the child's level of functioning, their strengths and needs. The profiling involves two distinct elements. One is related to the nature of the disability and the second is at the level of the child.

Studies of special populations enhance our understanding of the kinds of issues it is necessary to consider when addressing a child's intervention needs. One issue is the ways in which patterns of development could impact on intervention or indicate that the child requires specific support in another area. How might deficits in one area hinder the acquisition of other skills? These difficulties might be task constrained or affect more general processes of learning. For example, research suggests that children with otitis media can be less effective learners in the classroom because of distractibility, poor concentration spans and a high dependency on adults. Before an intervention is implemented to address a language problem in a child with otitis media one would need to investigate the child's learning strategies. In a similar vein the language problems of children with specific speech and language difficulties have ramifications for accessing the wider curriculum. Thus, the interventionist must possess an understanding of the relevant parameters for the particular child or group of children. These parameters can have important implications for how interventions are structured and have been outlined in previous chapters.

Children are individuals despite their generic difficulties, and the individual child's performance must also be looked at across a range of indicators. Wedell's (1995) conceptualization of best practice includes both cognitive and non-cognitive measures. Non-cognitive includes motivation, interest and affect. Perhaps unsurprisingly the predictive likelihood of success in any given environment is often influenced by these non-cognitive factors (see Chapter 7). Children who have experienced failure in communication or academic failure may doubt their own ability to succeed. They can come to view their efforts at achievement as futile. This in turn results in frustration and/or giving up very quickly, which contributes to further failure and the reinforcement of the belief that the child does not have the ability to succeed. With experience this cycle is strengthened and even successes can be viewed as luck or understood by perceiving the task as an 'easy' one. Often long-term educational benefits stem not from what children are specifically taught but from the effects on children's attitudes to learning, self-esteem and task orientation.

Summary

The suggested framework for intervention has explored developmental, contextual and individual factors. Interventions need to be constructed within an understanding of these different factors. So for example, a child with a hearing loss may compensate for this by developing positive strategies to

Some researchers have argued that there are specific interactions between a child's characteristics and the types of interventions that will benefit them the most. Commonly contrasted approaches are ones that use direct intervention in comparison to ones that use mediated intervention.

Direct	Mediated
Teacher initiated	Child initiated
Set rewards	Naturally occurring rewards
Elicited responses	Modelling
Predetermined sequence of instruction	Variable sequence of instruction
Didactic principles	Normal developmental patterns

Box 8.3: Matching children and interventions. Source: Cole et al. (1993)

clarify the input, e.g. sticking close to an adult, or they may influence development negatively by withdrawing. The environment might allow the individual to demonstrate their acquired skills and knowledge and develop further or it may limit this. Similarly, certain types of intervention approaches might be more appropriate for some children than others (see Box 8.3 as an example). The ways in which changes occur and impact on development will vary over time.

For example, children who have not mastered the communication skills expected of their age are likely to experience social problems. Their mis-understandings of the pragmatics of language, such as intonation or non-verbal cues, may make them appear defiant, rejecting or lacking in tact. This will not only influence their relationships with their peers, but over time may well result in reduced opportunities to use these skills, thereby further limiting the language-related experiences they acquire. Having established a set of questions which need to be addressed in framing the intervention, the factors involved in setting up the intervention need to be considered.

HOW SHOULD WE SET UP INTERVENTIONS?

The principles that have been identified provide a framework for considering the child's needs. Having determined the child's needs, an appropriate intervention needs to be devised. There are two core components to the intervention: what needs to be taught and how the child may be helped to learn the information and use the skills. Decisions about which language and communication skills are to be addressed need to be arrived at by a task analysis and subsequent targeting of specific aspects of the language system.

Aims and objectives

It is necessary to be specific about what the intervention is intended to achieve. This means setting aims and objectives, otherwise it will not be possible to assess the success of the intervention. Aims and objectives differ in their level of generality. Aims are not theory-driven; objectives are. Thus, in the case of a child with a speech and language difficulty, the aim of the intervention will be to improve the child's language. The objectives that are set to achieve this aim can differ, between someone who believes that speech processing is the cause of the difficulty and someone who believes that the difficulty is caused by a lack of understanding of pragmatic cues.

Objectives are statements about what the child should be able to do following intervention. Objectives should be set in the light of two criteria: the skills required for performance of the task and the current abilities of the learner. Cognitive task analysis is used to determine the skills required. The task analysis also serves as a basis for assessing the current abilities of the learner. By approaching the child's learning difficulty it is possible to discover which of the necessary components of skilled performance are currently possessed by the child and which are lacking, thereby being able to profile the child's educational needs.

Objectives need to be set in terms of pupil performance, and intervention procedures need to be carefully organized. A good objective states what it is that a child is expected to do and under what conditions the behaviour should occur. Moreover, objectives need to be explicit in terms of how well a task must be done so that they provide measurable indices of performance. For example, an objective that states that a child should *know the meaning of 'more' and 'less'* is inadequate since it fails to specify what criteria would constitute 'knowing'. On the other hand, an objective that states that a child, when presented with displays of different amounts, *should identify without error the array which contains 'more' amounts and identify the array which contains 'less' amounts* clearly specifies which responses are required from the child. In this case it would also be possible to devise more complex situations for demonstrating comprehension of 'more' and 'less'. Alternatively, the teacher might wish to include production of 'more' or 'less' as an objective. The level of precision with which an objective must be specified will vary according to the child and the task.

The content of the intervention
In general a first step in an intervention may involve a specification of what is carried out in the normal language learning environment. So for example, where a child is experiencing specific problems with phonological aspects of reading, a targeted approach to these skills might be the first approach. Often, for a variety of reasons, this is not done in a comprehensive and detailed fashion. For this reason, typical patterns of development may provide a structure for detailed interventions.

However, in some cases it may be inappropriate to use remediation processes that have been devised solely with reference to developmental processes that occur in children without language difficulties. This is not to say that the interventions should be fundamentally different. Rather, a greater emphasis may be placed on alternative routes to communication or areas

Low-key educational approaches – this involves increased incidental teaching such as:

- Providing opportunities for listening activities.
- Promoting the learning of new vocabulary.
- Promoting oral language use across all areas of the curriculum.
- Promoting self-organization and pre-literacy skills.

All of these activities involve aspects of good teaching practice but they are more focused and consciously addressed. The changes are valid extensions of normal patterns that occur in a range of situations.

Second-level intervention – interventions at this level involve:

- Profiling and focused language work.
- Additional time and input leading to over learning.
- Small group work.
- Concepts and skills broken down into small steps.

Box 8.4: Tiers of intervention. Source: Locke (1989)

which are commonly not directly addressed in normal development, such as sign language. As an example Ann Locke (1989) suggests a tier of interventions for children in primary school. These are presented in Box 8.4. She advises that if a child fails to improve following each of these stages that further advice should be sought from professionals such as psychologists. One of her main concerns is that pre-school and early primary-aged children do not receive sufficient opportunities to develop their oral language skills.

An important point to be aware of is that most programmes, even those focusing on multiple aspects of the language system, select target goals for production rather than comprehension. Deciding on the appropriate avenue to follow for a specific child depends on two key issues:

1. appropriate monitoring of the efficacy of an intervention;
2. reference to the wider intervention literature.

IMPLEMENTING THE INTERVENTION

A range of teaching methods exists to ameliorate language problems. These range from highly structured didactic teaching to naturalistic, child-orientated interventions closely resembling parent–child interaction. Many of these are only provided by specialists trained in speech and language therapy, but in other cases they are provided by teachers and carers. Issues related to *what* should be taught were considered in earlier sections (see section on task-based factors) here the major emphasis is on *how* the intervention is presented. At the structured end of the continuum are behavioural-didactic interventions designed to teach the formal aspects of language using

Learning theory has provided us with many ways to try and alter behaviour.

Modelling is a technique where a child is encouraged to copy an accurate model, for example the carer asks a question and the child is encouraged to model what the carer has said.

Reinforcement occurs when a child is rewarded for a behaviour and this reward acts as an incentive to maintain and/or increase the behaviour.

Stimulus control occurs when a behaviour is governed by a specific stimulus, for example a child might always respond in the same way after a particular word.

Box 8.5: Structured approaches to intervention

behaviourally based teaching such as modelling, stimulus control and reinforcement. In some cases the content is derived from current understanding of developmental and psycholinguistic knowledge while in others it is less clear what factors guide the choice of *what* is taught. The Portage intervention scheme is an example of this approach. It is one of a set of highly structured approaches using modelling and reinforcement (see Box 8.5). In the middle of the continuum are hybrid models of intervention that incorporate some aspects of behavioural language teaching methods but apply them in conversational contexts. Hybrid interventions, such as *milieu* or *incidental teaching,* emphasize the functional use of language in interaction while teaching new forms through modelling and reinforcement procedures.

At the other end of the continuum are responsive interaction interventions that facilitate the development of social communication while providing non-demanding models of appropriate language during interactions with adults. Two examples are the Hanen Early Language Parent Programme (Manolson, 1983) and the Swedish Early Language Intervention Programme (Johansson, 1994). Both of these programmes focus on early interactional patterns helping parents to be more responsive to their child by following the child's lead and encouraging child participation and turn taking. There is a current trend derived from theoretical perspectives to support conversationally embedded approaches as opposed to didactic ones (see Chapter 2). An alternative perspective is to use the principles outlined above and consider the child and the task in an interactive framework. This would mean that the most appropriate language teaching method would vary depending on the developmental level of the child, type and degree of the child's problem, and their language and communication goals.

The relationship between what is being modelled and what is being learnt in different environments needs to be examined. An important element for all of these approaches is the extent to which the child is guided by the instructor, that is the child's learning is *scaffolded.* Scaffolding refers to a situation in which someone who is more skilled at a task, for example a peer or a teacher, guides the child to greater levels of participation. Initially the expert takes major responsibility for solving the task and the novice is the onlooker. The expert models and explains the task, relinquishing responsibility as the novice becomes more competent. The practice of scaffolding children's learning has become an important tool across a range of tasks and situations.

A second issue concerns how to deal with errors. Learning is rarely error-free. In learning situations errors can serve a range of purposes. They can indicate where a child has failed to comprehend a distinction which is linguistically meaningful, such as the difference between the sounds *pr* and *pl*. Errors can reveal the way a child reasons about a task, such as interpreting a metaphor. Finally, they can identify inappropriate associations that may have been built over past encounters with the same set of problems. As a first step an analysis of the child's errors can provide useful information. In some cases feedback from the 'instructor' can help the child correct their performance, but it should be remembered that this is not always the case. Errors can often serve a useful role for the child in helping restructure their understanding of the processes. It is as yet unclear under which conditions a child should be allowed to 'discover' the processes for themselves as opposed to having their errors continually identified.

Finally it is necessary to address the consistency with which a particular intervention is carried out. There is mounting evidence that when intervention programmes are carried out consistently they are more effective. Recently Ilene Schwartz and her colleagues (1996) have investigated the extent to which variations in implementation affect children's progress. They found that children exposed to higher levels of recommended practices had higher rates of engagement and verbalization. There were greater gains in performance in these situations as well.

Monitoring interventions

One of the common failings of intervention programmes is that they are not presented regularly, systematically and for long enough. Ann Locke emphasizes the need for at least two to three months at the first level identified in Box 8.3 and a minimum of six months at the second level. An important aspect in monitoring is to keep records of the numbers of interventions and the child's progress. It is all too easy to say that no progress has been made over a term unless a clear baseline has been established documenting the child's skills. Box 8.6 outlines the key role played by baseline measurement. It is equally possible to assume lack of progress without realizing that the child has missed many sessions or they have been provided with an intervention that has been erratically presented, thereby failing to provide the child with the necessary experience and consolidation time. Monitoring is, therefore, an ongoing process. Not only does it allow evaluation of the effects of the intervention but in addition it can help identify additional factors that may be impinging on the success or otherwise of the intervention.

A baseline is the term used to describe the detailed information we have on an individual's behaviour prior to any intervention or change in the situation. Baselines allow us to compare a child's behaviour. A good baseline will take account of variation over sessions.

Consider a situation where we wanted to improve a child's use of verbs. First we would want to find out what kinds of verbs the child was using and in which situations; that is we would need a baseline. We would want to collect these data over a number of days to get a clear and consistent measure. We would then implement our intervention programme and monitor changes over time. The success (or not) of the programme would be measured in terms of the child's use of verbs at the end of the intervention.

When using a baseline it needs to be kept in mind that children might progress from a baseline without any intervention. A baseline analysis is not the same as a controlled experiment.

Box 8.6: Baselines

Other interventions

Other forms of intervention can be implemented when there is good reason to believe that the effects of a specific difficulty can be modified with alternative approaches. The choice of sign language for deaf youngsters is one such example. There is evidence to suggest that profoundly deaf children who have never learned a sign language have greater difficulty in learning speech than those who acquire it as a second language to signing (Jones and Crenan, 1986). There are similar examples when children are experiencing a visual impairment or a developmental delay. For example, the Portage project programme offers a structure for early intervention with children who are developmentally at risk. However, unlike the case of sign language there is little sound evidence of its efficacy (Sturmey and Crisp, 1986).

One of the exciting new developments in the last decade has been the increased focus on alternative and augmentative communication for a wide range of young people experiencing language and communication difficulties. Alternative communication replaces the standard form of speaking and writing, whereas augmentative communication is a way of communicating which supports speech or writing. Manual sign systems have been found to be a useful aid to language intervention, particularly with children experiencing severe language problems. Alternative forms of intervention can often have significant effects on other areas of communication. For example, Kiernan (1987) argues that children who receive forms of augmentative and alternative communication (AAC) frequently have been found to develop the ability to vocalize and to produce speech. Box 8.7 lists some of the advantages and disadvantages of AAC.

Advantages

- Visual information obvious and easier to analyse.
- Visual information captures attention.
- Can serve as a secondary support to oral language.
- Symbols can be transparent.

Disadvantages

- The system must be learned by everyone (parent, sibling, teacher or friend) who wishes to communicate with the child.
- AAC systems are slower than spoken language.
- Can require constant focused attention resulting in possible short cuts.

Box 8.7: Advantages and disadvantages of augmentative and alternative communication (AAC). Source: Locke (1997)

WHAT MAKES AN EFFECTIVE INTERVENTION?

It has been extremely difficult to identify which interventions work for what problems and under what conditions. Part of the problem rests with the difficulty with carrying out such studies. Equally problematic is the fact that learning is rarely a simple incremental progression. Learning can occur in a number of different ways. Recent detailed studies of development have provided very interesting information about differences in typical development. Sometimes development can proceed in a U-shape manner. In such cases the child appears to be successful with the task initially, then successful performance is replaced by errors and eventually success again. Closer investigation of the child's initial performance can reveal differences in their understanding, processing or representations related to the task. Children's over-regularization of the past tense, described in Chapter 2, is an example of this. Moreover, typical development often contains plateaux where learning seems to have ceased. Sometimes this occurs when children appear to be assimilating and reorganizing information that they have acquired. It is important to be aware that plateaux and regressions can be part of typical developmental processes and may be a positive sign in children with language difficulties, rather than a reason for despondency. While such differences in learning patterns are interesting and exciting they can cause major problems of interpretation for evaluating interventions.

Donaldson and Reid (1994), in their review of language intervention techniques, further stress the difficulty in identifying the efficacy of particular techniques. There is a paucity of published experimental studies in child language intervention, approximately 14 per year (Goldstein and Hockenberger, 1991). The vast majority are carried out with children with general learning difficulties or autism, thus providing a rather narrow focus to the available knowledge base. Data from individual studies suggest that in general there is a consensus that a variety of techniques can improve language skills. A technique which has gained considerable notoriety recently is auditory training (Merzenich *et al.*, 1996; Tallal *et al.*, 1996). Children are trained to discriminate stimuli on the basis of brief acoustic cues. Dramatic effects have been claimed for children with specific language impairment who received this relatively short but intensive training. Confirmation of these claims is needed through further evaluation studies.

However, there is general agreement that language interventions can be quite effective. Nye *et al.* (1987) reviewed 43 studies involving intervention and found that an average child with specific language impairment moved up 35 per cent on language measures as a result of language intervention. The average length of an intervention programme was 38 weeks or one school year. Grammatical rules exhibited the greatest improvement. Other forms of intervention have proved effective with populations of children with sensory impairments. For example, cued speech has been argued to have significant beneficial effects for the hearing impaired. In cued speech the speaker holds one hand near the mouth while speaking so the listener can see both lips and hands at the same time. Alegria and colleagues (unpublished) have suggested that being exposed to lip-reading with cued speech might develop mechanisms that help lip-reading processing and storing. This has important practical and theoretical consequences.

One of the most important questions that needs to be addressed is whether the skills acquired in a therapy or teaching settings generalize to other situations. This issue is often not addressed by interventions. Leonard (1981) reviewed language intervention studies with specifically language-impaired children over the previous eighteen years. Of the 32 studies he looked at, only five measured the occurrence of generalization and none attempted to investigate how to make generalization occur.

One of the problems with drawing conclusions from single studies, or reviews which include small numbers, is that it is difficult to get an overarching view of the general effectiveness of interventions. One of the ways around this problem is to carry out a meta-analysis. This is when a researcher or group of researchers pull together a range of studies to analyse the level of efficacy for different types of studies. Clearly defined criteria are set for the inclusion of studies in the analysis. A significant systematic review of the literature for children with language delay has been carried out by James Law and his colleagues (1998). The results of their analyses are extremely important. Firstly they show that for the studies they evaluated, there were positive and significant changes in all areas of language relative to children who received no intervention. Unfortunately, there were not enough studies to decide whether one form of intervention was better for particular forms of language problems or particular ages of children.

Their results also indicated that for expressive language and receptive language parent-administered intervention was as least as effective as direct clinician-administered treatment. This was not the case for articulation and phonological disorders where direct therapist treatment was more effective.

There are, however, few studies which address the long-term effects of these interventions. Moreover, it is unclear to what extent gains 'wash out' over time. Nor is it clear to what extent the nature of the child's difficulty alters over time. A problem that may initially present as a vocabulary deficit at 2 years of age may appear as a syntactic deficit at 5 and a pragmatic problem in adolescence.

Meta-analyses have also been used to assess the efficacy of interventions for students with learning disabilities (Lee Swanson *et al.*, 1996). While these studies are not directly related to language acquisition *per se,* they do provide valuable information about the sorts of factors we should be considering when examining the child's overall learning processes. The Swanson *et al.* review suggests that the effectiveness of interventions varies according to the area that is under investigation. For example, the most effective procedures for reading comprehension were direct instruction and cognitive strategy instruction, while word recognition and spelling were best influenced by phonetic/decoding strategies. Once again, their analysis suggests that considering the nature of the task that the child has to master is a key factor in the intervention process.

BARRIERS TO EFFECTIVE INTERVENTIONS

Interventions targeted at a child's language skills are designed to enhance their ability to use language as a tool for communication and learning. It is important that the skills generalize to their daily lives and that they can see themselves as effective communicators and learners. These goals are particularly difficult to achieve.

Generalization

Generalization is concerned with whether a newly acquired skill or set of knowledge can be transferred to new situations and contexts. There are different kinds of generalization. Generalization can occur across time, people, settings, tasks or situations, responses, modalities and new stimulus combinations. Training which focuses only on particular linguistic forms tends to yield effects limited to the child's use of those forms. In contrast, training with a more general focus usually results in broader linguistic gains (Leonard, 1981). Plans for generalization need to be built into an intervention programme from the beginning. It is important to verify that the knowledge and strategies the child does develop are applicable to processing language in normal contexts. This is reflected in both what is taught and how it is taught. One common suggestion is that failure to generalize is due to the child's lack of knowledge about usefulness of a particular skill or technique. Often children do not understand the relation between strategy use and level of performance on a task. It may be necessary to provide children with explicit information about why they should behave in a particular way. The effectiveness of this approach needs to be evaluated more carefully with children experiencing language and communication problems.

Self-esteem

There is a general view that children with difficulties of all kinds are vulnerable to developing low self-esteem. Our own observations of adolescents with specific speech and language difficulties would support this view. It is, however, not true in all cases. An important addition to understanding a child's communicative competence is to understand the child's learning history and the implications this may have for the approach taken to tasks. When children believe they can tackle a task, they will learn, given time and appropriate educational opportunities. Children with communication difficulties are often inattentive and seem to put little effort into tasks in the domain in which they have difficulty. This is sometimes interpreted as a problem within the child's attention. However, it is also possible that lack of attention and effort are the result, rather than the cause, of the learning difficulty. The developmental evidence suggests that early identification and support can moderate this negative cycle.

A final factor that needs to be addressed is the teacher's role in setting up and maintaining such negative views. The data concerning the consequences of teacher feedback are complex, but there are some initial conclusions which should be noted. There appears to be a developmental difference in the ways children respond to praise. Young children and children with learning difficulties appear to be motivated by praise. By contrast, when adults, teenagers and cognitively advanced primary schoolchildren are praised for poor work, they interpret the praise as implying they are low in ability. Thus, older children do not take praise at face value. To be effective in the long term praise should be contingent on effortful attempts and should convey specific information about what would lead to further improvements.

SUMMARY

Experimental investigations of child language interventions are the key to understanding children with language difficulties and how to help them develop communicative strategies most effectively. Interventions need to be targeted with the child as the governing factor. The interventions need to be grounded in a thorough understanding of developmental principles, the task, the child and the learning environment. Carefully planned and clearly evaluated interventions can significantly change a child's opportunities to communicate and learn. The case for intervening when children have language and communication difficulties rests not only on the direct impact on their language skills but by corollary on the impact on self-esteem, scholastic achievement motivation and social behaviour.

Chapter 9

Difficulties with Language and Communication: Identification, Understanding and Intervention

Difficulties with the language system occur for a variety of reasons and can be obscured by other factors. They are the most common problem found in preschool children. Oral language continues to develop in the primary and secondary school years, yet for a substantial minority language skills are still compromised at this point. When such problems continue they can impact on the child's ability to access the curriculum and benefit from later educational experiences The previous chapters have documented the range of difficulties that occur for children as they tackle the task of becoming competent language users. In this final chapter the central themes that have been highlighted in the previous chapters are reconsidered: patterns of development, identification, understanding and intervention.

PATTERNS OF DEVELOPMENT

It is important to realize that during the last 40 years we have gained a much deeper appreciation about the main milestones in typical and delayed development. The theories about these processes have become more sophisticated, and there is a much better appreciation of the way so many abilities and processes play a part in language development. Furthermore, no longer is it assumed that all children develop language and communication in exactly the same way, or that processes in typical development can be extrapolated to atypical development.

In the first chapter we considered findings about early social interaction, especially the way that early social interaction provides the basis for the development of relationships and the beginnings of an infants' appreciation of some of the broader features of communication within a particular culture. One reasonably clear message from studies of early interaction is that certain features help the development of speech. Adults who link their speech to children's interest appear to facilitate vocabulary acquisition, and for the moment it is perhaps best to assume that similar links will facilitate vocabulary acquisition in children with communication difficulties. However, an equally important message from this research is that adults need to be flexible in the way they interact with children. At the moment there is no instant fix or patterns of interaction that will radically alter the developmental process. Rather the whole research literature speaks against the use of set routines, and instead suggests that adults need to carefully monitor children's reactions and interest and allow children to sometimes take the lead in setting the agenda for the topic of interaction. The process of interaction needs to be a partnership.

Given the importance of language it is frustrating that we still have so little idea of the processes that allow most children to develop the use of speech without formal tuition, and why some groups of children find the process difficult. Nor is it clear why some components of the language system are more vulnerable to impairment. In general, receptive language is better preserved than expressive language, and the conceptual and social aspects of language are less likely to be impaired than the grammatical aspects. Neither of the major theoretical approaches, in our opinion, is particularly useful or comprehensive in their explanation of language acquisition when viewed from the perspective of children with communication or language difficulties. For example, neither the PPT nor connectionist explanations account for the difficulties children with Down syndrome have with productive speech, or why there should be such variability in the language development of children with autism. It should be admitted that part of the difficulty is formulating a detailed theory. There are now so many findings and local controversies in child language research that it is extremely difficult to integrate and understand all of them.

In contrast to research that has been driven by general theories about language acquisition there is also research which attempts to understand and explain specific features of the development of communication in children who are experiencing problems. Often this is of more relevance to practitioners and carers. Such research seeks both to explain why children have certain difficulties, and ultimately to provide interventions to assist these children. The interventions themselves can serve as a way of evaluating the initial explanations of the language problems. A good example of this approach is the work by Gina Conti-Ramsden (1997) and her colleagues. They describe the particular problems with verb learning by a group of children with specific speech and language difficulties. A useful way to evaluate their view would be to conduct an intervention study. Well-evaluated intervention work is an important source of data to analyse theories. Thus, if an intervention is based on a particular theoretical model and the children's performance improves, this provides support for the theory. If children fail to improve then the theory and the method of intervention should be re-evaluated.

IDENTIFICATION

To address the strengths and needs of the children we have been discussing it is important that their proficiency in language and communication are identified. This is true whether the language difficulties are seen as primary, as in the case of specific speech and language difficulties, or secondary as in the case of visual impairment, hearing impairment or general learning difficulties. Moreover as we have seen in the various chapters, when early appropriate interventions are in place, children's progress is markedly enhanced. Caretakers of blind children often establish a successful framework for language development by combining sound, touch, rhythm and movement to support verbal interactions. Appropriate interventions also have wider implications for the children's well-being. Establishing good language skills in sign and speech has important implications for socio-emotional development of deaf children (see Grove and Dockrell, forthcoming). Thus, early and accurate identification is of paramount importance for a child's successful development. This view is accepted in current legislation. The code of practice on the identification and assessment of special educational needs (DfE, 1994) stresses the need to identify children early so that appropriate action can be taken.

Identification should then lead to the use of detailed assessment procedures and appropriate interventions. As we saw in Chapter 7 children's language is often assessed at various developmental points prior to school entry. Screening procedures for language and communication can miss many children. This is partly because these measures are general and often imprecise thereby missing some of the more elusive problems; but also some pre-school children do not demonstrate difficulties which differentiate them from the norm at this point. Further, where other problems are primary, e.g. learning disabilities or sensory impairment, the subtle nuances of the language system can be overlooked while professionals and parents focus on more immediate demands. A critical aspect of pre-school identification is monitoring. If concern is raised a child's progress should be monitored, even if intervention is not deemed appropriate.

Parents are key players in the identification of pre-school problems and their perceptions and concerns should not be dismissed lightly. Where sensory or cognitive difficulties are identified it is important to monitor communication skills at all levels – phonological, syntactic, semantic and pragmatic. The early routines established between carer and child are key building blocks for the development of later communicative skills. The fact that deaf children of signing parents progress significantly better than deaf children of hearing parents supports this view. There is a continual need to retain a balanced and objective approach where typical variation is considered and difference is not necessarily equated with deficiency. For example, good evidence exists to support the view that the differences in the vocabularies of visually impaired children reflect different experiences rather than deficient language learning. This view is further substantiated by recent research evidence which indicates that while in English object words are acquired before action words, this is not the case in some other languages; in these cases action words precede object words in acquisition (Tardiff *et al.*, forthcoming).

Of major concern is the identification of the level of language skills on school entry. Conventionally, oral language is the medium by which the whole of the school curriculum is presented. Language and pragmatic skills are crucial in the child's interactions with teachers and peers. Children whose language skills are compromised in some way begin school with an inherent disadvantage. To some extent current government legislation has acknowledged these issues by introducing baseline assessment. The compulsory implementation of baseline assessment for all 5-year-olds in England could, in theory, go a significant way to identifying language-based problems. A key requirement is that the assessments be sufficiently detailed to identify individual children's learning needs, including special educational needs, in order to support effective and appropriate planning for teaching and learning. Unfortunately there are major limitations in the ways in which the schemes have been introduced (Lindsay and Desforges, 1998). Of particular concern, in relation to children with language and communication difficulties, is the failure to include formal assessments of language and communication skills as well as only the 'minimum focus on literacy and numeracy'. Even the well-standardized and constructed tools that are currently employed pay minimal attention to oral language.

Of equal importance is the low status of oral language skills within the curriculum. If we consider vocabulary as an example, the English national curriculum at best considers vocabulary as a marginal issue. Attainment target 1 for speaking and listening includes the following: 'Use a growing vocabulary' (Level 2); 'Use appropriately some of the features of Standard English vocabulary' (Level 4); and 'Use apt vocabulary' (Level 8). Such targets are imprecise and uninformative and difficult to evaluate. It is unlikely that a child with language and communication problems would have their needs met on the basis of such guidelines.

Effectively this means that teachers and parents have to use their own judgements about a child's language competence and the need for additional support or a modified curriculum. This can be problematic. There is no *a priori* reason that teachers should consider oral language skills. Firstly, there is a natural and not unreasonable assumption, that for many children oral language skills will be sufficiently developed at school entry. Secondly, the curricular emphasis is not on these skills. Moreover, few teachers have the training or expertise in normal and atypical language development to identify the range of language problems that exist. Even when problems are identified it can be hard to distinguish language and communication difficulties from the other difficulties that are evident in a large class. Given the tremendous demands on teachers' time with respect to other areas of the curriculum, there is no reason to assume that problems with oral language and communication skills will be identified.

UNDERSTANDING

Understanding the development of communication and language is fundamental to many of the issues that we have discussed in this book. We all have ideas about these processes and these ideas influence how we interact and relate to children, even if for some of us these are not formal scientific theories. Professionals use models and theory to provide a background to their actions. Having an understanding of usual patterns of development and of theories is important because at those points when we are no longer sure what we should do, there is a need to return to the core principles which can be used to guide our actions. Thus, understanding involves more than knowledge of the facts and theories of development; it means being able to see important principles that underlie these findings and theories.

We have already mentioned that there are no definitive theories or explanations about the mechanisms of typical language development. Even so we have a much better appreciation of the types of social interaction and communication that occur before children start to use language. We also have a much better idea of the major milestones in language development and when these occur. In addition, theories have been developed to try to explain these processes. Thus, our knowledge of typical development has considerably expanded. There is a similar story about the development of children with language and communication difficulties, progress has been made in identifying the main features of development in these children and theories have been formulated to explain why there are such difficulties. However, it should be admitted that often these findings are sketchier than we would like and that progress needs to be made in our understanding of the reasons for the language difficulties.

It is clear from common sense and more sophisticated scientific theories that the development of communication and language would not be possible without humans having innate capacities to enable these processes to occur. Furthermore, we have seen the way that genetic characteristics appear to influence the use of speech in children with Down syndrome, autism and Fragile X. However, this is not the same as genetic determinism. Very few psychological characteristics are known to be completely determined by a person's genes and uninfluenced by the characteristics of the person's environment. Thus, when thinking about intervention, there are strong arguments for examining the way that features of the environment can assist language development. As has been highlighted in the chapter on intervention, this should involve identifying the nature of the problem and then devising ways to support the child's progress.

What we would like to emphasize, which is in keeping with the theme of this book, is that there is little use in applying 'cookbook' methods of intervention based on our understanding of communication and language development. There are too many uncertainties to make this a satisfactory process. An understanding of typical development is always of use when we need to think about children with particular difficulties, as it is usually the case that more is known about typical than atypical development. This understanding provides us with information about the usual sequence in the development of a language skill and ideas about the mechanism that enables the development to take place. However, it always needs to be kept in mind that the process of development may not be the same for all children. For example, in the case of children with autism or Down syndrome there appears to be a difference in the way that children process information; in the case of children who have an absence of sensory input because of visual or hearing impairments, language development is different in a number of subtle but important ways. Thus, there always needs to be caution when using our understanding of typical development in relation to children with particular difficulties. It also needs to be borne in mind that different does not mean deficient; for example, children who are blind develop the ability to refer to events in the past at an earlier age than sighted children. This can be seen as a result of their need or ability to process information in a different way.

Even where we have 'understanding' of children who have similar difficulties there is a need for caution when applying this knowledge to a particular child whose development is the focus of our concern. Often the research findings that supply this understanding are based on relatively small samples; in addition it needs to be recognized that there can be wide variations in developmental patterns. Thus, it is important not to categorize or create low expectations that are based on a limited understanding of the condition. Equally importantly, it is rare for there to be a substantial set of findings that document the success or failure of specific forms of intervention with children who have a specific difficulty. Thus, we all should recognize that effective intervention needs to be based on a proper evaluation of the child who is the focus of attention. Although the need for a fuller understanding of typical and atypical development is always present this should not necessarily be taken as an insurmountable barrier. It can even be argued that the lack of a prescriptive theory allows interventions to be tailored and designed to fit in with a child's needs and requirements. Obviously this is a more difficult and costly process, but it may be more effective in meeting a child's individual needs.

In all this discussion of understanding it should also be remembered that the study of children with communication and language difficulties can play a significant part in our understanding of the processes which are important to typical development. Studies of children who have visual or hearing impairments can tell us a lot about the importance of these forms of sensory input, and how children are able to adapt to information being presented in different modalities. Similarly the work on children with autism provides the opportunity to identify the way that problems with the understanding of social understanding can affect the communicative process. Again caution is needed in the application of this knowledge, because there may be a number of differences between the atypical and typical children which should mean that conclusions are made when a number of pieces of evidence point to the same conclusion.

It might be thought that from our emphasis on the need for caution when applying understanding of communicative and language development to children with difficulties in these areas, that there is still such a long way to go before intervention can have a sound basis in research findings. One reason for our caution is examples of professionals applying either findings or theories in an uncritical way with no obvious benefit to the children in their care. Another reason is that we believe that the nature of children's development is not a simple deterministic process; knowing how a child is functioning at one age, or the type of environment a child experiences, cannot be used to predict with certainty what future characteristics a child will have. This is because children's future and abilities are very difficult to predict with a high degree of certainty. Thus, our understanding of language development needs to be coupled with the understanding that development is rarely a simple deterministic process. For example, recall the cases of isolation that were discussed in Chapter 5. Although this non-deterministic perspective might appear pessimistic, we believe a more pessimistic picture would be for child development to be so deterministic that future abilities were always predictable; part of the essence of being a human is that the future is not absolutely predictable from present abilities, or present experiences. Thus, we would argue that the understanding gained from research findings is of help in providing a set of ideas and principles that can be utilized within interventions that involve a problem-solving approach.

INTERVENTION

In Chapter 8 we considered a range of factors which need to be addressed when we intervene with children who have language problems. Here we would like to consider wider factors that can lead to the successful implementation of interventions. The primary concern of parents and teachers is what to do to help children develop successfully. Unfortunately, as we have shown, there is no single simple answer. Some practitioners and researchers have argued that if we can classify children the problems about choosing appropriate interventions will be reduced. To some extent this is true but classification can only ever serve as a rough guideline.

It is always possible to subclassify children who have a similar difficulty on the basis of other characteristics that vary within the population. However, the only justification for doing so is if the subclassification is relevant either to the nature of the difficulty that the child experiences or to the form of intervention that can be used with the difficulty. As we have seen there are very few homogeneous subtypes of language difficulty and performance is highly related to the context in which the child is developing. Thus, children's performance varies along a continuum; one cannot assume that a standard profile of abilities will occur in a particular child.

Educational legislation since the Warnock Report of 1978 has aimed to reduce the emphasis on categorization of pupils according to their difficulties and redirect attention towards assessment of their educational needs. We have in this book attempted to indicate the ways in which language difficulties can result in some quite specific educational needs. These needs have wider implications than simply providing specific interventions, though there is no doubt that this is important. Oral language skills can be supported at two distinct levels – general modification of the curriculum to support the learning of particular groups of children and more specific modifications to meet the needs of individual children. When modifications are made they need to be specific, measurable, attainable, realistic and time-limited.

The first step in any intervention must be the construction of an individual education plan. The plan should involve those skills that are determinants of performance in the particular linguistic contexts in which the child is experiencing the difficulty. Much emphasis has been placed recently on the social context of language and the need for context appropriate interventions. Such moves are entirely appropriate and reflect a wide base of psychological knowledge that has been acquired over the last few decades. However, such interventions cannot be seen to replace a more detailed understanding of the language system and those factors within the language system that can impede a child's performance. Vocabulary size appears to impact on the development of early grammatical utterances, and later vocabulary size impacts on school attainments. Thus a plan that considered context and language should focus on vocabulary development in an educationally appropriate environment. This would entail developing a situation where the adult supports the child's learning by adapting the educational setting. Performance can then be evaluated in terms of the child's acquisition of the relevant skills, their fluency with these skills, whether the skills are maintained over time, the child's ability to discriminate appropriate use of the skills, their ability to generalize to more than one context and their ability to adapt the skills appropriately. Such an analysis by necessity means a monitoring of an individual child's progress in context.

The principles for intervention that we outline have three rather different implications. The first is that providing access to the curriculum may mean modifying aspects of the curriculum. For many of the children we have considered, language skills go hand in hand with difficulties in literacy and numeracy and often a restriction in their access to other areas of the curriculum. This is not to say that such problems are inevitable and could not be changed by appropriate curricular or educational modifications. In fact the situation is quite the reverse. If we consider access as an example, Nicola Grove (1998) has shown how literary texts can be modified (including Shakespeare) for use with severe learning-disabled young people. Equally the work of Nunes and Moreno (discussed in Chapter 7) has demonstrated the scope for modifying the mathematics curriculum. The point is that these changes are often not made, and the failure to modify the curriculum comes from a difficulty in understanding the kinds of language and communication difficulties that are being experienced by the individual children.

The second point is that where children are educated is not the key issue. While we admire and in many cases support the views of those striving for inclusive education, what is of critical importance is that the child is receiving the support that they require at the appropriate point in time. Where this support is provided will depend on the child's needs, the provision and policies of the local education authority and the child's and parents' wishes. For some children this will be in be a mainstream classroom with additional resources; for others it will be in a unit, and yet others in wholly special provision.

Finally, we would argue that many of the issues that have been raised about the salience of language and communication are relevant for all children. Educational policy needs to consider the cognitive and social infrastructure on which literacy, numeracy and other educational tasks depend. Part of that infrastructure is the child's ability to use and understand language in diverse settings.

SUMMARY

Current educational practice is based on a philosophy of inclusive education. Teachers and children will be meeting, working with and playing with children who have language and communication difficulties. For these interactions to be positive and constructive it is important that there is an awareness of the key role played by language and communication in development. This book has aimed to describe the ways in which children's language can vary. Our view is that descriptions of variation need to be firmly grounded in an understanding of typical developmental trajectories. Charting developmental progress is a complex endeavour. We cannot assume that simply because a child has a hearing problem or a learning disability that they will develop in a similar fashion to other children with hearing or learning difficulties. Individual functioning is the product of an interaction among a variety of biological, social and personal factors, and meeting the needs of the children entails an awareness of this fact. What we wish to emphasize is that to assist the development of children with language and communication disorders involves a knowledge of many issues – particularly important is an awareness of the limitations of our understanding as well as an understanding of the way proper intervention techniques can make the best use of the knowledge that is available.

References and Further Reading

Chapter 1

Baron-Cohen, S. (1991) The theory of mind deficit in autism. *British Journal of Developmental Psychology*, 9, 301–14.

Bates, E. (1995) Individual differences and their implications for theories of language development. In P. Fletcher and B. MacWhinney (eds) *The Handbook of Child Language*. Oxford: Blackwell.

Bates, E., Bretherton, I. and Snyder, L. (1988) *From First Words to Grammar: Individual Differences and Dissociable Mechanisms*. Cambridge: Cambridge University Press.

Bates, E., Marchman, V., Thal, D., Fenson, L., Dale, P., Reznick J. S., Reilly, J. and Hartung, J. (1994) Developmental and stylistic variation in the composition of early vocabulary. *Journal of Child Language*, 21, 85–124.

Bertenthal, B. I. and Profitt, D. R. (1986) The extraction of structure from motion: implementation of basic processing constraints. Paper presented at the International Conference on Infant Studies, Los Angeles, 1986. Abstract in *Infant Behaviour and Development*, 9, 36.

Brown, R. (1973) *A First Language, the Early Stages*. Cambridge, MA: Harvard University Press.

Bushnell, I. W. R., Sai, F. and Mullin, J. T. (1989) Neonatal recognition of the mother's face. *British Journal of Developmental Psychology*, 7, 3–15.

Cazden, C. (1968) The acquisition of noun and verb inflections. *Child Development*, 39, 433–8.

Cooper, R. P. and Aslin, R. N. (1990) Preference for infant directed speech in the first month after birth. *Child Development*, 61, 1584–95.

Davis, H. (1978) A description of aspects of mother–infant vocal interaction. *Journal of Child Psychology and Psychiatry*, 19, 379–86.

DeCasper, A. J. and Fifer, W. P. (1980) Of human bonding: Newborns prefer their mothers' voices. *Science*, 208, 1174–6.

Dore, J. (1978) Conditions for the acquisition of speech acts. In I. Markova (ed.) *The Social Context of Language*. New York: Wiley.

Durkin, K. (1986) Language and social cognition during the school years. In K. Durkin (ed.) *Language Development in the School Years*. London: Croom Helm.

Fogel, A., Toda, S. and Kawai, M. (1988) Mother–infant face-to-face interaction in Japan and the United States: a laboratory comparison using 3-month-old infants. *Developmental Psychology*, 24, 398–406.

Fortescue, M. (1984/5) Learning to speak Greenlandic: a case study of a two-year-old's morphology in a polysynthetic language. *First Language*, 5, 101–13.

Gopnik, M. and Crago, M. (1991) Familial aggregation of a developmental language disorder. *Cognition*, 39:1, 1–50.

Goren, C. C., Sarty, M. and Wu, P. Y. K. (1975) Visual following and pattern discrimination of face-like stimuli by newborn infants. *Paediatrics*, 56, 544.

Halliday, M. (1975) *Learning How to Mean: Explorations in the Development of Language*. London: Edward Arnold.

Hobson, R. P. (1986) The autistic child's appraisal of expressions of emotion. *Journal of Child Psychology and Psychiatry*, 27, 321–42.

Hobson, R. P. (1991) Against the theory of 'Theory of Mind'. *British Journal of Developmental Psychology*, 9, 33–51.

Kaye, K. (1982) *The Mental and Social Life of Babies*. Chicago: University of Chicago Press.

Lock, A. (1980) *The Guided Reinvention of Language*. New York: Academic Press.

MacFarlane, A. (1975) Olfaction in the development of social preferences in the human neonate. In Ciba Foundation Symposium (ed.) *Parent–Infant Interaction*. New York: Elsevier.

Meltzoff, A. and Gopnik, A. (1993) The role of imitation in understanding persons and developing a theory of mind. In S. Baron-Cohen, H. Tager-Flushberg and D. Cohen (eds) *Understanding Other Minds – Perspective from Autism*. Oxford: Oxford University Press.

Meltzoff, A. N. and Moore, M. K. (1977) Imitation of and manual gestures by human neonates. *Science*, 198, 75–8.

Messer, D. (1994) *The Development of Communication: From Social Interaction to Language*. Chichester: Wiley.

Nelson, K. (1973) Structure and strategy in learning to talk. Monographs of the Society for Research in Child Development, No. 38.

Nelson, K. (1974) Concept, word and sentence: interrelations in acquisition and development. *Psychological Review*, 81, 267–85.

Nelson, K. (1988) Constraints on word learning? *Cognitive Development*, 3, 221–46.

Penman, R., Cross, T., Milgrom-Friedman, J. and Mears, R. (1983) Mothers' speech to prelingual infants: a pragmatic analysis. *Journal of Child Language*, 10, 17–34.

Piaget, J. (1932) *The Language and Thought of the Child*. London: Routledge and Kegan Paul.

Piaget, J. (1962) *Play, Dreams, and Imitation in Childhood*. New York: Norton.

Pine, J. M. (1992) The functional basis of referentiality: evidence from children's spontaneous speech. *First Language*, 12, 39–56.

Rabain-Jamin, J. and Sabeau-Jouannet, E. (1989) Playing with pronouns in French maternal speech to prelingual infants. *Journal of Child Language*, 16, 217–38.

Schaffer, H. R. (1977) *Studies in Mother–Infant Interaction*. London: Academic Press.

Scollen, R. (1976) *Conversations with a One Year Old: A Case Study of the Developmental Foundation of Syntax*. Honolulu: University Press of Hawaii.

Slobin, D. I. (1985) *The Cross-Linguistic Study of Language Acquisition, Vol. 1: The Data*. Hillsdale, NJ: Erlbaum.

Sylvester-Bradley, B. (1985) Failure to distinguish people and things in early infancy. *British Journal of Developmental Psychology*, 3, 281–92.

Sylvester-Bradley, B. and Trevarthen, C. B. (1978) Baby-talk as an adaptation to the infant's communication. In N. Waterson and C. E. Snow (eds) *The Development of Communication*. New York: Wiley.

Tomasello, M. and Farrar, J. (1986) Joint attention and early language. *Child Development*, 57, 1454–63.

Trevarthen, C. (1979) Communication and co-operation in early infancy: a description of primary inter subjectivity. In M. Bullowa (ed.) *Before Speech*. Cambridge: Cambridge University Press.

Younger, B. A. and Cohen, L. B. (1983) Infant perception of correlations among attributes. *Child Development*, 54, 858–67.

Chapter 2

Barnes, S., Gutfreund, M., Satterly, D. and Wells, D. (1983) Characteristics of adult speech which predict children's language development. *Journal of Child Language*, 10, 65–84.

Berko, J. (1958) The child's learning of English morphology. *Word*, 14, 150–77.

Bohannon, J. N. and Stanowicz, L. (1988) The issue of negative evidence: Adult responses to children's language errors. *Developmental Psychology*, 24, 684–9.

Bohannon, J. N., MacWhinney, B. and Snow, C. (1990) No negative evidence revisited: Beyond learnability or who has to prove what to whom. *Developmental Psychology*, 26, 221–6.

Brown, R. and Hanlon, C. (1970) Derivational complicity and the order of acquisition. In J. R. Hayes (ed.) *Cognition and the Development of Language*. New York: Wiley.

Chomsky, N. (1965) *Aspects of the Theory of Syntax*. Cambridge, MA: MIT Press.

Chomsky, N. (1981) *Lectures on Government and Binding*. Dordrecht: Foris.

Chomsky, N. (1986) *Knowledge of Language: Its Nature, Origins and Use*. New York: Praeger.

Clahsen, H. (1992) Learnability theory and the problem of development in language acquisition. In J. Weissenborn, H. Goodluck and T. Roeper (eds) *Theoretical Issues in Language Acquisition*. Hillsdale, NJ: Erlbaum.

Demetras, M. J., Post, K. N. and Snow, C. E. (1986) Feedback to first language learners: the role of repetitions and clarification questions. *Journal of Child Language*, 13, 275–92.

Farrar, M. J. (1992) Negative evidence and grammatical morpheme acquisition. *Developmental Psychology*, 28, 90–8.

Felix, S. (1992) Language acquisition as a maturational process. In J. Weissenborn, H. Goodluck and T. Roeper (eds) *Theoretical Issues in Language Acquisition*. Hillsdale, NJ: Erlbaum.

Ferguson, C. A. (1964) Baby talk in six languages. *American Anthropologist*, 66, 103–13.

Fernald, A., Taeschner, T., Dunn, J., Papousek, M., Boysson-Bardies, B. and Fukui, I. (1989) A cross-language study of prosodic modifications in mothers' and fathers' speech to preverbal infants. *Journal of Child Language*, 16, 477–501.

Furrow, D. and Nelson, K. (1986) A further look at the motherese hypothesis: a reply to Gleitman, Newport and Gleitman. *Journal of Child Language*, 13, 163–76.

Harris, M. (1992) *Language Experience and Early Development*. Hillsdale, NJ: Erlbaum.

Hirsch-Pasek, K., Treiman, R. and Schneiderman, M. (1984) Brown and Hanlon revisited: mothers' sensitivity to ungrammatical forms. *Journal of Child Language*, 11, 81–8.

McNeil, J. D. (1966) *The ABC Learning Activity: Language of Instruction*. New York: American Book.

Marfo, K. (1990) Maternal directiveness in interactions with mentally handicapped children: An analytical commentary. *Journal of Child Psychology and Psychiatry*, 31, 531–49.

Maurer, H. and Sherrod, K. B. (1987) Context of directives given to young children with Down's syndrome and nonretarded children: Development over two years. *American Journal of Mental Deficiency*, 91, 579–90.

Morgan, J. L. and Travis, L. L. (1989) Limits on negative information in language input. *Journal of Child Language*, 16, 531–52.

Murray, A. D., Johnson, J. and Peters, J. (1990) Fine-tuning of utterance length to preverbal infants: Effects on later language development. *Journal of Child Language*, 17, 511–25.

Ochs, E. and Schieffelin, B. B. (1984) Language acquisition and socialization. In R. A. Shweder and R. A. Levine (eds) *Culture Theory*. Cambridge: Cambridge University Press.

Ochs, E. and Schieffelin, B. (1995) The impact of language socialization on grammatical development. In P. Fletcher and B. MacWhinney (eds) *The Handbook of Child Language*. Oxford: Blackwell.

Penner, S. G. (1987) Parental responses to grammatical and ungrammatical child utterances. *Child Development*, 58, 376–84.

Pinker, S. (1987) The bootstrapping problem in language acquisition. In B. MacWhinney (ed.) *Mechanisms of Language Acquisition*. Hillsdale, NJ: Erlbaum.

Pinker, S. (1989) *Learnability and Cognition: The Acquisition of Argument Structure*. Cambridge, MA: MIT Press.

Pinker, S. and Prince, A. (1988) On language and connectionism: analysis of a parallel distributed processing model of language acquisition. *Cognition*, 28, 73–193.

Plunkett, K. (1995) Connectionist approaches to language acquisition. In P. Fletcher and B. MacWhinney (eds) *Handbook of Child Language*. Oxford: Blackwell.

Plunkett, K. and Marchman, V. (1991) U-shaped learning and frequency effects in a multi-layered perception: implications for child language acquisition. *Cognition*, 38, 43–102.

Plunkett, K. and Sinha, C. (1992) Connectionism and developmental theory. *British Journal of Developmental Psychology*, 10, 209–54.

Plunkett, K., Karmiloff-Smith, A., Bates, E., Elman, J. L. and Johnson, M. H. (1997) Connectionism and developmental psychology. *Journal of Child Psychology and Psychiatry*, 38, 53–80.

Power, D. J., Wood, D. J. and Wood, H. A. (1990) Conversational strategies of teachers using three methods of communication with deaf children. *American Annals of the Deaf*, 135, 9–13.

Rumelhart, D. E. and McClelland, J. L. (1986) On learning the past tense of English verbs. In McClelland, Rumelhart, and the PDP Research Group *Parallel Distributed Processing, Exploration in the Micro Structure of Cognition*. Cambridge, MA: MIT Press.

Sachs, J. and Johnson, M. L. (1976) Language development in a hearing child of deaf parents. In W. von Raffler-Enge and Y. Lebrun (eds) *Baby Talk and Infant Speech*. Lisse, Netherlands: Swets & Zeitlinger.

Saxton, M. (1997) The contrast theory of negative input. *Journal of Child Language*, 24, 139–61.

Scarborough, H. and Wyckoff, J. (1986) Mother. I'd still rather do it myself: Some further non-effects of 'motherese'. *Journal of Child Language*, 13, 431–8.

Shatz, M. and Gelman, R. (1973) The development of communication skills: Modification in the speech of young children as a function of the listener. *Monographs of the Society for Research in Child Development*, 38.

Snow, C. E. (1977) Mothers' speech research: From input to interaction. In C. E. Snow and C. A. Ferguson (eds) *Talking to Children*. Cambridge: Cambridge University Press.

Tomasello, M. and Farrar, J. (1986) Joint attention and early language. *Child Development*, 57, 1454–63.

Chapter 3

American Psychiatric Association (1994) *Diagnostic and Statistical Manual of Mental Disorders*, 3rd revised edition (DSM-IV). Washington, DC: American Psychiatric Association.

Aram, D. M., Ekelman, B. L. and Nation, J. E. (1984) Preschoolers and language disorders: 10 years later. *Journal of Speech and Hearing Research*, 27, 232–44.

Aram, D. M., Morris, R. and Hall, N. E. (1992) The validity of discrepancy criteria for identifying children with developmental disorders. *Journal of Learning Disabilities*, 25, 232–44.

Aram, D. M. and Nation, J. E. (1975) Patterns of language and behaviour in children with developmental language disorders. *Journal of Speech and Hearing Research*, 18, 229–41.

Baker, L. and Cantwell, D. P. (1987) A prospective psychiatric follow-up of children with speech/language disorders. *Journal of the American Academy of Adolescent Psychiatry*, 26, 546–53.

Bishop, D. V. M. (1987) The causes of specific developmental language disorder. *Journal of Child Psychology and Psychiatry*, 28, 1–8.

Bishop, D. V. M. (1997) *Uncommon Understanding: Development and Disorders of Language Comprehension in Children*. Hove, East Sussex: Psychology Press.

Bishop, D. V. M. and Adams, C. (1990) A prospective study of the relationship between specific language impairment, phonological disorders and reading retardation. *Journal of Child Psychology and Psychiatry*, 31, 1027–50.

Bishop, D. V. M. and Edmundson, A. (1987) Language impaired 4-year-olds: distinguishing transient from persistent impairment. *Journal of Speech and Hearing Disorders*, 52, 156–73.

Boucher, J. (1998) SPD as a distinct diagnostic entity: logical considerations and directions for future work. *International Journal of Language and Communication Disorders*, 33, 71–81.

Burden, V., Stott, C. M., Forge, J. and Goodyer, I. (1996) The Cambridge Language and Speech Project (CLASP): detection of language difficulties at 36–39 months. *Developmental Medicine and Child Neurology*, 38, 613–31.

Byers Brown, B. (1976) Language vulnerability, speech delay and therapeutic intervention. *British Journal of Disorders of Communication*, 11, 43–56.

Catts, H. and Kahmi, A. (1999) *Language and Reading Disabilities*. Needham Heights, MA: Allyn & Bacon.

Conti-Ramsden, G., Crutchley, A. C. and Botting, N. (1997) The extent to which psychometric tests differentiate subgroups of children with Specific Language Impairment. *Journal of Speech and Hearing Research*, 4, 765–77.

Conti-Ramsden, G., Donlan, C. and Grove, J. (1992) Children with Specific Language Impairment: curricular opportunities and school performance. *British Journal of Special Education*, 19, 75–80.

Conti-Ramsden, G. and Dykins, J. (1991) Mother–child interactions with language-impaired children and their siblings. *British Journal of Disorders of Communication*, 26, 337–54.

Conti-Ramsden, G., Hutcheson, G. D. and Grove, J. (1995) Contingency and breakdown: children with Specific Language Impairment and their conversations with mothers and fathers. *Journal of Speech and Hearing Research*, 38, 1290–302.

Department for Education (DfE) (1994) *The Code of Practice on the Identification and Assessment of Pupils with Special Educational Needs*. London: HMSO.

Dockrell, J. E. (1997) Acquiring a value system: the developmental perspective. In G. Lindsay and D. Thompson (eds) *Count Me In – Values into Practice in Special Education*. London: David Fulton.

Dockrell, J. E., George, R., Lindsay, G. and Roux, J. (1997) Problems in the identification and assessment of children with specific speech and language difficulties. *Educational Psychology in Practice*, 13, 29–38.

Dockrell, J. E. and Lindsay, G. (1998) The ways in which children's speech and language difficulties impact on access to the curriculum. *Child Language Teaching and Therapy*, 14, 117–33.

Dockrell, J. E. and Lindsay, G. (unpublished) Meeting the needs of children with special speech and language difficulties.

Dockrell, J. E., Messer, D., George, R. and Wilson, G. (1998) Children with word-finding difficulties – prevalence, presentation and naming problems. *International Journal of Disorders in Language and Communication*, 33, 445–54.

Donlan, C. (1993) Basic numeracy in children with specific language impairment. *Child Language Teaching and Therapy*, 9, 95–104.

Fazio, B. (1994) The counting abilities of children with specific language impairment: a comparison of oral and gestural tasks. *Journal of Speech and Hearing Research*, 37, 358–68.

Fazio, B. (1996) Mathematical abilities of children with Specific Language Impairment: a 2-year-follow-up. *Journal of Speech and Hearing Research*, 39, 839–49.

Fletcher, P. (1991) Subgroups in school-age language-impaired children. In P. Fletcher and D. Hall (eds) *Specific Speech and Language Disorders in Children*. London: Whurr.

Fletcher, P. and Ingham, R. (1995) Grammatical impairment. In P. Fletcher and B. MacWhinney (eds) *The Handbook of Child Language*. Oxford: Blackwell.

Fletcher, P. and Peters, J. (1984) Characterizing language impairment in children: an exploratory study. *Language Testing*, 1, 33–49.

Gallagher, T. (1991) *Pragmatics of Language*. San Diego, CA: Singular Publishing Company.

Gathercole, S. E. and Baddeley, A. D. (1990) Phonological memory deficits in language disordered children: is there a causal connection? *Journal of Memory and Language*, 29, 336–60.

Grove, J., Conti-Ramsden, G. and Donlan, C. (1993) Conversational interaction and decision-making in children with Specific Language Impairment. *European Journal of Communication Disorders*, 28, 141–52.

Grunwell, P. (1985) *Phonological Assessment of Child Speech (PACS)*. Windsor: NFER-Nelson.

Horne, M. D. (1985) *Attitudes Towards Handicapped Students: Professional, Peer and Parent Reactions*. Hillsdale, NJ: Erlbaum.

Hurtford, A. and Hart, D (1979) Social integration in a language unit. *Special Education Forward Trends*, 6, 8–10.

Ingram, T. T. S. (1972) The classification of speech and language disorders in young children. In M. Rutter and J. A. M. Martin (eds) *The Child with Delayed Speech*. London: William Heinemann Medical Books.

Joffe, V. (1998) Single word reading and contextual facilitation in relation to linguistic awareness in specific language-impaired children. Unpublished doctoral dissertation. Oxford: University of Oxford.

Johnston, J. R. (1991) Questions about cognition in children with Specific Language Impairment. In J. F. Miller (ed.) *Research on Child Language Disorders: A Decade of Progress.* Austin, TX: Pro-Ed.

Johnston, J. R. (1994) Cognitive abilities of children with language impairment. In R. Watkins and M. Rice (eds) *Specific Language Impairment in Children.* Baltimore: Brookes.

Johnston, J. and Smith, L. (1989) Dimensional thinking in language-impaired children. *Journal of Speech and Hearing Research,* 26, 33–8.

Lahey, M. (1988) *Language Disorders and Language Development.* New York: Macmillan.

Law, J., Harris, F., Boyle, J. and Harkness, A. (1998) *Screening for Speech and Language Delay: A Systematic Review of the Literature.* (Summary of main findings). London: City University.

Leonard, L. (1989) Language learnability and Specific Language Impairment in children. *Applied Psycholinguistics,* 10, 179–202.

Magnusson, E. and Naucler, K. (1990) Can preschool data predict language-disordered children's reading and spelling at school? *Folia Phoniatr,* 42, 277–87.

Mogford-Bevan, K. P. and Summersall, J. (1997) Emerging literacy in children with delayed speech and language. *Child Language Teaching and Therapy,* 13, 143–59.

Nelson, L., Kahmi, A. and Apel, K. (1987) Cognitive strengths and weaknesses in language-impaired children – one more look. *Journal of Speech and Hearing Disorders,* 52, 36–43.

Oakhill, J. (1994) Individual differences in children's text comprehension. In M. A. Gernsbacher (ed.) *Handbook of Psycholinguistics.* San Diego: Academic Press.

Paul, R. (1996) Clinical implications of the natural history of slow expressive language development. *American Journal of Speech and Language Pathology,* 5, 5–21.

Powell, R. and Bishop, D. V. M. (1992) Clumsiness and perceptual problems in children with Specific Language Impairment. *Developmental Medicine and Child Neurology,* 34, 755–65.

Rapin, I. and Allen, D. (1987) Developmental dysphasia and autism in preschool children: Characteristics and subtypes. Proceedings of the first international symposium on specific speech and language disorders in children. London: Afasic.

Rinaldi, W. (1996) The inner life of youngsters with specific developmental language disorder. In V. Varma (ed.) *The Inner Life of Children with Special Needs.* London: Whurr.

Rissman, A. S., Curtiss, S. and Tallal, P. (1990) School placement outcomes of young language impaired children. *Journal of Speech, Language, Pathology and Audiology,* 14, 49–58.

Scarborough, H. S. and Dobrich, W. (1990) Development of children with early language delay. *Journal of Speech and Hearing Disorders,* 33, 70–83.

Silva, P. A., Williams, S. M. and McGee, R. (1987) A longitudinal study of children with developmental language delay at age three: later intelligence, reading and behaviour problems. *Developmental Medicine and Child Neurology,* 29, 630–40.

Stackhouse, J. and Wells, W. (1997) *Children's Speech and Literacy Difficulties – A Psycholinguistic Framework.* London: Whurr.

Stone, C. A. and Connell, P. J. (1993) Induction of a visual symbolic rule in children with Specific Language Impairment. *Journal of Speech and Hearing Research,* 36, 599–608.

Stothard, S. E., Snowling, M., Bishop, D. V., Chipchase, B. B. and Kaplan, C. A. (1998) Language-impaired preschoolers: a follow up into adolescence. *Journal of Speech, Language and Hearing Research,* 41, 407–18.

Tallal, P. (1990) Fine grained discrimination deficits in language-learning impaired children are specific neither to the auditory modality nor to speech perception. *Journal of Speech and Hearing Research,* 33, 616–21.

Tallal, P., Miller, S. L., Bedi, G., Byma, G., Wang, X., Najarajan, S. S., Schreiner, C., Jenkins, W. M. and Merzenich, M. M. (1996) Language comprehension in language-learning impaired children improved with acoustically modified speech. *Science,* 271, 81–4.

Van der Lely, H. J. K. (1997) Narrative discourse in grammatical specific language impaired children: a modular deficit. *Journal of Child Language,* 24, 221–56.

Van der Lely, H. J. K. and Harris, M. (1990) Sentence comprehension strategies in specifically language impaired children. *Journal of Speech and Hearing Disorders*, 55, 101–17.

Watkins, R., Rice, M. L. and Moltz, C. (1993) Verb use by language-impaired and normally developing children. *First Language*, 13, 133–43.

Whitehurst, G. and Fischel, J. (1994) Practitioner review: early developmental language delay: what, if anything, should the clinician do about it? *Journal of Child Psychology and Psychiatry*, 35, 613–48.

World Health Organization (1990) *International Classification of Diseases and Disorders*, 10th edition. Geneva: World Health Organization.

Chapter 4

American Psychiatric Association (1994) *Diagnostic and Statistical Manual of Mental Disorders*. 4th edition (DSM-IV). Washington, DC: American Psychiatric Association.

Asperger, H. (1944) Die autistischen Psychopathen im Kindesalter, Archiv fur Psychiatrie und Nervenkrankheiten 117, 76–136. Translated by U. Frith in U. Frith (ed.) (1991) *Autism and Asperger Syndrome*. Cambridge: Cambridge University Press, 37–92.

Baron-Cohen, S., Baldwin, D. and Crowson, M. (1997) Do children with autism use the speaker's direction of gaze strategy to crack the code of language? *Child Development*, 68, 48–57.

Baron-Cohen, S., Leslie, A. M. and Frith, U. (1985) Does the autistic child have a 'theory of mind'? *Cognition*, 21, 37–46.

Bellugi, U., Marks, S., Bihrle, A. M. and Sabo, H. (1988) Dissociation between language and cognitive functioning in William's syndrome. In D. Bishop and K. Mogford (eds) *Language Development in Exceptional Circumstances*. London: Churchill Livingstone.

Bellugi, U., Wang, P. and Jerrigan, T. (1994) Williams syndrome: an unusual neuro-psychological profile. In S. H. Broman and J. Grafman (eds) *A Typical Cognitive Deficits in Developmental Disorders*. Hillsdale, NJ: Erlbaum.

Buckley, S. and Bird, G. (1993) Teaching children with Down's syndrome to read. *Down's Syndrome Research and Practice*, 1, 34–41.

Chapman, R. S. (1995) Language development in children and adolescents with Down's syndrome. In P. Fletcher and B. MacWhinney (eds) *The Handbook of Child Language*. Oxford: Blackwell.

Chapman, R., Schwartz, S. and Bird, E. K.-R. (1991) Language skills of children and adolescents with Down syndrome: 1 Comprehension. *Journal of Speech and Hearing Research*, 34, 1106–20.

Dykens, E. M., Hodapp, R. M. and Leckman, J. F. (1994) *Behavior and Development in Fragile X Syndrome*. Thousand Oaks, CA: Sage.

Frith, U. (1989) *Autism: Explaining the Enigma*. Oxford: Sage.

Greer, M. K., Brown. F. R. III, Pai, G. S., Choudry, S. H. and Klein, A. J. (1997) Cognitive, adaptive, and behavioral characteristics of Williams syndrome. *American Journal of Medical Genetics*, 7, 521–25.

Hobson, R. P. (1991) Against the theory of 'Theory of Mind'. *British Journal of Developmental Psychology*, 9, 33–51.

Hobson, R. P. (1993) *Autism and the Development of Mind*. Hove: Erlbaum.

Howlin, P. (1998) Psychological and educational treatments for autism. *Journal of Child Psychology and Psychiatry*, 39, 307–22.

Jarrold, C., Baddeley, A. D. and Hewes, A. K. (1998) Verbal and nonverbal abilties in the Williams syndrome phenotype: evidence for diverging developmental trajectories. *Journal of Child Psychology and Psychiatry*, 39, 511–24.

Jordan, R. and Powell, S. (1995) *Understanding and Teaching Children with Autism*. Chichester: Blackwell.

Kanner, L. (1943) Autistic disturbances of affective contact. *Nervous Child*, 2, 217–50.

Karmiloff-Smith, A., Grant, J., Berthoud, I., Davies, M., Howlin, P. and Udwin, O. (1997) Language and Williams syndrome: how intact is 'intact'? *Child Development*, 68, 246–62.

Marcell, M. and Cohen, S. (1992) Hearing abilities of Down syndrome and other mentally handicapped adolescents. *Research in Developmental Disabilities*, 13, 533–51.

Ozonoff, S., Pennington, B. F. and Rogers, S. J. (1991) Executive function deficits in high-functioning autistic individuals: relationship to theory of mind. *Journal of Child Psychology*.

Peeters, T. (1997) *Autism from Theoretical Understanding to Educational Intervention.* London: Whurr.
Powell, S. (1999) Autism. In D. Messer and S. Millar (eds) *Developmental Psychology: Contemporary Issues and Perspectives.* London: Arnold.
Reilly, J., Klima, E. and Bellugi, U. (1990) Once more with feeling: affect amd feeling in atypical populations. *Development and Psychopathology*, 2, 367–91.
Stevens, T. and Karmiloff-Smith, A. (1997) Word learning in a special population: Do individuals with Williams syndrome obey lexical constraints? *Journal of Child Language*, 24, 737–65.
Williams, J. C. P., Barratt-Boyes, B. G. and Lowe, J. B. (1961) Supravalvular aortic stenosis. *Circulation*, 24, 1311–18.
Wimmer, H. and Perner, J. (1983) Beliefs about beliefs: representation and constraining function of wrong beliefs in young children's understanding of deception. *Cognition*, 13, 103–28.
Wing, L. (1988) The continuum of autistic characteristics. In E. Schopler and G. Mesibov (eds) *Diagnosis and Assessment in Autism.* New York: Plenum Press.

Chapter 5
Andersen, E. S., Dunlea, A. and Kekelis, L. S. (1993) The impact of input: language acquisition in the visually impaired. *First Language*, 13, 23–49.
Baird, S. M., Mayfield, P. and Baker, P. (1997) Mothers' interpretations of the behaviour of their infants with visual and other impairments during interactions. *Journal of Visual Impairment and Blindness*, 91, 467–83.
Barraga, N. (1976) *Visual Handicaps and Learning: A Developmental Approach.* Belmont, CA: Wadsworth.
Brown, R., Hobson, P. R., Lee, A. and Stevenson, J. (1997) Are there autistic-like features in congenitally blind children? *Journal of Child Psychology and Psychiatry*, 38, 693–702.
Connelly, V. and Barlow-Brown, F. (forthcoming) The role of letter knowledge and phonological awareness when beginning braille. *Reading Research Quarterly.*
Curtiss, S. (1977) *Genie: A Psycholinguistic Study of a Modern-Day Wild Child.* London: Academic Press.
Davis, K. (1947) Final note on a case of extreme isolation. *American Journal of Sociology*, 52, 432–37.
DHSS (Department of Health and Social Security) (1988) Causes of blindness and partial sight among children aged under 16, newly registered as blind and partially sighted between 1985 and 1987. *Statistical Bulletin*, 3 September 1998. London: HMSO.
Dimcovic, N. and Tobin, M. J. (1995) The use of language in simple classification tasks by children who are blind. *Journal of Visual Impairment and Blindness*, 89, 448–59.
Dote-Kwan, J., Hughes, M. and Taylor, J. S. (1997) Impact of early experiences on the development of young children with visual impairments: revisited. *Journal of Visual Impairment and Blindness*, 91, 31–144.
Dunlea, A. (1989) *Vision and the Emergence of Meaning.* Cambridge: Cambridge University Press.
Fraiberg, S. (1977) *Insights from the Blind.* New York: Basic Books.
Kekelis, L. S. and Prinz, D. M. (1996) Blind and sighted children with their mothers: the development of discourse skills. *Journal of Visual Impairment and Blindness*, 90, 423–36.
Koluchova J. (1972) Severe deprivation in twins: a case study. *Journal of Child Psychology and Psychiatry*, 13, 107–14.
Koluchova, J. (1976) The further devlopment of twins after severe and prolonged deprivation: a second report. *Journal of Child Psychology and Psychiatry*, 17, 181–8.
Landau, B. (1983) Blind children's language is not 'meaningless'. In A. E. Mills (ed.) *Language Acquisition in Blind Children Normal and Deficient.* London: Croom-Helm.
Landau, B. (1997) Language and experience in blind children. In V. Lewis and G. M. Collis (eds) *Blindness and Psychological Development in Young Children.* Leicester: British Psychological Society.
Landau, B. and Gleitman, L. R. (1985) *Language and Experience: Evidence from the Blind Child.* Cambridge, MA: Harvard University Press.
Lennenberg, E. (1967) *Biological Foundations of Language.* New York: Wiley.

Lewis, V. and Collis, G. M. (1997) *Blindness and Psychological Development.* Leicester: BPS Books.

Locke, J. (1997) A theory of neurolinguistic development. *Brain and Language,* 58, 265–326.

Mason, M. K. (1942) Learning to speak after six and one-half years of silence. *Journal of Speech and Learning Disorders,* 7, 295–304.

McConachie, H. and Moore, V. (1994) Early expressive language and severely visually impaired children. *Developmental Medicine and Child Neurology,* 36, 230–40.

Mills, A. (1988) Visual Handicap. In D. Bishop and K. Mogford (eds) *Language Development in Exceptional Circumstances.* Edinburgh: Churchill Livingstone.

Mogford, K. (1988) Oral language development in prelinguistically deaf children. In D. Bishop and K. Mogford (eds) *Language Development in Exceptional Circumstances.* Edinburgh: Churchill Livingstone.

Moore, V. and McConachie, H. (1994) Communication between blind and severely visually impaired children and their parents. *British Journal of Developmental Psychology,* 12, 491–502.

Norgate, S. (1998) Research methods for studying the language of blind children. In N. H. Hornberger and D. Corson (eds) *Research Methods in Language and Education,* Vol. 8. The Netherlands: Kluwer Academic Publishers.

Norgate, S., Collis, G. M. and Lewis, V. (1998) The developmental role of rhymes and routines for congenitally blind children. *Cahiers de Psychologie Cognitive/Current Psychology of Cognition,* 17(2), 451–77.

Perez-Pereira, M. (1994) Imitations, repetitions, routines and the child's analysis of language: insights from the blind. *Journal of Child Language,* 21, 317–37.

Preisler, G. (1997) Social and emotional development of blind children: a longitudinal study. In V. Lewis and G. Collis (eds) *Blindness and Psychological Development in Young Children.* Leicester: BPS Books, 69–85.

RNIB (1994) *Blind and Partially Sighted Children in Britain: Volume 2.* Royal National Institute for the Blind and HMSO.

Skuse, D. (1988) Extreme deprivation in early childhood. In D. Bishop and K. Mogford (eds) *Language Development in Exceptional Circumstances.* Edinburgh: Churchill Livingstone.

Warren, D. (1984) *Blindness and Early Childhood Development,* 2nd edition. New York: American Foundation for the Blind.

Webster, A. and Roe, J. (1998) *Children with Visual Impairments: Social Interaction, Language and Learning.* London: Routledge.

Chapter 6

Andrews, J. F. and Mason, J. M. (1986) How do deaf children learn about pre-reading? *American Annal of the Deaf,* 131, 210–17.

Belmont, J. and Krachmer, M. (1978) Deaf people's memory: there are problems in testing special populations. In M. M. Gruneberg, P. E. Morris and R. N. Sykes (eds) *Practical Aspects of Memory.* New York: Academic Press.

Bishop, D. V. M. (1983a) Comprehension of English syntax by profoundly deaf children. *Journal of Child Psychology and Psychiatry,* 24, 415–34.

Bishop, D. V. M. (1983b) *Test for Reception of Grammar.* Available from the author, Department of Psychology, University of Manchester.

Bonvillian, J. D. (1999) Sign language development. In M. Barrett (ed.) *The Development of Language.* Hove: Psychology Press.

Cromer, R. F. (1978) The basis of childhood dysphasia: a linguistic approach. In M. A. Wykes (ed.) *Developmental Dysphasia.* New York: Academic Press.

Davis, J. M., Elfbein, J., Schum, R. and Bentler, R. (1986) Effects of mild and moderate hearing impairments on language, educational and psychosocial behaviour in children. *Journal of Speech and Hearing Disorders,* 51, 53–62.

Dawson, S. (1991) Educational progress profiles of children with cochlear implants. Paper presented at the Annual Convention of the American Speech Language and Hearing Association.

Dodd, B. (1980) The spelling abilities of profoundly pre-lingually deaf children. In U. Frith (ed.) *Cognitive Processes in Spelling.* New York: Academic Press.

Dodd, B., Woodhouse, L. and McIntosh, B. (1992) The linguistic abilities of young children with hearing impairment: First report of longitudinal study. *Australian and New Zealand Journal of Developmental Disabilities*, 18, 17–34.

Emanuel, R. and Herman, R. (1992) The early identification and the effects of impaired hearing on language development. In J. Law (ed.) *The Early Identification of Language Impairment in Children*. London: Chapman and Hall.

Friel-Patti, S. (1990) Otitis media with effusion and the development of language: a review of the evidence. *Topics Language Disorders*, 11, 11–22.

Friel-Patti, S. (1992) Research in child language disorders: what do we know and where are we going? *Folia Phoniatrica*, 44, 126–42.

Friel-Patti, S. and Finitzo, T. (1990) Language learning in a prospective study of otitis media with effusion in the first two years of life. *Journal of Speech and Hearing Research*, 33, 188–94.

Gilbertson, M. and Kahmi, A. G. (1995) Novel word learning in children with hearing impairments. *Journal of Speech and Hearing Research*, 38, 630–42.

Gregory, S. and Mogford, K. (1981) Early language development in deaf children. In B. Woll, J. G. Kyle and M. Deuchar (eds) *Perspectives on BSL and Deafness*. London: Croom Helm.

Gross, R. N. (1970) Language used by mothers of deaf children and mothers of hearing children. *American Annals of the Deaf*, 115, 93–6.

Hall, D. (1996) *Health for all Children*, 3rd edition. Oxford: Oxford University Press.

Hanson, V. L., Shankweiler, D. and Fischer, F. W. (1983) Determinants of spelling ability in deaf and hearing adults: access to linguistic structure. *Cognition*, 14, 323–44.

Harris, M. and Beech, J. R. (forthcoming) Implicit phonological awareness and early reading development in pre-lingually deaf children. *Journal of Deaf Studies and Deaf Education*.

Hirsch-Pasek, K. (1987) The meta linguistics of finger spelling: an alternative way to increase reading vocabulary in congenitally deaf readers. *Reading Research Quarterly*, 22, 455–74.

Kyle, J. and Woll, B. (1985) *Sign Language: The Study of Deaf People and their Language*. Cambridge: Cambridge University Press.

Levitt, H., McGarr, N. and Geffner, D. (1988) Development of language and communication skills in hearing impaired children. ASHA Monographs No. 26.

Marschark, M. and Harris, M. (1996) Success and failure in learning to read: the special (?) case of deaf children. In C. Cornoldi and J. Oakhill (eds) *Reading Comprehension Difficulties: Processes and Intervention*. Hillsdale, NJ: Lawrence Erlbaum Associates.

Mayberry, R. I. and Eichen, E. B. (1991) The long-lasting advantage of learning sign language in childhood: another look at the critical period for language acquisition. *Journal of Memory and Language*, 30, 486–512.

Meadow-Orleans, K. P. (1987) An analysis of the effectiveness of early intervention programmes for hearing-impaired children. In M. J. Guralnick and F. C. Bennett (eds) *The Effectiveness of Early Intervention for At-risk and Handicapped Children*. New York: Academic Press.

Merrills, J. D., Underwood, G. and Wood, D. J. (1994) The word recognition skills of profoundly prelingually deaf children. *British Journal of Psychology*, 12, 365–84.

Mogford, K. (1988) Oral language development in prelinguistically deaf children. In D. Bishop and K. Mogford (eds) *Language Development in Exceptional Circumstances*. Edinburgh: Churchill Livingstone.

Northern, J. L. and Downs, M. P. (1984) *Hearing in Children*, 3rd edition. Baltimore: Williams and Wilkins.

Nunes, T. and Moreno, C. (1997) Is hearing impairment a cause or difficulty in learning mathematics? *Equals*, 3, 15–16.

Nunes, T. and Moreno, C. (forthcoming) Solving problems with different mediators: how do deaf children perform? *Educational Studies in Mathematics*.

Somerset Education Authority (1981) *Ways and Means – Hearing Impairment*. Hampshire: Globe Education.

Wallace, I. F., Gravel, J. S., Schwartz, R. G. and Ruben, R. G. (1996) Otitis media, communication style of primary caregivers and language skills of two year olds, preliminary report. *Journal of Developmental and Behavioural Pediatrics*, 17, 29–35.

Waters, G. S. and Doehring, D. G. (1990) Reading acquisition in congenitally deaf children who communicate orally: insights from an analysis of component reading, language and memory skills. In T. H. Carr and B. A. Levy (eds) *Reading and its Development.* San Diego, CA: Academic Press.

Wood, D., Wood, H., Griffiths, A. and Howarth, I. (1986) *Teaching and Talking with Deaf Children.* London: Wiley.

Wood, D. J., Wood, H. A. and Howarth, S. P. (1983) Mathematical abilities in deaf school leavers. *British Journal of Developmental Psychology,* 1, 67–74.

Chapter 7

Anthony, A., Bogle, D., Ingram, T. T. S. and McIsaac, M. (1971) *Edinburgh Articulation Test.* Edinburgh: Livingstone.

Armstrong, D., Galloway, D. and Tomlinson, S. (1993) *British Journal of Sociology,* 14, 399–408.

Bain, B. and Olswang, L (1995) Examining readiness for learning two-word utterances: dynamic assessment validation. *Journal of Speech-Language Pathology,* 4, 81–91.

Baron-Cohen, S., Allen, J. and Gillberg, C. (1992) Can autism be detected at 18 months? The needle, the haystack and the CHAT. *British Journal of Psychiatry,* 161, 839–43.

Bates, E., Dale, P. and Thal, D. (1995) Individual differences and their implications for theories of language development. In P. Fletcher and B. MacWhinney (eds) *The Handbook of Child Language.* Oxford: Blackwell.

Bishop, D. V. M. (1983) *Test for Reception of Grammar.* Available from the author, Department of Psychology, University of Manchester.

Bishop, D. V. M. (1989) *Test for Reception of Grammar,* 2nd edition. Manchester: The Author, Age and Cognitive Performance Research Centre, University of Manchester.

Bishop, D. V. M. (1997) *Uncommon Understanding: Development and Disorders of Language Comprehension in Children.* Hove, East Sussex: Psychology Press.

Bishop, D. V. M. and Edmundson, A. (1987) Language impaired 4-year-olds: Distinguishing transient from persistent impairment. *Journal of Speech and Hearing Disorders,* 52, 156–73.

Brambring, M. and Troster, H. (1994) The assessment of cognitive development in blind infants and preschoolers. *Journal of Visual Impairment and Blindness,* 88, 9–18.

Chazen, M., Laing, A., Shackleton Bailey, M. and Jones, G. (1980) *Some of our Children.* London: Open Books.

Cicchetti, D. and Wagner, S. (1990) Alternative assessment strategies for the evaluation of infants and toddlers: an organizational perspective. In S. J. Meisels and J. P. Shonkoff (eds) *Handbook of Early Childhood Intervention.* New York: Cambridge University Press.

Dale, P., Bates, E., Reznick, J. and Morisset, C. (1989) The validity of a parent report instrument of child language at twenty months. *Journal of Child Language,* 16, 239–249.

Dewart, H. and Summers, S. (1988) *Pragmatic and Early Communication Profile.* Windsor: NFER.

Dockrell, J. E., George, R., Lindsay, G. and Roux, J. (1997) Professionals' understanding of specific language impairments – implications for assessment and identification. *Educational Psychology in Practice,* 13, 27–35.

Dunn, L. M., Whetton, C. and Burley, J. (1997) *The British Picture Vocabulary Scales.* Windsor: NFER-Nelson.

Elliot, C. D., Smith, P. and McCulloch, K. (1997) *British Ability Scales II.* Windsor: NFER-Nelson.

Fischel, J., Whitehurst, G., Caulfield, M. and De Baryshe, B. (1989) Language growth in children with expressive language delay. *Pediatrics,* 82, 218–27.

Fletcher, J., Francis, D., Rourke, B., Shaywitz, S. and Shaywitz, B. (1993) Classification of learning disabilities: relationships with other childhood disorders. In G. Reid Lyon, D. Gray, J. Kavanaugh and N. Krasnegor (eds) *Better Understanding Learning Disabilities: New Views from Research and Their Implications for Education and Public Policies.* Baltimore: Paul H. Brookes Publishing Co.

Frederickson, N., Frith, U. and Reason, R. (1997) *Phonological Assessment Battery* (PhAB) Standardised Edition. Windsor: NFER-Nelson.

Howlin, P. and Cross, P. (1994) The variability of language test scores in 3- and 4-year-old children of normal non-verbal intelligence: a brief research report. *European Journal of Disorders of Communication*, 29, 279–88.

Lahey, M. (1990) Who shall be called language disordered? Some reflections and one perspective. *Journal of Speech and Language Disorders*, 55, 612–20.

Largo, R. H., Graf, S., Kundw, S., Hunziker, U. and Molinari, L. (1990) Predicting developmental outcome at school age from infant tests of normal, at-risk and retarded infants. *Developmental Medicine and Child Neurology*, 32, 40–5.

Law, J. (1992) The process of early identification. In J. Law (ed.) *The Early Identification of Language Impairment in Children*. London: Chapman Hall.

Lindsay, G. and Desforges, M. (1998) *Baseline Assessment: Practice, Problems and Possibilities*. London: David Fulton.

Lunt, I. (1993) The practice of assessment. In H. Daniels (ed.) *Charting the Agenda*. London: Routledge.

McCauley, R. J. and Demetras, M. J. (1990) The identification of language impairment in the selection of specifically language impaired subjects. *Journal of Speech and Hearing Disorders*, 55, 468–75.

McCauley, R. J. and Swisher, L. (1984) Use and misuse of norm-referenced tests in clinical assessment: a hypothetical case. *Journal of Speech and Hearing Disorders*, 49, 338–48.

Messick, S. (1983) Assessment of children. In P. H. Mussen (ed.) *Handbook of Child Psychology*, Vol. 1, 4th edition. New York: John Wiley and Sons, 475–526.

Olswang, L. and Bain, B. (1996) Assessment information for predicting upcoming change in language production. *Journal of Speech and Hearing Research*, 39, 414–23.

Plante, E. and Vance, R. (1994) Selection of preschool language tests: a data-based approach. *Language Speech and Hearing Services*, 25, 15–24.

Renfrew, C. E. (1972) *The Bus Story*. Bicester: Winslow Press.

Reynell, J. (1985) *Reynell Language Development Scales*. Revised edition. Windsor: NFER.

Rice, M. L., Buhr, J. C. and Nemeth, M. (1990) Fast mapping word-learning abilities of language-delayed preschoolers. *Journal of Speech and Hearing Disorders*, 55, 33–42.

Rust, J. (1995) *Wechsler Objective Language Dimension*. London: The Psychological Corporation.

Sattler, J. M. (1992) *Assessment of Children's Intelligence and Ability*. Boston: Allyn and Bacon.

Schery, T. K. (1985) Correlates of language development in language disordered children. *Journal of Speech and Hearing Disorders*, 50, 73–83.

Semel, E. M., Wiig, E. and Secord, W. (1987) *Clinical Evaluation of Language Fundamentals – Revised*. San Antonio, TX: Psychological Corporation.

Siegel, L. (1992) Reproductive, perinatal and environmental factors as predictors of the cognitive and language development of pre-term and full-term infants. *Child Development*, 53, 963–73.

Stark, R. E., Mellits, E. D. and Tallal, P. (1983) *Behavioural Attributes of Speech and Language Disorders*. New York: Academic Press.

Tellegen, P. and Laros, J. (1993a) The construction and validation of a non-verbal test of intelligence: the revision of the Snidjers-Oomen Tests. *European Journal of Psychological Assessment*, 9, 147–57.

Tellegen, P. and Laros, J. (1993b) The Snijders-Oomen non-verbal intelligence tests: general intelligence or tests of learning potential? In J. H. M. Hamers, K. Sijtsma and A. J. J. M. Ruijssenaars. *Learning Potential Assessment*. Amsterdam: Swets and Zeitlinger.

Terman, L. M. and Merrill, M. A. (1960) *Stanford-Binet Intelligence Scale*. Boston: Houghton-Mifflin.

Thurlow, M. L. and Ysseldyke, J. E. (1979) Current assessment and decision making practices in model LD programs. *Learning Disability Quarterly*, 6, 172–83.

Torgeson, J. K. (1986) Learning disabilities theory: its current state and future perspectives. *Journal of Learning Disabilities*, 19, 399–407.

Van der Lely, H. (1990) Sentence comprehension processes in specifically language-impaired children. Unpublished PhD thesis. London: University of London.

Vess, S. and Gregory, L. (1985) Best practices in the assessment of hearing impaired children. In A. Thomas and J. Grimes (eds) *Best Practices in School Psychology*. Kent, Ohio:

National Association of School Psychologists.

Watkins, M. (1996) Diagnostic utility of the WISC-III Developmental Index as a predictor of learning disabilities. *Journal of Learning Disabilities*, 29, 305–12.

Wright, J. (1993) Assessment of children with special needs. In J. Beech, L. Harding and D. Hilton-Jones (eds) *Assessment in Speech and Language Therapy*. London: Routledge.

Chapter 8

Alegria, J., Charlier, B. L. and Mattys, S. (unpublished) The role of lip-reading and cued speech in the processing of phonological information in deaf children.

Bates, E., Dale, P. and Thal, D. (1995) Individual differences and their implications for theories of language development. In P. Fletcher and B. MacWhinney (eds) *The Handbook of Child Language*. Oxford: Blackwell.

Bronfenbrenner, U. (1979) *The Ecology of Human Development: Experiments by Nature and Design*. Cambridge, MA: Harvard University Press.

Cole, K. N., Dale, P., Mills, P. and Jenkins, J. (1993) Interaction between early interventions curricula and student characteristics. *Exceptional Children*, 60, 17–28.

Donaldson, M. L. and Reid, J. (1994) Strategies for intervention: goals, techniques and settings. In J. Watson (ed.) *Meeting Special Educational Needs: Working with Communication Difficulties*. Edinburgh: Moray House Institute of Education.

Garbarino, S. (1982) Sociocultural risk. In C. B. Kopp and J. B. Krakow (eds) *The Child: Development in a Social Context*. Reading, MA: Addison-Wesley.

Gerber, A. (1987) Collaboration between SLPs and educators: a continuing education process. *Journal of Communication Disorders*, 11, 107–23.

Goldstein, H. and Hockenberger, E. H. (1991) Significant progress in child language intervention: an 11-year retrospective. *Research in Developmental Disabilities*, 12, 401–24.

Johansson, I. (1994) *Language Development in Children with Special Needs – Performative Communication*, translated by E. Thomas. London: Jessica Kingsley.

Jones, P. and Crenan, A. (1986) *Sign and Symbol for Mentally Handicapped People*. London: Croom Helm.

Kiernan, C. (1987) Non-vocal communication systems: a critical survey. In W. Yule and M. Rutter (eds) *Language Development and Disorders*. Oxford: Blackwell/MacKeith Press.

Law, J., Boyle, J., Harris, F. and Harkness, A. (1998) Screening for speech and language delay. National Dissemination seminar. London: City University.

Lee Swanson, H., Carson, C. and Sasche-Lee, C. (1996) A selective synthesis of intervention research for students with learning disabilities: is there general support for a strategy deficit model? *Advances in Learning and Behavioural Disabilities*, Vol. 10B. Greenwich, CT: JAI Press Inc.

Leonard, L. (1981) Facilitating linguistic skills in children with specific language impairment. *Applied Psycholinguistics*, 2, 89–148.

Locke, A. (1989) Screening and intervention with children with speech and language difficulties in mainstream. In K. Mogford and J. Sadler (eds) *Child Language Disability*. Clevendon: Multilingual Matters.

Locke, D. (1997) *Augmentative Communication*. Distance Learning Materials. Human Communication Sciences: University of Sheffield.

Manolson, A. (1983) *It Takes Two to Talk*. Toronto: Hanen Early Language Resource Centre.

Merzenich, M. M., Jenkins, W. M., Johnstone, P., Schreiner, C., Miller, S. L. and Tallal, P. (1996) Temperal processing deficits of language-learning impaired children ameliorated by training. *Science*, 271, 77–81.

Nye, C., Foster, S. and Seaman, D. (1987) Effectiveness of language intervention with language-learning disabilities. *Journal of Speech and Hearing Disorders*, 52, 1026–36.

Paul, R. (1996) Clinical implications of the natural history of slow expressive language development. *American Journal of Speech and Language Pathology*, 5, 5–21.

Pearl, R., Donahue, M. and Bryan, T. (1986) Social relationships of learning-disabled children. In J. K. Torgeson and B. Y. L. Wong (eds) *Psychological and Educational Perspectives on Learning Disabilities*. Orlando, FL: Academic Press.

Schwartz, I., Carta, J. and Grant, S. (1996) Examining the use of recommended language intervention practices in early childhood special education classrooms. *Topics in Early Childhood Special Education*, 16, 251–72.

Sturmey, P. and Crisp, A. G. (1986) Portage guide to early education: a review of research. *Educational Psychology*, 6, 139–57.

Tallal, P., Miller, S. L., Bedi, G., Byma, G., Wang, X., Najarajan, S. S., Schreiner, C., Jenkins, W. M. and Merzenich, M. M. (1996) Language comprehension in language-learning impaired children improved with acoustically modified speech. *Science*, 271, 81–4.

Wedell, K. (1995) *Putting the Code of Practice into Practice: Meeting Special Educational Needs in the School and Classroom*. Institute of Education, University of London.

Wolfendale, S. (1987) *Special Needs in Ordinary Schools*. London: Cassell.

Chapter 9

Conti-Ramsden, G. and Jones, M. (1997) Verb use in specific language impairment. *Journal of Speech, Language and Hearing Research*, 40, 1298–313.

Department for Education (DfE) (1994) *The Code of Practice on the Identification and Assessment of Pupils with Special Educational Needs*. London: HMSO.

Grove, N. (1998) *Literature for All*. London: David Fulton.

Grove, N. and Dockrell, J. E. (forthcoming) Growing and learning with sensory impairments. In D. Messer and S. Millar (eds) *Developmental Psychology*. London: Arnold.

Lindsay, G. and Desforges, M. (1998) *Baseline Assessment: Practice, Problems and Possibilities*. London: David Fulton.

Tardiff, T. (forthcoming) Nouns are not always learned before verbs: evidence from Mandarin speakers' early vocabularies. *Developmental Psychology*.

Warnock report (DES) (1978) *Special Educational Needs*. London: HMSO.

Name Index

Subject Index